Yearbook of the ILA Italian Branch

ILA Italy

BRILL | NIJHOFF

LEIDEN | BOSTON

Typeface for the Latin, Greek, and Cyrillic scripts: "Brill". See and download: brill.com/brill-typeface.

ISBN 978-90-04-72765-6 (hardback)
ISBN 978-90-04-72766-3 (e-book)
DOI 10.1163/9789004727663

This book is printed on acid-free paper and produced in a sustainable manner.

Contents

Book Review

ILA *Italy Activities*

Notes on Contributors

Christine Chinkin
FBA, CMG, previously Professor of International Law, is currently Professorial Research Fellow at the Centre for Women Peace and Security at the London School of Economics. She is co-author of *The Boundaries of International Law: A Feminist Analysis* (Manchester University Press 2000), *The Making of International Law* (Oxford University Press 2007), *International Law and New Wars* (CUP 2017), *Gendered Peace through International Law* (Hart Publishing 2024) and author of *Women, Peace and Security and International Law* (CUP 2022).

Roberta Clerici
previously Professor of Private International Law at the University of Milan, is the author of over one hundred publications, particularly on issues of Private Inter-national Law. She is also co-director of the journal *Rivista di diritto internazionale privato e processuale*, member of the Scientific Committee of the online journal *Freedom Security Justice. European Legal Studies*, and member of the Editorial Committee of the journal *Diritto, immigrazione, cittadinanza*. Prof. Clerici is also coordinator of the Board of Directors of the Italian International Lawyers (In-ternational Chamber), member of the Scientific Committee of the National *School* of Specialization for *Corporate Lawyers*, as well as member of Italian and international prestigious scientific institutions.

Nikos Lavranos
is the first Secretary-General of the European Federation for Investment Law and Arbitration (EFILA). He is founder & owner of NL-Investmentconsulting, external Legal Advisor for numerous law firms. He is also Partner at Herreveld van der Hurk & Partners, Senior Advisor at Grayston & Company (Brussels) and Of Counsel at Wöss & Partners (Vienna).

Antonio Leandro
is Full Professor of International Law at the University of Bari Aldo Moro. Lawyer qualified to practice before the Italian Supreme Court. Member of the Group of Experts on Restructuring and Insolvency Law and former member of the Group of Experts on European Freezing of Bank Accounts appointed by the DG Justice of the European Commission. Author of four monographs and some 200 papers, as well as editor, or co-editor, of six collective books.

Maria Chiara Malaguti
is Full Professor of International law at Catholic University of the Sacred Heart, Rome. She was appointed President of UNIDROIT since 1 September 2020. An international arbitrator for commercial disputes and foreign direct investments included in various rosters, she supports the General Attorney's Office of Italy in the procedures opened against Italy as for international investment law. Prof. Malaguti holds degrees in law and in economics, an LLM from Harvard Law School and a PhD from the EUI in Florence. She has various publications, mainly focusing on financial markets and sovereign debt, harmonization of law and international investment law.

Michael Mcilwrath
is the founder and CEO of MDisputes, a company devoted to providing in-house dispute resolution support to private and public enterprises. He spent 22 years as in-house litigation counsel, most recently as Vice President of Litigation of Baker Hughes Company, and previously as the head of litigation for GE Oil & Gas. Michael is adjunct professor at Bocconi School of Law in Milan, and an Officer at Large of the IBA's Mediation Committee. He was the Chair of the Global Pound Conference in 2016–17 and a Board Member of the International Mediation Institute (IMI) from 2008 to 2020, as well as IMI's President in 2009–10. Michael is the co-author of two textbooks *Negotiating International Commercial Contracts: Practical Exercises* (2020 Eleven Publishing) and *International Mediation and Arbitration: A Practical Guide* (Kluwer 2010), and numerous articles about international mediation and arbitration. He is a regular contributor to OGEMID and the Kluwer Arbitration Blog.

Cameron Miles
is an international lawyer and barrister practicing from 3 Verulam Buildings in London, UK.

Facundo Pérez-Aznar
is an Adjunct Professor of International Economic Law at the University of Buenos Aires (UBA) and a Senior Researcher at the Geneva Centre of International Dispute Settlement (CIDS). He worked for several years as a legal counsel in the Department of International Affairs of the General Attorney's Office of Argentina, which represents Argentina's interests in international investment disputes. He previously worked as a legal officer in the Latin American Economic Integration Directorate at Argentina's Ministry of Foreign Affairs. Facundo has advised different governments and international organisations

on international investment and trade law matters as an independent expert and consultant.

Luca G Radicati di Brozolo
is a partner of the litigation and arbitration boutique law firm ArbLit – Radicati di Brozolo Sabatini Benedettelli Torsello, a tenant at Fountain Court Chambers in London and a leading academic in the fields of private international law and arbitration law. He was a tenured professor of Private International Law at the Catholic University of Milan until 2019 and is the author of several books and over 250 publications. He has a very active practice in commercial and investor-State arbitration as arbitrator, counsel and expert. He is a past Vice-President of the LCIA and a former member of the Court of the ICC.

Attila M Tanzi
President of the Italian Branch of the International Law Association, is Full Professor of International Law at the Alma Mater University of Bologna and an Associate Member of 3 Verulam Buildings, London. A Legal Adviser of the Italian Ministry for Foreign Affairs (1987 to date), he has a long-standing experience in international litigation, both as counsel and arbitrator. Formerly, Chairman of the Legal Board of the 1992 Water Convention of the United Nations Economic Commission for Europe (2004–2012) and President of its Implementation Committee (2013–2024).

Chiara Tondini
is an International Disputes Counsel at MDisputes, where she provides strategic in-house litigation support to private and public organizations involved in complex international disputes. In her role, she assists clients in arbitration, mediation, and other dispute resolution mechanisms primarily in the commercial context. Chiara also serves as a legal advisor for programs aimed at enhancing access to justice globally. Before joining MDisputes, Chiara was an international arbitration and mediation Counsel for an international law firm in Italy, and previously she was the founder and manager of the Florence International Mediation Chamber (FIMC) and the Florence International Dispute Resolution Academy (FIDRA). She had been representing the FIMC at the UNCITRAL WG II (Dispute Settlement) sessions for the preparation of the Singapore Convention on mediation. She is Co-Rapporteur of the International Law Association (ILA) Committee on ADR in International Law. She is a member of the International Bar Association (IBA), Mediation Committee.

Gabriella Venturini
is Professor Emerita of International Law at the University of Milan, Italy. She is Associate Member of the Institute of International Law/Institut de Droit International and Council Member of the International Institute of Humanitarian Law. She was President of the Italian Branch (ILA Italy) of the International Law Association from 2013 to 2021. Being full Professor of International Law at the University of Milan, she taught and wrote extensively in the field of public international law including International Humanitarian Law and Human Rights Law, International Disaster Law, Disarmament and Non-proliferation, Space Law, International Trade Law and EU Law.

Foreword

In the first two decades of the new millennium, international law has experienced an unprecedented phase of development in almost all of its branches. Several landmark events have stirred the waters of international law: multilateralism – whose advancement seemed unchallenged after the end of the Cold War – has gradually entered a crisis due to widespread nationalist trends that have undermined liberal institutions and international cooperation from within worldwide. This season of landslides has shaped an international community divided into regional macro-areas, in which various hotbeds of conflict have (re)ignited also right into the heart of Europe.

We live in a time when the language of international law has never been so widely spoken, considering that almost every faction in a conflict invokes international law to justify its actions and reactions. Whilst this may suggest the growing importance of the discipline and the work done by internationalists, in their different capacities, it may also generate the frustrating impression that international law lends itself to be cynically co-opted and is therefore ultimately perceived as useless: when everyone seems to be right, no one is right.

Against such a backdrop, ILA Italy wishes to enhance its efforts in joining forces with the international community of the willing in the building of bridges that bring scholars, practitioners, peoples, and possibly decision makers closer together beyond conflicting national interests, through the language of international law. To that end, we decided to start the Yearbook of the Italian Branch of the ILA precisely to provide an effective contribution to safeguarding the legitimacy of the discipline and of the international legal system, more broadly, with a view to testifying to the Branch's activities and those of its associates within the ILA Committees and Study Groups.

The project intends to take on legal analysis of the latest developments and major contemporary challenges of international law, public and private, and European Union law through the combined lenses of Academia and practice. As reflected in the composition of its Board, the Italian Branch is fostering its efforts in offering a permanent forum for dialogue and cross-fertilisation between different professional quarters for whom international law and relations are of relevance. For the same purpose, English is the language of the Yearbook.

This project also intends to acknowledge the significant contribution Italian internationalists have made – and continue to make – to the development and codification of international law, including by engaging within the ILA and its bodies.

Gabriella Venturini, former President of ILA Italy, presents an overview of the history of the Italian Branch since its foundation just a century ago, in 1925. The editorial of Christine Chinkin, current Chair of the ILA, offers an important reflection on women, peace and security in international law, as an important contribution fostering gender balance within our Association.

The Section devoted to 'Articles and Essays' hosts multiple contributions on alternative dispute resolution, namely by Roberta Clerici, Nikos Lavranos, Antonio Leandro, Maria Chiara Malaguti, Facundo Pérez-Aznar, next to a co-authored piece by Michael McIlrwath and Chiara Tondini. These articles are the written elaboration of the authors' presentations given at the ILA Italy Biennial Conference held at the University of Ferrara on November 16, 2023. Credit for the excellent organisation of the event goes to Serena Forlati, Head of the Department of Law of Ferrara University and a most pro-active member of the Branch.

In the following Section, 'Views from International Lawyers', Luca Radicati di Brozolo, a former Secretary-General of ILA, a highly reputed scholar and arbitrator, offers an overview of the history of the works carried out by the ILA Committee on International Commercial Arbitration, of which he has been an active member and (co-)Rapporteur, assessing its contribution to the codification of key procedural legal institutions, with special regard to the *lis pendens* and *res judicata* principles. In the same Section, Cameron Miles, a barrister and an inter-State counsel, wrote an inspiring and witty piece catering especially to young readers embarking, or wishing to embark on, an international law career.

In order to keep our members, but also the wider legal community, up to date with the works conducted by the ILA Committees and Study Groups, Giovanna Adinolfi and Mirko Sossai, ILA Italy board members, edited a Section of the Yearbook containing reports by Italian members of those bodies.

A separate Section is devoted to the assessment of the impact of the ILA works on international judicial and arbitral practice, for which credit goes to the members of the Yearbook Editorial Board: Carlotta Ceretelli, Donato Greco, Mariangela La Manna, Giuliana Lampo and Andrea Mensi.

In the last Section, Alberto Malatesta reviewed the book *To the Benefit of International Law* (Panthéon-Assas and Pedone 2023), edited by Catherine Kessedjian, Olivier Descamps, and Teodolinda Fabrizi at the occasion of the 150th anniversary of the ILA.

Given the especially troublesome present juncture in international affairs, the issue opens with an article by Attila Tanzi, who identifies societal weaknesses and political incapacity rather than law inherent limits as the main factors undermining the effectiveness of international law in the 21st century.

Finally, we would like to take this opportunity to express our gratitude to Gianni & Origoni and Watson Farley & Williams, among the top international law firms active in Italy, not only for the generous support they provided to ILA Italy in the realisation of this Yearbook but also for embracing our effort to enhance relations between Academia, public and private international law scholars and legal practitioners.

Milan, September 15, 2024.

Alberto Malatesta
Secretary-General of ILA Italy

Attila M Tanzi
President of ILA Italy

The Italian Branch of the International Law Association

*Gabriella Venturini**

Writing an introduction to the first volume of the Yearbook of the Italian branch of the International Law Association makes me rather emotional, thinking back to all the years that I have been a member and participated in the works of the ILA international committees and study groups. The ILA gave me the opportunity of working close to eminent colleagues and learning a great deal from them. Indeed, the majority of international research collaborations I have taken part in had their origin in the ILA community.

We should remember and be proud that Italian lawyers intensely participated to the activities of the ILA since its inception. One of the driving forces behind the initiative was Pasquale Stanislao Mancini, the eminent Italian jurist, diplomat and statesman who was also a co-founder and the first President of the *Institut de Droit International*. It is notable that two of the first ILA biennial conferences were held in Italy. In 1883, the Milan conference was devoted to everlasting maritime issues such as the slave trade and collisions at sea, as well as to jurisdictional matters like the rules for the execution of foreign judgements. In 1892, in Genoa, the ILA conference especially focused on the many aspects of state jurisdiction in territorial waters. The conference's president was senator Paolo Boselli, later to become minister of the Kingdom of Italy and head of the Italian government.

For decades, the Italian members of the ILA carried out their collaborative activities on an informal basis. As a consequence of this, records or documents related to the domestic initiatives are rarely found. Eventually, the first statutes of the Italian branch were approved in 1925. Their articles provided that the branch was ruled by a president and a secretary-general, the latter also serving as treasurer. They were assisted by a board of ten members designated by co-optation and with no time limits. The nomination of the Italian members who would join the ILA international committees was the exclusive prerogative of the president.

The 1925 statutes, only slightly amended in 1945, governed the activity of ILA Italy up to few less than one century. Since their adoption, prominent jurists

* Professor Emerita, University of Milan; Associate Member, Institut de Droit International; Council Member, International Institute of Humanitarian Law; Former President, ILA Italy.

 | DOI:10.1163/9789004727663_002

served as president, secretary-general and members of the board. Among them were Tomaso Perassi, whose seminal works delved into the relationship between international law and the domestic legal system as well as on the law of the United Nations. Eminent specialists in the fields of commercial law and company law like Torquato Carlo Giannini and Tullio Ascarelli also contributed to the activities and prestige of the branch.

It must be recognized that he unlimited duration of terms of office was a source of stability for the Italian branch. Renowned academics and specialists, who also held important international positions in both domestic institutions and international organisations, served with continuity and for extended periods of time as branch presidents, secretaries-general and members of ILA committees. Mario Scerni served as president of the Italian branch from 1966 to 1982 and, since 1972, he was assisted by Giuseppe Guerreri, attorney at law in Rome, who acted as secretary-general of the branch for the following thirty years. While Professor Scerni first served in the committee on deep sea mining, piracy, air and sea, and subsequently in the committee on the law of the sea, Mr Guerreri was a member of the committees on air law and on legal aspects of air traffic control. In consideration of his longstanding and worthwhile activity in both the Italian branch and in the ILA committees, Mr. Guerreri was then co-opted as a member of the ILA Executive Council, in which he assiduously participated until his passing. Francesco Capotorti served for forty years, from 1958 until 1998, first in the committee on family law and then in the committee on the formation of customary international law. In 1984, he succeeded Mario Scerni to the presidency of the Italian branch that he held until 2000. Afterward Luigi Ferrari Bravo became the president of the branch and remained in office until 2012.

The Italian doctrine of international law, traditionally embracing public international law as well as studies on conflict of laws, has constantly been part of the long-lasting activities of the ILA international committees straddling the 20th and the 21st centuries. Thus, Italian members have significantly contributed to the development of the ILA declarations, resolutions and other legal documents. Gaetano Morelli served in the committee on international company law in the 1950s. From 1950 until the late 1970s Roberto Ago served first in the committee on human rights, then in the committee on international commercial arbitration. In the 1950s and 1960s Riccardo Monaco served in the committees on the United Nations charter and on the succession of new states to the treaties. Giuseppe Sperduti served for thirty years in the committees on state immunity and on human rights. Francesco Capotorti served first in the family law committee and then in the committee on the formation of customary international law.

The membership of Tullio Treves in the international monetary law committee, starting from 1970, continued uninterrupted for more than forty years. He was succeeded by Chiara Zilioli, then director of the Legal office and now general counsel of the European Central Bank (ECB). Giorgio Sacerdoti served in the ILA committees on international terrorism, international commercial arbitration, on the legal aspects of the international economic order and international trade law, starting in 1972 and until 2004. Manlio Frigo has been serving since 1990 in the cultural heritage law committee and in its successor committee on participation in global cultural heritage governance. Natalino Ronzitti chaired the committee on reparation for victims of armed conflict, which in 2014 adopted the ILA Declaration of international law principles on reparation for victims of armed conflict, later presented at the Accademia nazionale dei Lincei in Rome. Tens of members of the Italian branch, professors of international law, international lawyers or officers of international institutions, are presently serving in the ILA committees and study groups in the fields of both public and private international law.

I first became a member of the Italian branch in the mid-eighties. I remember with great feeling president Capotorti and secretary-general Guerreri, who governed the branch in great accord. In the nineties, my experience as member of the Italian delegation at the Committee on the Peaceful Uses of Outer Space (COPUOS) of the United Nations (UN) favoured my participation in the committee on space law, where I had the privilege to work with Karl-Heinz Böckstiegel, Maureen Williams and Stephen Hobe. Later on, I joined the committee on nuclear weapons, non-proliferation and international law. In the wake of its initiatives, I contributed with chapters to several volumes of the Springer series on *Nuclear non-proliferation in international law* directed by Jonathan Black-Branch and Dieter Fleck, chair and rapporteur of the ILA committee. I also participated in the study group on the conduct of hostilities under international humanitarian law, the final report of which was published by the U.S. Naval College in its periodical *International Legal Studies*. This is how the substantive work done in the ILA committees reverberates on the scholarly activity of their members.

Assuming the presidency of the Italian branch in 2013 was a privilege and a challenge that I accepted with some trepidation. I am deeply grateful to Alberto Malatesta for his constant support and cooperation as well as to Mariangela La Manna, who put her talent and enthusiasm at the service of ILA Italy. Our goal has been to foster initiatives by branch members and to intensify cooperation with other branches in Europe and overseas. In a short time, the growth in the number of members resulted in the increase of ILA Italy's involvement in the

ILA endeavours. I am glad to say that in parallel the number of women in the branch grew up to reach substantive gender equality.

In the following years, ILA Italy was able to organise or sponsor a number of seminars and conferences in the field of public international law addressing topics such as sovereign states' insolvency and international crises' management; international commercial and investment arbitration and its contribution to the development of international law; developments of the international justice, with special regard to World Trade Organization (WTO) case-law; international trade law and the green economy; United Nations sanctions; protection of persons in times of disaster; protection of cultural property and United Nations Educational, Scientific and Cultural Organization (UNESCO) World Heritage; sustainable natural resources governance; and many others. As for private international law subjects such as international contracts law as well as private international law relating to civil procedure were extensively covered. National research and study groups were active on rural sustainability and food security, cross-border insolvency, and identification of customary international law, this latter at the invitation of the Codification division of the UN Office of Legal Affairs. Intersessional meetings of ILA committees and study groups were also held in Pisa at the Sant'Anna school of advanced studies on the topic of human rights in times of emergency, and in Florence on individual responsibility in international law, in cooperation with the French branch. ILA Italy actively developed cooperation with universities and other academic institutions and professional associations, such as the Italian association for arbitration, the Interuniversity centre on the law of international organizations, and the International Institute for the Unification of Private Law (UNIDROIT).

Eventually we felt it was time to revise and update our statutes dating back to the past century. We drafted the new Statutes in accordance with the ILA Constitution, which sets the purpose of furthering the study and development of international law, both public and private. ILA Italy undertakes to support ILA's activities through participation in the committees and study groups of the association, as well as by means of research, meetings, seminars and conferences on related topics. The branch is governed by the president, who is responsible for the relations with the ILA Headquarters and for designating the Italian members in committees and study groups. He is assisted by the secretary-general, who also performs the functions of treasurer, and by a board entrusted with the preparation of national events and initiatives. All bodies are elected by the assembly of members for a four-years period, renewable once. The assembly also elects the three members of the internal audit committee.

The text of the new statutes were submitted to the members of the branch and approved after extensive discussion on 8 November 2019.

I am pleased to say that the new statutes proved to be effectively workable. Since 2021 Attila Tanzi, who succeeded me as branch president, together with Alberto Malatesta who continues as secretary-general and treasurer, further incremented both the number and the credentials of the branch members, attracting diplomats and cross-border lawyers along with young and dynamic academics. This fostered initiatives in the areas of alternative dispute resolution in international and European Union (EU) law; sustainable international investment law; climate change and the energy transition; migration and international law; advisory competence of international tribunals; international crimes and state immunity; and many others. Finally, and in line with the long-standing tradition of the branch, some members have been called to act in the international arena. I mentioned Chiara Zilioli as general counsel of the ECB. Besides, Maria Chiara Malaguti is currently serving as president of the UNIDROIT; Ida Caracciolo has been appointed as judge of the International Tribunal for the Law of the Sea and Giuseppe Nesi is a member of the International Law Commission (ILC).

It is now appropriate to share ILA Italy's experience and achievements not only among the branch's members, but also with all those committed to promoting research in, and development of international law. I am confident that this new-born Yearbook will soon find its way to becoming an effective tool to enhance research on international law and practice, by consolidating and renewing the long tradition of our branch.

Editorial

Women, Peace and Security: Where Now?

*Christine Chinkin**

I am delighted to have been invited to contribute to the inaugural Italian Yearbook of International Law, established to celebrate the 100th anniversary of the Italian branch of the International Law Association and congratulate the Italian branch on this achievement.

1 Introduction[1]

In 2022 my monograph *Women Peace and Security in International Law* was published by Cambridge University Press. The book is a revised version of the Hersch Lauterpacht Memorial Lectures I delivered in 2016 where I reflected on Women, Peace and Security (WPS) as a widely recognised global agenda involving multiple actors, at both the national and international levels. WPS has emerged as a foreign and defence policy initiative in many Countries, as evidenced by the adoption of National Action Plans (NAPS) for domestic implementation by over 100 States, including Italy.[2] It is the subject of extensive writing by scholars within international relations, peace and conflict studies[3] and is the subject of much activism by non-governmental organisations (NGOs).[4] There is an annual WPS open debate in the Security Council of the United Nations (UN) and regional organisations including the European Union, the African Union and NATO have integrated WPS principles into their policies and operations. But WPS remains scarcely referenced in international

* Professorial Research Fellow, London School of Economics; Executive Chair, International Law Association.

1 This contribution has been written with support from a European Research Council Advanced Grant on 'Gendered Peace' under the European Union's 2020 Horizon Research and innovation programme (Grant Agreement No, 786494).

2 Italy adopted its first NAP in 2010, followed by further NA s in 2014, 2016 and 2020; see <https://www.wpsnaps.org/nap/italian-national-action-plan-ii/> accessed 23 September 2024.

3 See for instance the many contributions in Sara E Davies and Jacqui True (eds), *Oxford Handbook of Women, Peace and Security* (OUP 2019); *Soumita Basu, Paul Kirby and Laura J Shepherd (eds), New Directions in Women, Peace and Security (Bristol UP 2020).*

4 The NGO Working Group on WPS is 'a consensus-based coalition of 19 international non-governmental organizations (NGOs) working to advance the Women, Peace and Security agenda at the United Nations and around the world' <https://www.womenpeacesecurity.org/about/> accessed 23 September 2024.

 | DOI:10.1163/9789004727663_003

legal literature and seems largely unknown to – or at least discounted by – 'mainstream' international lawyers.[5] In the lectures and the book I sought to understand why this is the case and to redress this silence by examining WPS through the lens of international law and querying whether it could be understood as a special regime of international law grounded in customary international law. In this article I discuss developments since the book's publication and consider the tensions that are created by an agenda that is seen as progressive by its civil society proponents but which does not fit easily within the institutional space of the UN. I ask from the perspectives of advancement of women's rights and peace: where now?

2 The WPS Agenda 2000–2019

2.1 *The Pillars of WPS*

This first section sets the scene by briefly recapping the WPS agenda.[6] WPS as a UN Security Council agenda comprises ten Security Council resolutions commencing with Resolution 1325 in 2000,[7] supplemented by Presidential Statements. Resolution 1325 was the first Council resolution 'to expressly consider the impact of wars and conflicts on women and the contribution of women to conflict resolution and lasting peace.'[8] It implicitly recognises that conflict – like all other social interactions – is gendered. Women and men have different roles, experiences, needs and priorities in conflict and post-conflict but traditionally it has been the experiences of men that have formed the basis of decision and policy making, including law making while those of women and girls and of socially marginalised groups are silenced or discounted. WPS is about

5 There are of course exceptions; see Gina Heathcote and Dianne Otto (eds), *Rethinking Peacekeeping, Gender Equality and Collective Security* (Palgrave Macmillan 2014); Hilary Charlesworth, 'Are Women Peaceful? Reflections on the Role of Women in Peace-Building' (2008) 16 Feminist Legal Studies 347.

6 Christine Chinkin, *Women, Peace and Security and International Law* (CUP 2022) 1 ff.

7 UNSC Res 1325 (31 October 2000) UN Doc S/RES/1325(2000); UNSC Res 1820 (9 June 2008) UN Doc S/RES/1820(2008); UNSC Res 1888 (30 September 2009) UN Doc S/RES/1888(2009); UNSC Res 1889 (5 October 2009) UN Doc S/RES/1889(2009); UNSC Res 1960 (16 December 2010) UN Doc S/RES/1960; UNSC Res 2106 (24 June 2013) UN Doc S/RES/2106(2013); UNSC Res 2122 (18 October 2013) UN Doc S/RES/2122(2013); UNSC Res 2242 (13 October 2015) UN Doc S/RES/2242(2015); UNSC Res 2467 (23 April 2019) UN Doc S/RES/2467(2019); UNSC Res 2493 (29 October 2019) UN Doc S/RES/2493(2019).

8 Inter-Ministerial Committee for Human Rights, 'Italy's IV Plan of Action on Women, Peace and Security (2020–2024), in accordance with UN Security Council Resolution 1325 (2000)' (Rome, 10 December 2020) 6.

promoting a concept of peace and of security that is relevant to women as well as to men and giving effect to a gendered analysis of conflict and post-conflict that provides stakeholders – States, international and national institutions and local communities – with the basis for inclusive gender-sensitive policy making and operations. Although the language of gender is used throughout the resolutions. the agenda is 'women, peace and security' not 'gender, peace and security'. The Security Council conflates gender with women and assumes the binary women/men. The WPS resolutions are not inclusive and do not address how conflict impacts upon LGBTQI people.[9]

Founding Resolution 1325 has three major themes. First, after reaffirming what it called 'the important role of women in the prevention and resolution of conflicts and in peace-building' it urges gender balance in participants in all processes for conflict prevention, management and resolution, in UN field operations and in positions such as special envoys or representatives of the UN Secretary-General. For the Security Council this entails increasing women's participation in peace processes, UN peace operations and special procedures. Second, Resolution 1325 calls on all actors involved in post-conflict reconstruction to ensure a gender perspective in all decision and policy-making about armed conflict and its aftermath. In effect this requires gender mainstreaming: making the concerns, perceptions and experiences of women and men, girls and boys 'an integral dimension of the design, implementation, monitoring and evaluation of policies and programmes in all political, economic and societal spheres so that women and men benefit equally and inequality is not perpetuated.'[10] Third, the Council expresses its concern that 'civilians, particularly women and children, account for the vast majority of those adversely affected by armed conflict, … and increasingly are targeted' in armed conflict. It demands accountability and an end to impunity for perpetrators of sexual violence against women and girls that constitutes a war crime and crime against humanity.

Resolution 1325 was not followed up for 8 years until Resolution 1820 was adopted in 2008.[11] This resolution shifted the focus to deal explicitly with sexual

---

9 The Special Representative of the Secretary-General on Conflict-Related Sexual Violence does note the incidence of such crimes against those who identify as LGBTQI persons; Report of the Secretary-General, 'Annual Report on Conflict-Related Sexual Violence' (2022) UN Doc S/2022/272 para 24. See more generally Dianne Otto (ed), *Queering International Law Possibilities, Alliances, Complicities, Risks* (Routledge 2019).

10 Office of the Special Adviser on Gender Issues and Advancement of Women, 'Gender Mainstreaming: An Overview' (UN 2002) V-VI.

11 Six Security Council Presidential Statements on WPS were adopted between Resolution 1325 and Resolution 1820: UNSC Presidential Statement 32 (2002) UN Doc S/PRST/2002/32;

violence and protection of women and girls from sexual violence in armed conflict.[12] It recognises that women are disproportionately targeted and asserts that 'when used or commissioned as a tactic of war in order to deliberately target civilians or as a part of a widespread or systematic attack against civilian populations, sexual violence can significantly exacerbate situations of armed conflict and may impede the restoration of international peace and security'. Accordingly, 'effective steps to prevent and respond to such acts of sexual violence can significantly contribute to the maintenance of international peace and security'. Resolution 1820 is also a landmark resolution in that it elucidates that rape and sexual violence are not inevitable and unfortunate byproducts of war but may be – and are – used as a deliberate tactic and weapon of war. Security Council Resolution 2242 adopted in 2015 extended the understanding of rape and sexual violence as a tactic of war to encompass a tactic of terror, highlighting its deliberate use as part of the ideology and strategic objectives of certain terrorist or violent extremist groups to increase their power through supporting, financing, recruitment, and the destruction of communities.[13]

The subsequent eight WPS resolutions picked up and developed these initial themes so that taken together it is often said that WPS comprises four pillars:

- Participation and representation of women and girls in decision and policy making about conflict and post-conflict;
- Prevention of sexual violence against women and girls and prevention of conflict;
- Protection against sexual violence through measures such as enhancing military discipline and ensuring women's access to justice mechanisms;
- Post-conflict relief including through humanitarian delivery and long-term recovery through post-conflict reconstruction, disarmament, demobilization and reintegration (DDR) processes and reparations.

UNSC Presidential Statement 40 (2004) UN Doc S/PRST/2004/40; UNSC Presidential Statement 52 (2005) UN Doc S/PRST/2005/52; UNSC Presidential Statement 42 (2006) UN Doc S/PRST/2006/42; UNSC Presidential Statement 5 (2007) UN Doc S/PRST/2007/5; UNSC Presidential Statement 40 (2007) UN Doc S/PRST/2007/40.

12 As a non-permanent member of the Security Council at the time Italy 'played a leading role in the negotiations to assure that the connection between international security and sexual violence was finally recognized.' Inter-ministerial Committee on Human Rights General Directorate for Political Affairs and Security, 'National Action Plan of Italy on "Women, Peace and Security" 2010–2013' (Rome, 23 December 2010) 2.

13 UNSC Resolution 2242 was adopted against the backdrop of the extreme violence committed by ISIS and other terrorist and extremist groups; Report of the Secretary-General, 'Conflict-related sexual violence' (2015) UN Doc S/2015/203; Report of the Secretary-General, 'Women and peace and security' (2015) UN Doc S/2015/716.

The resolutions portray women without explanation as 'good at peace' and as having 'special needs' in conflict, primarily for protection against sexual violence. Women's multiple other experiences of conflict are not explored, nor are the intersections between gender and other axes of discrimination such as race, ethnicity or sexuality. Men are similarly essentialised through being simultaneously implicitly labelled as perpetrators of sexual violence and as protectors of women through peacekeeping and military operations. Only two resolutions refer to the possibility of men and boys as victims of sexual violence[14] but these do not address their 'special needs'. Later WPS resolutions modify to some extent the depiction of women as passive victims of violence in conflict through emphasising the importance of their empowerment,[15] leadership[16] and a survivor-centred approach to decision-making about sexual violence in conflict.[17] The Security Council calls on States to build the capacity of civil society groups so as to enhance community-level protection mechanisms and to hold civil society briefings on local contexts.

The WPS resolutions[18] have led to the growth of what might be called a WPS industry in conflict-affected areas with new posts and positions instituted within the UN, for instance: women protection officers and teams of experts on rule of law and criminal investigation to work with national authorities and with peacekeeping missions to collect and collate evidence. In 2009 Resolution 1888 established the post of the Special Representative of the Secretary-General (SRSG) on Sexual Violence in Armed Conflict to 'provide coherent and strategic leadership' in strengthening coordination within UN mechanisms and advocating for more effective measures in tackling sexual violence in armed conflict.[19] The SRSG is responsible for the Secretary-General's annual report to

14 UNSC Res 2106 (24 June 2013) UN Doc S/RES/2106(2013); UNSC Res 2467 (23 April 2019) UN Doc S/RES/2467(2019).

15 'Beijing Declaration and Platform for Action', Fourth World Conference on Women (Beijing, 4–15 September 1995) A/CONF.177/20 (1995)/Rev.1 para 7: States dedicated themselves to enhancing the 'empowerment and advancement of women all over the world'; empowerment first enters the WPS lexicon in UNSC Res 1888 (30 September 2009) UN Doc S/RES/1888(2009) preamble: 'promotion and empowerment of women and … support for women's organizations and networks are essential in the consolidation of peace'.

16 Women's leadership is introduced in UNSC Res 1889 (5 October 2009) UN Doc S/RES/1889(2009) principle 1: urging 'further measures to improve women's participation during all stages of peace processes, … including by enhancing their engagement in political and economic decision-making at early stages of recovery processes, through inter alia promoting women's leadership and capacity'.

17 UNSC Res 2467 (23 April 2019) UN Doc S/RES/2467(2019) paras 8 and 16.

18 See especially UNSC Res 1888 (30 September 2009) UN Doc S/RES/1888(2009).

19 Ibid principle 4.

the Security Council which provides detailed information on and lists parties to armed conflict that are credibly suspected of committing or being responsible for acts of rape or other forms of sexual violence with the possible outcome of the Council imposing targeted sanctions against them.[20]

The four WPS pillars are grounded in existing special regimes of public international law:

- International Humanitarian Law which prohibits rape and enforced prostitution in international armed conflict[21] and outrages on personal dignity, humiliating and degrading treatment in non-international armed conflict;[22]
- International Criminal Law which recognises forms of conflict-related sexual violence as constituting war crimes and crimes against humanity when the other required elements for these crimes are present;[23]
- International Human Rights Law, in particular the Convention on the Elimination of All Forms of Discrimination (CEDAW) which is explicitly brought into resolution 1325 and resolution 2467 in 2019.[24]
- Refugee law, through the 1951 Refugee Convention.[25]

2.2 *The Genealogy of WPS*

Women, peace and security is a thematic agenda of the Security Council. It is not a response to an identified threat to international peace and security or act of aggression under UN Charter Chapter VII, triggered by Article 39. It is not directed at a named country mandating measures to be undertaken

20 UNSC Res 1960 (16 December 2010) UN Doc S/RES/1960 (2010) principle 17(c).

21 Convention Relative to the Protection of Civilian Persons (adopted 12 August 1949, entered into force 21 October 1950) 75 UNTS 287 (Fourth Geneva Convention) art 27; Protocol Additional to the Geneva Conventions of 12 August 1949 and relating to the Protection of Victims of International Armed Conflicts (adopted 8 June 1977, entered into force 7 December 1979) 1125 UNTS 3 (Additional Protocol I) art 76.

22 Fourth Geneva Convention art 3; Protocol Additional to the Geneva Conventions of 12 August 1949 and relating to the Protection of Victims of Non-International Armed Conflicts (adopted 8 June 1977, entered into force 7 December 1978) 1125 UNTS 609 (Additional Protocol II) art 4(2)(e).

23 Rome Statute of the International Criminal Court (adopted 17 July 1998, entered into force 1 July 2002) 2187 UNTS 3 (Rome Statute) art 7 (1)(g) ('rape, sexual slavery, enforced prostitution, forced pregnancy, enforced sterilization or any other form of sexual violence of comparable gravity' as crimes against humanity); art 8(b)(xxii) (the same crimes as violations of the laws and customs of war in international armed conflict); and art 8(e)(vi) (violation in non-international armed conflict).

24 UNSC Res 1325 (31 October 2000) UN Doc S/RES/1325 (2000) principle 9; UNSC Res 2467 (23 April 2019) UN Doc S/RES/2467 (2019) principle 18.

25 UNSC Res 1325 (31 October 2000) UN Doc S/RES/1325 (2000) principle 9.

by Member States but is non-specific, directed at conflict situations in general. The resolutions are presumably adopted under Chapter VI of the Charter although this is not spelled out. It is one of several themes taken up by the Council in the past decades. Other thematic resolutions include those relating to children and armed conflict, protection of civilians in armed conflict, HIV AIDS, food security, youth, peace and security and, most recently, the impact of COVID-19. In common with all these agendas, WPS comes within the Security Council's primary responsibility for the maintenance of international peace and security, as stipulated in Article 24 of the Charter.

WPS however has a different genealogy from other thematic agendas in that the impetus and lobbying for Resolution 1325 did not come from within the UN and was not State-driven. It emanated from civil society through a number of NGOs working together.[26] While the NGOs advocating for Resolution 1325 had different priorities, this first WPS resolution was lobbied for as a woman's rights agenda and a women's peace agenda. This dual agenda is reflected in the opening words of the UK's 2018–2022 NAP which asserts that 'the global WPS agenda exists to promote and fulfil women's human rights and achieve gender equality as part of efforts to build more peaceful and stable societies for all.'[27] It may be described as a human security agenda for women.

But this dual character has produced institutional tension. Within the UN, human rights and social justice come within the authority of the General Assembly, the Economic and Social Council and the Human Rights Council, a subsidiary body of the General Assembly. Women's advancement and gender equality are the domain of the Commission on the Status of Women (CSW) and UN Women. The Security Council has no mandate relating to gender, gender mainstreaming or human rights except in so far as these issues are pertinent to the maintenance of international peace and security. Nor does it have the appropriate expertise.[28]

Why then it might be asked was 1325 lobbied for within the Security Council? The answer lies in frustration at previous attempts at securing women's interests within international institutions and in the growing strength of women's global networking, coalition building and lobbying within international

26 Sanam Naraghi Anderlini, 'Civil Society's Leadership in Adopting 1325 Resolution' in Sara E Davies and Jacqui True (eds), Oxford Handbook of Women, Peace and Security (OUP 2019) 38–52.

27 UK Government, 'National Action Plan on Women, Peace & Security 2018–2022' (London, 16 January 2018) 3.

28 Jennifer Klot, 'The United Nations Security Council's Agenda on Women, Peace and Security: Bureaucratic Pathologies and Unrealised Potential' (PhD thesis, London School of Economics and Political Science 2015).

fora. The last were especially forged through the global summits on women that were held throughout the UN Decade for Women, 1975–1985.[29] These were the primary place for the pursuit of a women's agenda within the UN with the specified objectives of equality, development and peace.[30] The conferences formed a new – institutional – episode in the long history of women's activism for peace and women's rights. Ten years after the end of the Decade, the immediate forerunner to resolution 1325 was the Beijing Declaration and Platform for Action (PFA) adopted by the 4th World Conference on Women in 1995. PFA Critical Area of Concern E addressed women and armed conflict and included among its strategic objectives that States and other international actors should increase women's participation in conflict resolution.[31]

Frustration followed at the disconnect between Beijing and power politics that was exemplified by the Dayton peace process[32] where there was a single woman participant – a UK Foreign and Commonwealth representative – and no provision with respect to the widespread and systematic sexual violence committed throughout the war in Bosnia-Herzegovina. This led NGO attention to turn from the General Assembly and CSW (the UN bodies responsible for implementation of the PFA) to the more powerful Security Council, seeking that body's stamp of authority and legitimacy for advancement of women's interests.[33] Support for a Security Council resolution was given by some States, notably Namibia and Bangladesh with the UK and Canada also to the fore and by the UN Development Fund for Women (UNIFEM) which acted as a conduit between the NGOs and the Council. The adoption of 1325 – the first Security Council resolution explicitly appertaining to women – was widely celebrated

29 The three World Conferences of Women were convened in Mexico City (in 1975), Copenhagen (in 1980) and Nairobi (in 1985).

30 The Decade objectives were proclaimed in UNGA Res 3010 (XXVII) (18 December 1972) UN Doc A/RES/3010(XXVII) and were continued through to the Fourth World Conference on Women held in Beijing in 1995.

31 Participation in peace processes had long been a demand of women's activists. See for instance the resolution that 'representatives of the people' should participate in the post-World War I peace settlement, including women; 'Resolutions Adopted at the Hague Congress' in Jane Addams, Emily Greene Balch and Alice Hamilton (eds), Women at The Hague: The International Congress of Women and Its Results (MacMillan 1915) at <https://documents.alexanderstreet.com/d/1000674016> accessed 23 September 2024.

32 The General Framework Agreement for Peace for Bosnia and Herzegovina was negotiated at Dayton in the autumn of 1995 and signed in Paris 14 December 1995 just months after the Beijing Conference.

33 There was no role envisaged for the Security Council in the PFA; Jennifer Klot, 'The United Nations Security Council's Agenda on Women, Peace and Security: Bureaucratic Pathologies and Unrealised Potential' (PhD thesis, London School of Economics and Political Science 2015).

by women activists and scholars as having successfully raised the profile of matters of concern to women by bringing them into the power base of the UN.

This unorthodox process and outcome – a civil society inspired Security Council thematic resolution – has had significant consequences for women's NGOs and the Council. Women's NGOs have sought to keep some ownership of WPS through the activities of the NGO Working Group on Women, Peace and Security and of specific NGOs, notably the Women's League for International Peace and Freedom (WILPF). The former prepares monthly action points for the Council, provides briefings and monitors the Council's implementation of WPS. WILPF has a dedicated programme, PeaceWomen, on WPS and similarly monitors Security Council (in)action[34] and State NAPs. Advocacy by these and other NGOs has enhanced provision for civil society engagement with the Council notably in Resolution 2242 in 2015.[35]

Adoption of Resolution 1325 brought 'women and armed conflict' from the Beijing PFA into the Council's security agenda, dominated by the power dynamics of the five permanent members (P5) and where security is understood in terms of militarised national security, not human security. This has seen the securitisation of threats including those emanating from terrorism and violent extremism, justifying surveillance, the establishment of military bases and military intervention, all of which impact adversely on women's security. Other measures included in the Beijing strategic objectives on women and armed conflict concerning the reduction of military expenditures, disarmament of both nuclear and conventional weapons, non-violent methods of dispute resolution and fostering a culture of peace find no place in the WPS resolutions.[36] This is unsurprising considering the P5's status as nuclear weapon States and leading arms dealers. These additional measures had been

34 Eg., Sarah Kenny Werner and Elena B Stavreska, 'Where are the Words? The Disappearance of the Women, Peace and Security Agenda in the Language of Country-Specific UN Security Council Resolutions' (WILPF 2020) (discussing the Security Council's omission of the language of WPS from UN Charter chapter VII mandates).

35 UNSC Res 2242 (13 October 2015) UN Doc S/RES/2242 (2015) principle 5(a): 'Expresses its intention to convene meetings of relevant Security Council experts as part of an Informal Experts Group on Women, Peace and Security to facilitate a more systematic approach to Women, Peace and Security within its own work and enable greater oversight and coordination of implementation efforts'; principle 5(c) expressed the Council's intention to 'to invite civil society, including women's organizations, to brief the Council in Country-specific considerations and relevant thematic areas'.

36 The UNGA designated 2000 as the International Year for the Culture of Peace; UNGA Res 52/15 (15 January 1998) UN Doc A/RES/52/15. UNSC Res 1325 (31 October 2000) UN Doc S/RES/1325 (2000) makes no reference to this.

lobbied for by at least some NGOs[37] but were dropped as part of the price for achieving Security Council validation of the relevance of women's interests; the linguistic move from 'equality, development and peace' to 'women, peace and security' was perhaps too little remarked but it signified the new concentration on security. The transformative potential of WPS that had been hoped for was thus lost at the outset as it became subsumed into the Security Council's security agenda. WPS has enabled the Council to co-opt women and to be used to legitimate its actions for instance in the context of counter-terrorism rather than WPS changing the Council's militaristic mindset.

Zeynep Kaya has aptly summarised the WPS agenda as having 'one foot planted in traditional [SC] security conceptions and structures and the other in transnational and feminist peace activism'.[38] This has created a tension between the 'urge to reflect existing international power structures and normative frameworks and the desire to eliminate, or at least reduce, gender inequalities and include women in peacebuilding.' WPS 'does not represent feminist peace or feminist security, mainly because of this dual position of being both an agenda for feminists and for the UN Security Council.' The former is better strived for within the GA and the human rights bodies despite their weaker authority. The latter's objective appears to be limited to making conflict safer and more humane for women and girls through condemning sexual and gender-based violence and offering reparation rather than to preventing conflict through tackling its root causes, advancing women's rights or securing peace.

The location of WPS within the Security Council has not however been considered appropriate by all its members. Russia and China have expressed their opinion that the Council is overstepping its mandate and process. For instance in the open debate in 2015 which followed the adoption of Resolution 2242, the most progressive of the WPS resolutions,[39] Russia reiterated that the Beijing Declaration and PFA remained 'key guidelines' for expanding women's rights and opportunities and that the Council should maintain the allocated 'division

37 The Women's International League for Peace and Freedom (WILPF), the oldest women's peace and human rights NGO established following the 1915 Women's Congress in the Hague and the Hague Appeal for Peace; Jennifer Klot, 'The United Nations Security Council's Agenda on Women, Peace and Security: Bureaucratic Pathologies and Unrealised Potential' (PhD thesis, London School of Economics and Political Science 2015).

38 Zeynep Kaya, 'Feminist Peace and Security in the Middle East and North Africa', in 'Transforming Power to Put Women at the Heart of Peacebuilding: A Collection of Regional-Focused Essays on Feminist Peace and Security' (Oxfam 2020) at <https://oxfamilibrary.openrepository.com/bitstream/handle/10546/621051/dp-feminist-peace-security-essay-collection-210920-en.pdf> accessed 23 September 2024.

39 UNSC Res 2242 (13 October 2015) UN Doc S/RES/2242(2015) is progressive for example in its linkage between WPS and other security threats including climate change and potential global health pandemics.

of labour' within the UN.[40] The Russian delegate also expressed concern about the procedural innovation in Resolution 2242 to set up an informal expert group to brief the Council: a 'dubious approach that is aimed at establishing more and more auxiliary bodies covering various items on the agenda.' China too referred to the Beijing Conference for its 'great and far-reaching significance for the development of the global cause of women'.[41] It also argued that the existing UN mechanisms should each play their own role, that the Security Council should strengthen its coordination with the General Assembly, ECOSOC and UN Women but that it should perform fully its primary role for the maintenance of international peace and security. There should, the Chinese representative stated, be caution about setting up new mechanisms.

3 The Fracturing of WPS

Despite their reservations both China and Russia voted with the other members of the Security Council for the unanimous adoption of Resolution 2242, as had been the case with all the previous WPS resolutions. But in 2019 this consensus was fragmented and what remain to date the final two WPS resolutions[42] were adopted in what had become a changed social and political environment. There had been no new WPS resolution since Resolution 2242 in 2015 until in 2019 a new resolution was proposed by Germany. The context was not promising. In 2015 a Global Study on the Implementation of resolution 1325[43] had concluded that lack of implementation of its central pillars was the major weakness of WPS and that States did not match their rhetorical approval of the agenda with action or financial commitment. Sexual violence and other forms of gender violence in conflict continued at high rates[44] and women remained only sparsely represented in peace processes. The Secretary-General reported that between 1992 and 2019, women had constituted on average 13 per cent

40 UNSC Verbatim Record (13 October 2015) UN Doc S/PV/7533 21–23.

41 Ibid 20–21.

42 UNSC Res 2467 (23 April 2019) UN Doc S/RES/2467(2019); UNSC Res 2493 (29 October 2019) UN Doc S/RES/2493(2019).

43 Radhika Coomaraswamy and others, 'Preventing Conflict, Transforming Justice, Securing the Peace. A Global Study on the Implementation of Security Council Resolution 1325' (United Nations 2015).

44 'Despite important progress on the policy and operational fronts, we face an increasingly complex global security environment in which sexual violence remains a cruel tactic of war, torture, terror and political repression, and a brutally effective tool of displacement and dehumanization', Report of the Secretary-General, 'Conflict-related sexual violence' (2020) UN Doc S/2020/4873 para 3.

of negotiators, 6 per cent of mediators and 6 per cent of signatories in major peace processes worldwide and that the percentage of peace agreements with gender equality provisions had increased since 1995 but remained at 22 per cent. As of May 2020, 5.4 per cent of United Nations military personnel and 15.1 per cent of civilian police personnel were women, compared with 3 and 10 per cent, respectively, in 2015.[45] There had thus been some improvement but it was progress at a glacial rate.

By 2019 the pushback against human rights in general and against women's sexual and reproductive rights in particular was making itself felt. It was evidenced in record levels in 2019 of political violence targeting women.[46] The UN Special Rapporteur on the situation of human rights defenders reported that 'In the current political climate, in which there is a backlash against human rights, women defenders are often the first to come under attack.'[47] Violent resistance to their work was fuelled by the rise of populism, fundamentalism and extremism and the 'worrying rise in misogynistic, sexist and homophobic speech by prominent political leaders' normalised violence against women and non-binary persons'.[48] He also reported that funding for women's rights organisations had significantly dropped.[49] WPS – a progressive agenda for women despite its shortcomings – was confronted by authoritarian governments promoting an abusive gender ideology,[50] closing of political and civic space, by attempted erosion of human rights standards and by persistent and violent racism, homophobia, transphobia and misogyny.

For the first time consensus in adoption of WPS resolutions was fractured in 2019 when Russia and China abstained from Resolution 2467. The United States (under the first Trump administration) threatened to veto the Resolution and only voted in favour when language relating to women's sexual and

45 Report of the Secretary-General, 'Women and peace and security' (2020) UN Doc S/2020/946 para 7.

46 Report of the Secretary-General, 'Women and peace and security' (2019) UN Doc S/2019/800 para 4(b).

47 OHCHR, 'Report of the Special Rapporteur on the situation of human rights defenders. Situation of women human rights defenders' (2019) UN Doc A/HRC/40/60 para 7.

48 Ibid para 24.

49 Ibid para 25.

50 'Gender equality and the Istanbul Convention: a decade of action. Conference Report' Council of Europe Conference on 'Gender equality and the Istanbul Convention: a decade of action' (Berlin, 11 May 2021) discussing how attacks on the Convention on Preventing and Combating Violence against Women and Domestic Violence (adopted 11 May 2011, entered into force 1 August 2014) 3010 UNTS 107 (Istanbul Convention) are part of a 'wider, well organised and extremist global movement against the concept of gender that seeks to roll back human rights in Europe, specifically women's sexual and reproductive rights and LGBT+ rights.'

reproductive rights was removed.[51] Resolution 2467 was however progressive in some aspects; it emphasised a 'survivor-centred' approach; made strong provision for access to justice and for 'children born as result of sexual violence in conflict.'[52] Consensus was again secured for a second resolution in 2019[53] but it was bland, added little of substance and was primarily directed at preparing the ground for a new resolution on the 20th anniversary of 1325 in 2020.

There was however scepticism about celebrating this anniversary, which coincided with the 25th anniversary of the Beijing Conference. In the lead up to the 2020 annual debate on WPS, women's NGOs were expressing the view that the normative agenda was adequate, that a new resolution would be a distraction, that there was a risk of back sliding and that what was needed was political commitment to effective implementation and allocation of appropriate resources to this end.[54] A draft resolution put forward by the Russian Federation,[55] which held the presidency of the Council at the crucial time, was not adopted through failure to gain the required 10 affirmative votes. Objections to the draft resolution included that it did not meet the minimum standard with regard to the indispensable role of civil society in the implementation of the WPS agenda on the ground; there was insufficient reference to existing normative frameworks including CEDAW and the Committee's General Recommendation 30;[56] lack of meaningful language on the implementation of or

51 The German draft of UNSC Res 2467 (23 April 2019) UN Doc S/RES/2467(2019) included provision for emergency contraception, the safe termination of pregnancy and HIV prevention and treatment. UNSC Res 2467 has no language on sexual health and reproductive rights; principle 16(b) notes the 'link between sexual violence in armed conflict and post-conflict situations and HIV infection, and the disproportionate burden of HIV and AIDS on women and girls as a persistent obstacle and challenge to gender equality'.

52 Christine Chinkin and Madeleine Rees, 'Commentary on Security Council Resolution 2467 Continued State Obligation and Civil Society Action on Sexual Violence in Conflict' (LSE 2019) at <http:s//www.lse.ac.uk/women-peace-security/assets/documents/2019/Final-WPS-Commentary Report.pdf> accessed 23 September 2024.

53 UNSC Res 2493 (29 October 2019) UN Doc S/RES/2493 (2019).

54 Eg. 'it is not normative frameworks, civil society effort, or a lack of understanding of the gaps and challenges of WPS implementation that impede progress on the agenda. On the contrary, extensive blueprints exist, civil society actors have been working tirelessly towards building just, equitable, and sustainable communities, and report after report has shown where the problem lies ... What is missing in this picture is actionable commitment through structural shifts by powerful actors, including the UNSC, the UN, and Member States'; Women's International League for Peace & Freedom, 'UNSCR 1325 at 20 Years Perspectives from Feminist Peace Activists and Civil Society' (WILPF 2020) 41.

55 UNSC Draft Resolution (30 October 2020) UN Doc S/2020/1054.

56 UN Committee on the Elimination of Discrimination against Women, 'General Recommendation No. 30 on women in conflict prevention, conflict and post-conflict situations' (18 October 2013) UN Doc CEDAW/C/GC/30. The Committee reiterated 'the need for a concerted and integrated approach that places the implementation of the Security Council

accountability for WPS; and inadequate mention of the need for financing the agenda and overcoming structural barriers to gender equality.[57] In summarising these objections and explaining its decision to abstain, Belgium stated that 'Should the draft resolution be adopted, it would erode the hard-won gains of our predecessors'.[58]

There have been no new WPS resolutions since 2019 and the environment was further worsened by the onset of the Covid-19 pandemic the effects of which were already evident by the time of the October 2020 rejection of Russia's draft resolution. The pandemic and restrictions imposed in response – curfews, isolation, lockdown – increased rates of violence against women including in conflict-affected areas. Conflict and displacement are vectors of disease and gender-based violence. Restrictive measures prevented humanitarian aid bodies from bringing services to survivors; resources were diverted away from the health needs of those who had been subjected to sexual violence; protection measures that had been introduced were undermined or entirely withdrawn; monitoring and investigations were no longer possible with missions depleted by illness. Women who constitute the bulk of front-line health-care workers and shoulder most of the burden of care faced serious economic consequences of the crisis.[59]

The UN Secretary-General has described WPS as being at its core a crisis-prevention agenda[60] that centres the importance of women's human rights and women's leadership in preventing and responding to other forms of crisis, not just conflict. It could have been a blueprint for policy-making throughout the pandemic and its aftermath, thereby enhancing its significance This did not happen and women were largely excluded from State decision-making about responses to the pandemic. The Secretary-General cited a survey of 30 Countries that showed that on average only 24 per cent of members of COVID-19 task

---

agenda on women, peace and security into the broader framework of the implementation of the Convention and its Optional Protocol.' Ibid para 26.

57 See the summary of concerns about the draft resolution, NGO Working Group on Women, Peace and Security, 'Security Council members unite to protect the Women, Peace and Security agenda on its 20th anniversary' (30 October 2020) at <https://www.womenpeacesecurity.org/blog-unsc-protect-wps-agenda-20th-anniversary/> accessed 23 September 2024.

58 UNSC 'Letter dated 30 October 2020 from the President of the Security Council addressed to the Secretary-General and the Permanent Representatives of the members of the Security Council' (3 November 2020) UN Doc S/2020/1076 annex 17 (Statement by the Permanent Representative of Belgium to the United Nations, Philippe Kridelka).

59 Report of the Secretary-General, 'Women and peace and security' (2020) UN Doc S/2020/946 para 2.

60 Ibid para 4.

forces were women and in conflict-affected areas it was still lower, at 18 per cent.[61] Despite the Secretary-General's call for a global ceasefire during the pandemic, violent conflict continued and it was business as usual with respect to women's exclusion and marginalisation in peace processes. For instance, prior to the Taliban takeover in Afghanistan in August 2021 there was only one woman among the Taliban and Afghan government delegates that met in Moscow in March 2021 for attempted peace negotiations.[62] It was also business as usual with respect to the arms trade and militarism. In September 2021 – that is before the February 2022 invasion of Ukraine – the Secretary-General reported that 'amid a global pandemic, unprecedented stress in meeting people's social, economic and health needs and a 3.3 per cent contraction of the global economy, global military expenditure increased by 2.6 per cent, totalling nearly $2 trillion in 2020. Military spending as a share of gross domestic product saw the largest increase since the global financial crisis in 2009'.[63] We might well ask with the Secretary-General 'whose peace?' and 'whose security?' is being upheld.[64]

It has not been the peace or security of women in Afghanistan. The divided Council was shameful in its non-invocation of WPS and its inaction over the Taliban's seizing of power that put women, especially those who had participated in public life and advocated for democratic rights, at heightened risk. Civil society stepped in, compiling details of women at risk, seeking and arranging safe passage and evacuation routes for them. Many were not able to leave Kabul with accounts of women activists being killed or arrested while awaiting evacuation while 'resettlement schemes favoured those who supported the military rather than those who built peace and advanced human rights and democracy and were thus biased towards men.'[65] In December 2022 a range of UN human rights experts made a joint statement that Afghan women are being completely erased from the public sphere.[66]

---

61 Ibid para 3.

62 Report of the Secretary-General, 'Women and peace and security' (2021) UN Doc S/2021/827 para 4.

63 Report of the Secretary-General, 'Women and peace and security', (2021) UN Doc S/2021/827 para 7; '2023 saw global military expenditures increase for the ninth consecutive year, to reach an all-time high of $2.44 trillion'; Report of the Secretary-General, 'Women and peace and security', (2024) UN Doc S/2024/671 para 51.

64 Ibid para 2.

65 Report of the Secretary-General, 'Women and peace and security', (2022) UN Doc S/2022/740 para 16.

66 OHCHR, 'Afghanistan: Taliban's targeting of women and NGOs preventing delivery of life-saving assistance is deplorable, say UN experts' (30 December 2022) at <https://www.ohchr.org/en/statements/2022/12/afghanistan-talibans-targeting-women-and-ngos-preventing-delivery-life-saving> accessed 23 September 2024.

Afghanistan – like Yemen, Tigray, Iran, Syria, the Occupied Palestinian Territory and many other places worldwide – demonstrates again that violence is gendered, that peace without taking account of its gendered nature is meaningless and that the Security Council is unwilling to insist upon the principles that it has enunciated over two decades. In the Secretary-General's summation: 'The juxtaposition of violence targeting women and their rights, on the one hand, and their extreme marginalization and exclusion, on the other, still encapsulates the women and peace and security agenda.'[67] With respect to Afghanistan, the Council appears unable to do more than repeat its 'deep alarm' at the worsening situation and reiterating its support for UN bodies with mandates relating to the Country (UN Assistance Mission in Afghanistan (UNAMA) and the Special Representative of the Secretary-General and UNAMA) and being kept apprised of the situation.[68]

4 WPS: Glimmers of Hope?

In this dispiriting picture glimmers of hope for the future of WPS might be sought in the over 100 States that have adopted NAPs, including Italy's 2020 NAP completed under the auspices of the Inter-ministerial Committee on Human Rights with input from civil society. Critics have noted that NAPs concluded by States in the global North are directed toward external foreign policy justifying interventions in the global South and reinforcing the global racialised status quo while failing to address racial, gender and other inequalities at home.[69] Conversely those from the global South tend to be more inward looking addressing their own situation. Italy sets out four objectives in its NAP that to some extent follow this pattern in that they concern women's participation in peace processes and operation and enhancement

67 Report of the Secretary-General, 'Women and peace and security' (2021) UN Doc S/2021/827 para 4.

68 UNSC 'Security Council Press Statement on Afghanistan' (27 December 2022) Press Release SC/15165. The Council held a closed session on Afghanistan on 13 January 2023 amidst calls for it to focus on how to reverse the Taliban's decrees: Amnesty International, 'Afghanistan: UN Security Council must take concrete steps to end the 'systemic decimation' of women and girls' rights in the Country' (13 January 2023) at <https://www.amnesty.org.uk/press-releases/afghanistan-un-security-council-must-take-concrete-steps-end-systemic-decimation> accessed 23 September 2024.

69 Toni Haastrup and Jamie J Hagen, 'Global Racial Hierarchies and the Limits of Localization via National Action Plans' in Soumita Basu, Paul Kirby and Laura J Shepherd (eds), New Directions in Women, Peace and Security (Bristol UP 2020) 133.

of women's rights in conflict and post-conflict affected areas, although these should encompass European conflicts. It recognises that implementation of WPS is linked to the 'general promotion and protection of equality and human rights of women and girls, within the framework of the Beijing Declaration and Programme of Action-1995', international human rights standards and treaties for combatting violence against women and girls thereby integrating WPS principles into its domestic policy. Like many other NAPS there is no budget, although the Italian Parliament allocated resources for implementation of the previous NAP.

A second potential area of hope for WPS is that more countries are committing to a feminist foreign policy. UN Women reported in July 2022 that these include Sweden (2014), Canada (2017), France (2019), Mexico (2020), Spain (2021), Luxembourg (2021), Germany (2021) and Chile (2022) and that the Netherlands and Belgium are in the process of developing such policies.[70] There are commonalities but also differences in scope and understanding about what a feminist foreign policy might entail. Italy is not within this list and is an exporter of arms.[71] In January 2021 at the behest of civil society that exposed human rights violations in the war in Yemen the government halted arms exports to Saudi Arabia and the United Arab Emirates.[72] Foreign policies (like domestic implementation of the NAP) are subject to the political agendas of a new government following electoral change.

Another positive step is the Statement of Shared Commitment to WPS[73] made by Niger, Norway, the United Arab Emirates, the United Kingdom, Albania, Brazil, Ecuador, France, Gabon, Japan, Malta, and Switzerland. These States have pledged that while they hold the presidency of the Security Council they will make WPS a top priority and ensure its implementation in concrete and tangible ways. And in 2022 more than 50 Countries, including Italy, have signed up to a new Political Declaration on Conflict-Related Sexual Violence. This UK initiative comprises four themes: strengthening the global

---

70 UN Women, 'Feminist Foreign Policies: an Introduction' (UN 2022) at <https://www.unwomen.org/sites/default/files/2022-09/Brief-Feminist-foreign-policies-en.pdf> accessed 23 September 2024.

71 The 'militarism-trade nexus' is an area of debate among advocates of a feminist foreign policy; ibid.

72 'Italy blocks sale of missiles to Saudi Arabia and UAE' Reuters (29 January 2021) at <https://www.reuters.com/article/us-yemen-security-gulf-italy-idUSKBN29Y1VV/> accessed 23 September 2024.

73 'Statement of Shared Commitments' (4 April 2022) at <https://www.norway.no/contentassets/1b036f2777f74bd3b8ff473555c63a98/statement-of-shared-commitments-2022.pdf> accessed 23 September 2024.

response; preventing conflict-related sexual violence; promoting justice and accountability; and supporting survivors.[74] But, as throughout the two decades of WPS resolutions, these commitments lack legal force and do not extend to examining the structural causes of inequalities that fuel violence,[75] to arms reduction, or despite much hand wringing, any forceful condemnation of the attacks on the extraordinarily brave actions of women protesting their countries' policies in Iran, Myanmar, Afghanistan and elsewhere. Sexual violence whether committed in conflict or in peacetime remains more readily attributed to individual perpetrators rather than to State policies.

Women's NGOs face a dilemma; should they continue to support the WPS agenda within the Security Council or should they turn their attentions elsewhere, perhaps back to the General Assembly and human rights bodies? In October 2022 in an open letter to UN Permanent Representatives to the UN in advance of the annual Open Debate on WPS the NGO Working Group on WPS implored the Council to take concrete steps to enhance the practical application of WPS. One such step was a demand for accountability not just of those who directly deny women's human rights but of the Security Council itself, through urging the Council to reject actions that undermine the core tenets of its own agenda. For instance, the Council should ensure that peace operations are mandated to incorporate WPS, as should country specific resolutions that are binding on Member States under UN Charter Article 25. It could reject reports from country specific special envoys and representatives that do not address meaningfully WPS principles and insist on their resubmission. The Council has not shown any inclination to take any such forceful steps and current divisions within it make further progress unlikely.

As the 25th anniversary of Resolution 1325 approaches the situation is bleak. In his review of WPS in September 2024 the Secretary-General recounted that '[a]mid record levels of armed conflict and violence, progress made over decades is vanishing before our eyes.' The backlash against women's rights is escalating. At the same time after a gap of 6 years a new resolution would be timely: the CEDAW Committee for instance has emphasised the need to adapt

74 UK Government, 'Preventing Sexual Violence in Conflict Initiative (PSVI) Conference 2022: a political declaration on conflict-related sexual violence' (London, 28–29 November 2022) at <https://www.gov.uk/government/publications/conflict-related-sexual-violence-political-declaration-at-the-2022-preventing-sexual-violence-in-conflict-initiative-conference/preventing-sexual-violence-in-conflict-initiative-psvi-conference-2022-a-political-declaration-on-conflict-related-sexual-violence> accessed 23 September 2024.

75 The Declaration does commit to addressing drivers of conflict-related sexual violence 'such as gender inequality and harmful social norms' but does not acknowledge their structural basis in patriarchal systems of power.

and extend the WPS agenda to the changing nature of conflict and new threats to peace and security, and to apply it holistically as a women's human rights agenda in all decision-making and policymaking situations.[76] In the current political environment it seems unlikely that the Committee's progressive recommendations will be heeded.

5 Where is Peace in WPS?

WPS has three components: women, peace and security. This article has said a lot about women and about security but little about peace. The same is true of the Security Council where there are only passing references in the WPS resolutions to conflict prevention[77] and no substantive actions about peace. The 2015 Global Study on the implementation of Resolution 1325 reported that women from around the world that had been consulted in the preparation of the Report overwhelmingly called for an end to militarisation and for prevention and protection through nonviolent means to be emphasized by the international system.[78] The Security Council has not heeded this call throughout the WPS resolutions.

This absence of any conceptualisation of peace is similarly applicable to international law: where is peace in international law, in international law texts, courses or curricula despite the centrality of the discipline's objective 'to save future generations from the scourge of war'?[79] Where peace is discussed it is usually in conjunction with some other concept: peacekeeping, peace-building and peace-making, peaceful settlement of disputes[80] rather

76 UN Committee on the Elimination of Discrimination against Women, 'General Recommendation No. 40 on the equal and inclusive representation of women in decisionmaking systems' (25 October 2024) UN Doc CEDAW/C/GC/40 paras 58-61. The Committee also urges parity – 50/50 women and men – in all relevant decision-making.

77 UNSC Res 1325 (31 October 2000) UN Doc S/RES/1325 (2000) and subsequent resolutions urge women's increased representation in processes for conflict prevention but do not develop what those processes might require. The assumption is that peace is simply the absence of conflict.

78 Radhika Coomaraswamy and others, 'Preventing Conflict, Transforming Justice, Securing the Peace. A Global Study on the Implementation of Security Council Resolution 1325' (United Nations 2015) 25.

79 Charter of the United Nations (adopted 26 June 1945, entered into force 24 October 1945) preamble.

80 A good example is the 1992 Agenda for Peace and its 1995 Supplement; Report of the Secretary-General, 'An Agenda for Peace Preventive diplomacy, peacemaking and peace-keeping' (1992) UN Doc A/47/277-S/24111; Report of the Secretary-General,

than as a stand-alone concept and with more discussion of process than of the objective of developing international law as a tool for peace. And in general peace is deemed only relevant to territories in or emerging from conflict. We must ask why international law says a lot about conflict but not much about peace; or why courses on the use of force or the laws of war flourish but there is a paucity of courses on peace. Is it because of the inherent violence of a discipline that is founded upon colonial, racist, heterosexual and patriarchal oppression? In arguing for decolonisation of the international law curriculum Al Attar and Abedkarim argue that 'to teach international law is to augment Eurocentrism within its praxis, and the alternatives are limited and unsatisfactory'.[81] This paradox – the maintenance of international peace as the purpose of a discipline that is founded in colonial, racist, heterosexual and patriarchal oppression – may go some way to explaining why peace is not generally a component of any branch of public international law.

Centring peace instead of conflict could open new perspectives and shift mindsets: what would the Security Council look like if it had been named as the Peace Council in 1945?[82] Could 'peace' cut across and reduce the siloing of international legal regimes? Could promotion of peace potentially be a unifying concept across traditional principles of the prohibition of the use of force; peaceful settlement of disputes; universality of human rights; environmental law; terrorism; the law of public commons; or as the underlying rationale for accepted international crimes such as aggression, genocide, and crimes against humanity and for emerging (or debated) international crimes such as ecocide, drug, arms and people trafficking and use of nuclear weapons; or for other evolving areas such as animal rights, the rights of rivers and other natural features, or protection of the planet itself? The marginalisation of peace in public international law – a subject committed to the maintenance of international peace and security – demonstrates how securitised and masculinised international legal discourse is; maybe international lawyers should join with feminist NGOs and activists to 'reclaim peace' as an emancipatory concept. These questions are especially relevant appropriate for the ILA, an organisation that was founded to seek peace and justice though the study, clarification, and development of international law.[83]

'Supplement to an Agenda for Peace: position paper of the Secretary-General on the occasion of the 50th anniversary of the United Nations' (1995) UN Doc A/50/60, S/1995/1.

81 Mohsen Al Attar and Shaimaa Abedlkarim, 'Decolonising the Curriculum in International Law: Entrapments in Praxis and Critical Thought' (2021) 34 Law and Critique 41.

82 I thank Dianne Otto for this thought.

83 <https://www.ila-hq.org/en> accessed 23 September 2024.

Essays and Articles

In Defense of International Law in Times of Crisis

*Attila M Tanzi**

1 Introductory Remarks[1]

When confronted with a world of cascading and intersecting crises involving human atrocities, increasingly battered by natural disasters following from the unstoppable climate change phenomenon, where more than a quarter of its population is deprived of fundamental freedoms, the natural reaction from the general public is that of questioning the effectiveness, if not the mere relevance, of international law. Inevitably, the United Nations (UN), which is an integral part of the international legal system, is also indicted.

The present article will argue that, however understandable, this attitude is flawed as it conflates cause and effect. Most international legal rules are silently complied with as a matter of routine. There is no denying that the fundamental rules and principles aimed at ensuring international peace and security are increasingly abused or plainly infringed upon. However, the point will be made that the increase in international (and national) illegality is not attributable to ostensible flaws in the law, but a consequence of the poor state of health of the international society. In fact, next to its rules-making and enforcement connotation, international law will be considered as a thermometer of the state of health of the international society.

This article is organised in four parts, next to the present introductory remarks. First, reference is made to the current critical state of global affairs. Second, the relationship between law and society is addressed against the backdrop of the contemporary international social malaise. Thirdly, the focus will turn to the sense to be made of the quest for reform coming from different quarters, with special regard to the UN as the main institutional pillar of the international legal system. In the concluding remarks, the aspirational value of the rule of law will be emphasised together with a call on states to engage in the avoidance of following or allowing to follow a double standard approach to international legality.

* Full Professor of International Law, Alma Mater University of Bologna; President, ILA Italy; Associate Member, 3 Verulam Buildings, London.

1 A version of this paper was published as 'International Law in the Times of Crises: Imperatives and Prerogatives' (2024) 24 *IPRI* Journal 15. The present article summarises a number of ideas advanced by the Author during the IPRI Margalla Dialogue of 2024.

 | DOI:10.1163/9789004727663_004

2 Global Malaise

As recently put it by Shivshankar Menon, '[t]he world […] is adrift'.[2] Indeed, international relations are increasingly characterised by a widespread 'revisionist' attitude with respect to the multilateralist approach to an international order based on global cooperation through international institutions. Major powers now rather 'pursu[e] their own ends to the detriment of the international order and seek […] to change the order itself'.[3]

This gloomy picture depicted in 2022 was confirmed a year later in his speech to the General Assembly by current UN Secretary-General António Guterres, as follows:

> [D]ivides are deepening. Divides among economic and military powers. Divides between North and South, East and West. We are inching ever closer to a Great Fracture in economic and financial systems and trade relations; one that threatens a single, open internet; with diverging strategies on technology and artificial intelligence; and potentially clashing security frameworks.[4]

And from Ukraine to Gaza, we are witnessing increasing security clashes, on both cyber and physical spaces. But international divisions and conflicts go hand in hand, or, rather, are the reflection of the increasing polarization of cultural, social and political divisions at the national level in many countries. Whilst social and cultural diversity represents an immense potential asset in any society, lack of dialogue and competing attitudes by the diverse social components are ever more leading to disruptive social and political outcomes on the domestic level in many nations. The widening chasm between rich and poor adds to domestic instability around the world, rendering populations ever more vulnerable to economic and financial criminality, and the governmental response increasingly authoritarian.

The expanding level of social and political malaise in an increasing number of countries was also stressed by the UN Secretary-General in his address to the General Assembly in its 2023 session: '[D]ivides are also widening within

---

2 Shivshankar Menon, 'Nobody Wants the Current World Order. How All the Major Powers – Even the United States – Became Revisionists' (Foreign Affairs, 22 August 2022) <www.foreignaffairs.com/world/nobody-wants-current-world-order> accessed 17 June 2024.

3 Ibid.

4 'Secretary-General's address to the General Assembly', 19 September 2023, available at <www.un.org/sg/en/content/sg/speeches/2023-09-19/secretary-generals-address-the-general-assembly> accessed 17 June 2024.

countries. Democracy is under threat. Authoritarianism is on the march. Inequalities are growing. And hate speech is on the rise. In the face of all these challenges and more, compromise has become a dirty word'.[5]

Such security, social and economic challenges put international law – with special regard to its rules on the use of force, genocide, warfare, human rights, international trade, the environment and poverty – under an extraordinarily heavy stress test.[6]

3 International Law in Societal and Political Crisis

As stressed by the great Master of international law of the last century Louis Henkin, '[t]he health of the law (…) will depend largely on the health of the society, on its ability to contain explosive forces and mobilize creative ones for general welfare'.[7]

It is thus inevitable that, with the international society, and domestic societies alike, in such a state of ill health and turmoil as referred to above, international law may not now enjoy good health. This fully reflects the observation made more than a century ago by the great Russian lawyer and diplomat Friedrich de Martens, also one of the fathers of the two Peace Conferences held in The Hague in 1899 and 1907,[8] to the effect that 'the flaws of international law […] are only the inevitable consequence of the imperfections and instability that characterise the domestic legal system that has prevailed in all states to date'.[9]

Being international law the result of the social and political process no less than in any domestic legal system, the more homogenous the social

5 Ibid.

6 See Stefan Lehne, 'After Russia's War Against Ukraine: What Kind of World Order?' (Carnegie Endowment for International Peace, 28 February 2023) <https://carnegieeurope.eu/2023/02/28/after-russia-s-war-against-ukraine-what-kind-of-world-order-pub-89130> accessed 17 June 2024 and Oona A Hathaway, 'War Unbound: Gaza, Ukraine, and the Breakdown of International Law' (Foreign Affairs, 23 April 2024) <www.foreignaffairs.com/ukraine/war-unbound-gaza-hathaway> accessed 17 June 2024.

7 Louis Henkin, How Nations Behave (2nd edn, Columbia University Press 1979) 44.

8 On the historical relevance of the two Hague Conferences, see Betsy Baker, 'Hague Peace Conferences (1899 and 1907)', in Max Planck Encyclopaedia of Public International Law (online edn, OUP 2009). See also Yves Daudet (ed), Actualité de la Conférence de La Haye de 1907, Deuxième Conférence de la Paix: colloque La Haye, 6–7 septembre 2007 (Martinus Nijhoff Publishers 2008).

9 Friedrich de Martens, Traité de droit international (vol 1, Libraire Marescq Aine 1883) 287 (English translation by the present Author).

components and their shared values, the smoother the legal process, as opposed to a conflictual scenery characterised by a highly fragmented society. Homogeneity would ease the law-making process. And, since the ensuing rules would reflect generally shared social and political values, they would be naturally met by spontaneous compliance.

In international relations, just like in any national society, when the law is recurrently violated, this is hardly because the law is bad, but because of the social, ethical and political circumstances prevailing in that country at any given point in time. Suffice to consider a country plagued by organised crime, drug cartels and corruption, money laundering and even terrorism. When the population is raided by criminal gangs, the national financial system is undermined by widespread financial crimes, and law-abiding business falls victim of blackmail, this can seldom be said to be the fault of the rules of criminal law and procedure in that particular country. Criminal law reform, in and of itself, can hardly be the solution to the problem. And even where appropriate legislation is lacking, again, the problem is a political one, to the extent that there is no sufficient identity of views, or political will, among lawmakers for new suitable legislation to be adopted.

Theories equating the international legal order to the collective expression of the sovereign wills,[10] or updated conceptions of international law based on natural law of the kind revived in the 1990s – when, once the Cold War was over, political globalisation even seemed to lead to the reduction, if not demise, of national sovereignty[11] – sit increasingly uncomfortably in today's divided world, ever more characterised by nationalistic unilateralism and cross-regional antagonistic alliances. In line with the above reasoning, the current difficulties impinging dramatically on the effectiveness of fundamental rules of international law appear to be but a reflection of the lack of political capacity, or willingness, by the major and mid-sized powers to engage in multilateral diplomacy and international cooperation. The latter represents the indispensable framework and catalyst through which to collectively address the global challenges – from climate change to migration flows, demographic growth, pandemics, poverty, use of cyber space and of increasingly advanced digital technology, and the finite character of vital natural resources – that individual states, however powerful, cannot solve alone.

10 Paul Gragl, Legal Monism: Law, Philosophy, and Politics (OUP 2018) 34.

11 From a strictly legal standpoint, see for all Oscar Schachter, 'The Decline of the Nation-State and Its Implications for International Law' (1998) 36 Columbia Journal of Transnational Law 7 and Christoph Schreuer, 'The Waning of the Sovereign State: Towards a New Paradigm for International-Law?' (1993) 4 European Journal of International Law 447.

4 Breaching the Law, Invoking the Law

Even though it is of meagre consolation, one is to note that the most serious breaches of international law today on the ban on the use of force, on genocide, or international humanitarian law, are accompanied by attempts at legal justification. The two main justifications recurrently invoked are self-defence and humanitarian intervention.[12] Both arguments have been invoked by Russia – concerning its attack and ongoing use of force against Ukraine[13] – and, in different variations, by Israel with regard to the military operations in Gaza.[14] From a legal, and a political, communication perspective, this attitude renders the disputes arising from the events in question akin to domestic litigation of a criminal law character, where assessment of the facts of the case are predominant, for the disputes in question do not stem from differences about the contents of the applicable rules.

Even though it may be of little solace, this self-justificatory attitude should not be taken as foregone. For it comes in contrast to previous governmental attitudes aiming at dismantling the legal authority of the key legal pillars of international law in question. One may recall the initial stand taken by the

---

12 An earlier example can be found in the case Military and Paramilitary Activities in and against Nicaragua (Nicaragua v USA) (Merits) [1986] ICJ Rep 14, where the US justified its activities in support of the Contras guerrillas as acting in collective self-defence for the benefit of El Salvador, Honduras and Costa Rica against alleged hostile activities carried out by the Sandinista government of Nicaragua. However, the Court excluded on the basis of the evidence produced that the circumstances of the case justified the actions of the US.

13 One should recall the speech in which Russian President Vladimir Putin tried to provide justification under international law for the Russian invasion of Ukraine in February 2022, as follows: '[I]n accordance with Article 51 of Part 7 of the UN Charter, with the sanction of the Federation Council of Russia and in pursuance of the treaties of friendship and mutual assistance ratified by the Federal Assembly on 22 February this year with the Donetsk People's Republic and the Luhansk People's Republic, I decided to conduct a special military operation. Its goal is to protect people who have been subjected to bullying and genocide by the Kiev regime for eight years', 'Full text: Putin's declaration of war on Ukraine', English translation by The Spectator, 24 August 2022, <www.spectator.co.uk/article/full-text-putin-s-declaration-of-war-on-ukraine/> accessed 17 June 2024.

14 See the remarks by Israeli Prime Minister Benjamin Netanyahu, who insisted on Israel's right to self-defence in the face of growing criticism from the US and other allies on the conduct of military operations in Gaza after Hamas' terrorist attack on 7 October 2023, Eugenia Yosef and Eyad Kourdi, 'Netanyahu insists Israel will defend itself even if "forced to stand alone"' (CNN, 6 May 2024) <https://edition.cnn.com/2024/05/05/middleeast/netanyahu-icc-warrants-israel-intl-latam/index.html> accessed 17 June 2024.

George Bush Jr. US Presidency in 2001, advocating the abrogation of the UN Charter Chapter VII and of the customary law constraints on the use of force exclusively for the US, in pursuit of a hegemonic design aimed at administering some kind of *Pax Americana*, reminiscent of the imperial *Pax Romana*,[15] and based on the US self-perception of being the sole global superpower.[16]

In legal terms, the meagre consolation that we can draw from the self-justificatory attitude in question follows the reasoning the International Court of Justice (ICJ) put forward in its landmark case on the *Military and Paramilitary Activities in and against Nicaragua* between Nicaragua and the US, whereby:

> For a rule to be established as customary, the corresponding practice must be in absolutely rigorous conformity with the rule. In order to deduce the existence of customary rules, the Court deems it sufficient that the conduct of States should, in general, be consistent with such rules, and that instances of State conduct inconsistent with a given rule should generally have been treated as breaches of that rule, not as a recognition of a new rule. If a state acts *prima facie* incompatible with a recognized rule, but defends its conduct by appealing to exceptions or justifications contained within the rule itself, then whether or not the State's conduct is in fact justifiable on that basis, the significance of that attitude is to confirm rather than to weaken the rule.[17]

This reasoning does not prevent a widespread deep demand for innovation and development of international law.

5 The Quest for Reform

The need for new international law-making addressing unregulated areas of international social interactions or phenomena is increasingly invoked in

---

15 See, amongst others, James MacDonald, When Globalization Fails: The Rise and Fall of Pax Americana (Farrar, Straus & Giroux 2015) and Marcos T Berger, 'From Pax Romana to Pax Americana? The History and Future of the New American Empire', (2009) 46 International Politics 140.

16 See Nico Krisch, 'International Law in Times of Hegemony: Unequal Power and the Shaping of the International Legal Power' (2005) 16 European Journal of International Law 369, José E Álvarez, 'Hegemonic International Law Revisited' (2003) 97 American Journal of International Law 873 and Detlev F Vagts, 'Hegemonic International Law' (2001) 95 American Journal of International Law 843.

17 Military and Paramilitary Activities in and against Nicaragua (n 12) 98.

authoritative quarters as a matter of urgency.[18] However, in such a divided world as the one we are currently confronted with, it is very difficult to find the necessary widespread consent to produce new multilateral legally-binding instruments, perhaps, with the rare exception of politically neutral topics.[19]

One such topic could for example be that of the protection of persons in the event of disasters, which has been thoroughly addressed by the UN International Law Commission (ILC) through an authoritative set of draft-articles acknowledged by the UN General Assembly in 2016.[20] States are still discussing the recommendation by the ILC that a Convention be elaborated on the basis of the draft-articles, and a decision is due to be taken by the UN General Assembly Sixth Committee at the seventy-ninth session of the Assembly in 2024.[21]

The difficulty in cajoling the necessary widespread consent towards multilateral conventional law-making in the present days is also generally testified by increasing resort to some kind of quasi-law-making through the use of soft-law instruments.[22] In times of less international political fragmentation,

---

18 Daniel Bethlehem, 'The End of Geography: The Changing Nature of the International System and the Challenge to International Law' (2014) 25 European Journal of International Law 9. From the same Author see also, more recently, 'Project 2100 – Is the International Legal Order Fit for Purpose?' (EJIL Talk!, 29 November 2022) <https://www.ejiltalk.org/project-2100-is-the-international-legal-order-fit-for-purpose/> accessed 17 June 2024.

19 One may recall the significant challenges encountered in the reform of international economic law, particularly with respect to investment law and arbitration. The production of new legally binding instruments in this domain has proven to be particularly contentious. By way of example, mention should be made of the still ongoing discussions within the UN Commission on International Trade Law (UNCITRAL) Working Group III, set up in 2017 with the task of exploring reforms in the field of investor-state dispute settlement (ISDS). Its last report of April 2024 confirms the difficulties to reach a consensus on hard and fast solutions, let alone in a conventional format. The fate of various free trade agreements negotiated by the European Union (EU), which include provisions for the establishment of permanent investment courts, as an alternative to the existing arbitration system – such as the Comprehensive Economic and Trade Agreement (CETA) with Canada and the Transatlantic Trade and Investment Partnership (TTIP) with the US – illustrates the broader struggles in achieving comprehensive reform in the field. The TTIP negotiations have long been suspended, if not discontinued. More recently, EU Members States have shown reluctance to ratify Chapter 8 of CETA establishing an Investment Court System (ICS). A similar fate has been followed by the dispute settlement chapter in other free trade agreements, such as those between the EU and Vietnam, and Singapore, respectively, with the ad-hoc Agreements on Investment Protection still to enter into force.

20 UNGA Res 71/141 (13 December 2016) UN Doc A/RES/71/141 para 2.

21 UNGA Res 76/119 (9 December 2021) UN Doc A/RES/76/119 point 2.

22 On the importance of soft-law instruments in the dynamics of international law see, for all, Mariolina Eliantonio, Emilia Korkea-aho and Ulrika Mörth (eds), Research Handbook on Soft Law (Edward Elgar Publishing 2023).

reliance on the latter kind of instruments could prove to be an expeditious way to produce international law through complementary widespread spontaneous compliance with the soft-law standards in question, which would thus evolve into customary law. Conversely, nowadays going down the route of negotiating international instruments falling short of a conventional format is pursued primarily as a diplomatic means for states to engage into exercises whose end-product is characterised by its non-legally binding nature as such.[23]

6 The Reform Discourse in the UN

As far as international institutions are concerned, significantly the UN Secretary-General Guterres has recently launched an appeal for reform in dramatic terms, arguing that 'the alternative to reform is not the status quo. The alternative to reform is further fragmentation. It is reform or rupture'.[24]

However, the same considerations made above on the difficulties in the present time about international law-making in general would inevitably apply with specific regard to the UN Charter. And this is all the more so, given the weighted procedure under articles 108 and 109 of the Charter – requiring the consent of two-thirds of the member states and, especially, that of all Permanent Members of the Security Council – for either 'amendment' or 'revision' of the Charter, respectively.[25]

Under such procedural framework, a review process may be set in motion that could well lead to the *adoption* of a change by a two-thirds majority. But the process could risk stopping in the middle of the ford if not obtaining the ratification of the five Permanent Members within the required two-thirds ratifying member states. In the not unlikely worst-case scenario, the mere adoption of a new text would clearly undermine the authority of the original text of the Charter while falling short of the *entry into force* of the adopted text.

In fact, the above appeal for reform by the UN Secretary-General does not seem to be one involving the review of the Charter, but rather one addressing the deeper attitude of major and middle-sized powers currently inclined towards

23 Attila M Tanzi, 'The Role of the UN in the Codification and Progressive Development of International Law' in Vesselin Popovski and Ankit Malhotra (eds), Reimagining the International Legal Order, (Routledge 2024) 95.

24 'Secretary-General's address to the General Assembly' (n 4).

25 Cf Attila Tanzi, 'Notes on the "Permanent Conference of Revision" of the United Nations Charter at the 50th Anniversary of the Organization' (1995) 78 Rivista di diritto internazionale 723.

unilateralism, thus abandoning that international cooperative approach in multilateral forums which is the precondition for the functioning of the UN system in the pursuit of the Charter's goals, with special regard to the peaceful settlement of international disputes. Indeed, by way of example, considering Chapter VIII of the Charter on the 'regional organizations first' principle, the Conference on Security and Co-operation in Europe, later Organization for Security and Co-operation in Europe (OSCE), comes to mind regarding its powerful role as a multilateral forum for negotiation and mutual understanding key to containing the East-West confrontation during the Cold War, to the extent of catalysing its end.[26] Against such a backdrop, it is regrettable that similar precious multilateral forums for a rules-based dispute-preventive and confidence-building dialogue would be neglected before, and especially after, the Crimean crisis of 2014, which could have prevented the 2022 Ukrainian invasion.

Reverting to the UN Secretary-General's appeal for reform, the view that it is not aimed at an exercise of amendment, let alone revision, of the Charter, but an attempt to resuscitate a multilateral cooperative spirit in the member states, emerges from the language on the UN website pertaining to the preparation of the 'Summit of the Future' to be held on 22–23 September 2024, according to which 'the Summit of the Future is a once-in-a-generation opportunity to enhance cooperation on critical challenges and address gaps in global governance'.[27] Rather than a context for discussing the review of the UN Charter, the Summit appears to have been conceived as a solemn opportunity to 'reaffirm existing commitments including to the Sustainable Development Goals (SDGs) and the United Nations Charter, and move towards a reinvigorated multilateral system'.[28]

The rationale of the Secretary-General's call for change in terms referring to the attitude of member states, rather than to amending the Charter, can also

26 See, amongst others, Ulrich Fastenrath and Christian Fastenrath, 'Organization for Security and Co-operation in Europe (OSCE)' in Max Planck Encyclopaedia of Public International Law (online edn, OUP 2019), Roberto Dominguez (ed), The *OSCE*: Soft Security for a Hard World: Competing Theories for Understanding the *OSCE* (Peter Lang 2014), David Galbreath and Malte Brosig, 'OSCE' in Knud Erik Jørgensen and Katie Verlin Laatikainen (eds), Routledge Handbook on the European Union and International Institutions: Performance, Policy, Power (Routledge 2013) 271. See also, with a more political overtone, Vincent Chetail (ed) Conflits, sécurité et cooperation/Conflicts, security and co-operation, Liber amicorum, Victor-Yves Ghebali (Bruylant 2007).

27 <https://www.un.org/en/summit-of-the-future> accessed 17 June 2024.

28 Ibid.

be found to have been clearly expressed in the 2023 policy brief 'A New Agenda for Peace', as follows:

> In the declaration on the commemoration of the seventy-fifth anniversary of the United Nations, heads of State and Government undertook to promote peace and prevent conflicts. Honouring this pledge will require major changes by Member States, in their own actions and in their commitment to uphold and strengthen the multilateral system as the only viable means to address an interlocking set of global threats and deliver on the promises of the Charter of the United Nations around the world.[29]

The message to treasure the existing UN system as originally envisaged and pursue its realisation has been sent across by other UN Secretary-Generals in topical moments. One may recall Kofi Annan's address to the plenary session of the UN General Assembly in 2003, when, after recalling the fundamental aims of the Charter, he stated: 'The world may have changed, Excellencies, but those aims are as valid and urgent as ever. We must keep them firmly in our sights'.[30] Going back in time to January 1992, it is most relevant to recall that, precisely in the peak of the impulsion for reform, Secretary-General Boutros Boutros-Ghali underscored that:

> The powerful must resist the dual but opposite calls of unilateralism and isolationism if the United Nations is to succeed. For just as unilateralism at the global or regional level can shake the confidence of others, so can isolationism, whether it results from political choice or constitutional circumstance, enfeeble the global undertaking. Peace at home and the urgency of rebuilding and strengthening our individual societies necessitate peace abroad and cooperation among nations.[31]

Reverting to the present day, there is a passage in Secretary-General Guterres' speech to the plenary session of the 2023 UN General Assembly, however, where he made reference to an aspect which would bring into question action

29 <https://dppa.un.org/en/a-new-agenda-for-peace> accessed 17 June 2024.

30 'Secretary-General's address to the General Assembly', 23 September 2003, available at <www.un.org/sg/en/content/sg/statement/2003-09-23/secretary-generals-address-the-general-assembly> accessed 17 June 2024.

31 Boutros Boutros-Ghali, An Agenda for Peace: Preventive Diplomacy, Peacemaking and Peace-keeping (United Nations 1992) 46.

requiring some kind of formal review of the Charter. Namely, the question of the reform of the Security Council.[32]

In fact, the issue of the revision of the Charter was in the mind of its drafters since the San Francisco Conference, precisely with a view to reconsidering the veto power of the five Permanent Members and the membership of the Council. So much so that article 109(3) provided that the proposal to convene a conference of revision of the Charter should be placed on the agenda of the 10th annual session of the General Assembly in case such a conference had not taken place by then. The package deal conceived at the constituent San Francisco Conference was meant to assuage the concerns of small and medium-sized states about the privileged status of the five Permanent Members, as well as their right of veto, to the effect that such setting would only be provisional, just until a conference of revision would be held.

The issue was actually placed on the agenda of the 10th annual session of the General Assembly, but the votes of two-thirds of the Assembly, together with the concurring vote of nine members of the Security Council, required to convene the conference of review were clearly out of reach. Therefore, the issue was not put to vote and it was decided that such a conference should be held 'at an appropriate time'.[33]

Next to considerations of substance concerning the options for revision, there were, and possibly are, important considerations of a procedural nature that militate against embarking on the route of a conference of revision. The most important of such considerations has already been mentioned with regard to the highly weighed procedure for the entry into force of the would-be revised text. Even if a new negotiated text managed to obtain the two-thirds of the votes necessary for its adoption, its entry into force would remain hostage of the collective attitude of the member states necessary to reach the minimum two-thirds ratifications, including especially that of each and all of the five Permanent Members, thus risking to dent the authority of the original text.

Combined with this there is the other procedural consideration militating against convening a general conference of revision of the Charter under article 109, that is the strict time constraints typical of a diplomatic conference, within which to close the negotiations, with success or failure. Convening a second session providing further latitude for reaching general consent is not unusual – one may recall the two sessions of the diplomatic conference leading to the 1969 *Vienna Convention on the Law of Treaties*. However, given the fundamental

32 'Secretary-General's address to the General Assembly' (n 4).

33 UNGA Res 992 (21 November 1995) UN Doc A/RES/992.

political stakes involved in the Charter review discourse, the risk of a double failure within a strict temporal framework would be extremely high.

It is fair to say that it is against this procedural backdrop that changes to the Charter, with special regard to change in the composition of the UN organs, including the Security Council, have realistically been discussed within the framework of the General Assembly under article 108 on amendments, without the above discussed time constraints required under article 109. To that end, one may recall the well-known amendments to articles 23 and 27 enlarging the composition of the Security Council and adjusting its voting procedure accordingly, as well as the membership of the Economic and Social Council (ECOSOC) under article 61 of the Charter, adopted by the General Assembly in December 1963 and entered into force in August 1965. A further amendment to article 61 was adopted by the General Assembly in December 1971, which entered into force in September 1973.[34] Article 109 itself was amended in December 1965, so that its first paragraph now provides that a general conference of member states for the purpose of revising the Charter may be held at a date and place to be fixed by a two-thirds vote of the members of the General Assembly and a vote of nine members of the Security Council.[35]

Based on these somewhat loose procedural boundaries, with special regard to the temporal framework, the General Assembly has provided the forum for some kind of a 'permanent conference of revision' under article 108, instead of an ad-hoc diplomatic conference under article 109.

The negotiation process has been revived since the early 1990s, under the impulsion of the end of the Cold War, leading however to no tangibly formal results, and, since 2016, it has focused on the Security Council within the Intergovernmental Negotiations framework (IGN), which is composed of international groupings characterised by different views for reform. Namely, the African Union, supporting a procedural approach centred around a 'treaty based negotiations' and informal top-down 'quick-fix;' the G4 nations (Brazil, Germany, India and Japan), aiming at acquiring permanent membership, possibly with the right of veto; the Uniting for Consensus Group (UfC) – coordinated by Italy and including Argentina, Malta, Mexico, Pakistan and South Korea, amongst others – which procedure-wise calls for the required consensus before engaging into any decision process, while it substance-wise shows openness to the addition of new seats for non-permanent members, provided

34 See the amendments in 'United Nations Charter: Amendments to Articles 23, 27, 61, 109', <www.un.org/en/about-us/un-charter/amendments> accessed 17 June 2024.

35 Ibid.

this be through general consensus to be expressed in the negotiation process; the L.69 Group of Developing Countries – involving states from Africa, Asia, Latin America and the Caribbean, and Pacific Small Island States – united by the common intent of reaching an expansion of permanent and non-permanent seats with a view to attaining a more equitable representation in the Council; and the Arab League, expressing a mild inclination towards a comprehensive reform of the Council based on consensus. The common Chinese-Russian position is also worth noting, which is mildly open towards informal consensus-based formulas, provided consensus goes clearly beyond the two-thirds majority, and is averse to imposed quick timelines.

Against the above divergencies on formulas of reform concerning composition and voting procedure of the Security Council, a recent significant development is noteworthy. Namely, a non-legally binding, but authoritative instrument like a General Assembly resolution, aiming to enhance the accountability of the Security Council, and especially of the Permanent Members placing their veto. It provides some form of residual competence by default for the General Assembly on the issues with respect to which the Security Council could not act because of the veto in question. This is Resolution 262/76, adopted by the General Assembly in April 2022, which, in the relevant part for our purposes, states that:

1. The General Assembly shall convene a formal meeting of the General Assembly within 10 working days of the casting of a veto by one or more permanent members of the Security Council, to hold a debate on the situation as to which the veto was cast, provided that the Assembly does not meet in an emergency special session on the same situation;
2. Also decides, on an exceptional basis, to accord precedence in the list of speakers to the permanent member or permanent members of the Security Council having cast a veto;
3. Invites the Security Council, in accordance with Article 24 (3) of the Charter of the United Nations, to submit a special report on the use of the veto in question to the General Assembly at least 72 hours before the relevant discussion in the Assembly [...].[36]

This resolution is reminiscent of the so-called 'Uniting for Peace' resolution adopted in 1950 at the time of the Korean War in order to sidestep the Soviet veto against a draft-resolution in the Security Council aimed at taking enforcement action against North Korea which had invaded South Korea.[37] However,

---

36 UNGA Res 76/262 (28 April 2022) UN Doc A/RES/76/262.

37 UNGA Res 377 A (V) (3 November 1950) UN Doc. A/RES/377 (V). For a doctrinal commentary from the time this resolution was adopted, see Keith S Petersen, 'The Uses of the

Resolution 262/76 clearly falls short of any attempt at residually affording the General Assembly with enforcement powers with which the Security Council is vested under Chapter VII on the collective security system. After all, the 'Uniting for Peace' never achieved its original objective of introducing some kind of unwritten modification to the Charter by way of constitutional customary law, since it was immediately contested by the Soviet delegation and soon abandoned by the proposing Western delegations themselves, once they lost their majority in the General Assembly with the fast-unfolding decolonisation process.

7 Conclusion

The article has argued and tried to illustrate how, in the relationship between law and society, the former is the by-product of the latter and its political process. Therefore, societal crisis cannot be attributed to alleged shortcomings of the law. Blaming the law for not being able to fix major social conflicts and crisis flows from a misrepresentation of reality where putative limitations of the law become the scapegoat of the political incapacity, or unwillingness, to properly address such conflicts and crisis in the pursuit of the general interest.

A harmonious society and its government can produce good law for the community at large in a long-term perspective, which may easily adjust to evolving social needs, becoming effective through spontaneous compliance and functional enforcement mechanisms generally regarded as authoritative and legitimate. On the other hand, whatever in the abstract may be good law, it cannot change a troublesome society.[38]

In the international society the issue is doubly complex, for the difficulties around the international balance intersect with those in a plurality of national societies, which are inevitably reflected on the international sphere. And it has already been stressed how the fact that we are living in times of increasingly divided and polarised societies which produce authority and legitimacy crisis in many nation-states and, consequently, on the international level cannot but impact on international law and its effectiveness as ever.[39]

Uniting for Peace Resolution since 1950' (1959) 13 International Organization 219 and Juraj Andrassy, 'Uniting for Peace' (1956) 50 American Journal of International Law 563.

38 See also 'Addendum to Attila M. Tanzi, A Concise Introduction to International Law, Second Edition' 4–14, <www.giappichelli.it/media/catalog/product/aggiornamenti/9788892145337_Tanzi_Addenda.pdf> accessed 17 June 2024.

39 See Friedrich de Martens' remarks above (n 9).

The Gaza and Ukrainian crises are taking an extremely heavy toll on international peace and security, as well as on international legality and on confidence in it. The Ukrainian conflict, apart from its dramatic humanitarian aspects, has reintroduced the East-West confrontation to an unprecedented degree, catalysing further fragmentation on the international scene.

The attack by Hamas on Israel on 7 October 2023 has also represented an attack on the diplomatic peace process in the Middle East which was being conducted by a number of Islamic countries, especially from the Gulf. The ripple effect of this attack and of the disproportionate military reaction by Israel, in combination with the other internal and international, ongoing and potential, conflicts around the world may be beyond imagination.

Against the backdrop of the gloomy international and domestic picture worldwide described above, one may think of international law and international lawyers at the time preceding the two World Wars, between and during them. The following words by Judge Anzilotti in his individual opinion in the 1931 Permanent Court of International Justice Advisory Opinion in *Customs Regime between Germany and Austria* may come to mind with a degree of disenchantment:

> Independence [...] is really no more than the normal condition of States according to international law; it may also be described as sovereignty (*suprema potestas*), or external sovereignty, by which is meant that the State has over it *no other authority than that of international law*.[40]

Upon further reflection, also prompted by the positive thinking by one of the most authoritative successors of Judge Anzilotti, based on the recurrent lessons of history, such disenchantment may be tempered by the objective consideration that no war or systemic atrocity has prevented international law to resuscitate and grow each time stronger than before. Indeed, as authoritatively stated by ICJ Judge, and former President, Abdulqawi Yusuf:

> History teaches us that the manner in which humanity engages with international law depends on the nature and scale of the challenges that it faces. When faced with the cruelty and inhumanity of slavery in the nineteenth century, States adopted in 1890 and 1926 binding legal instruments to prohibit slavery and to cooperate with a view to its suppression. When faced with the death of 75 million civilians during the

40 Customs Regime between Germany and Austria (Advisory Opinion) PCIJ Rep Series A/B No 41, Individual Opinion by M Anzilotti, 57.

> Second World War, States adopted the Fourth Geneva Convention in 1949 devoted to the protection of civilians in times of international armed conflicts. When faced with the uprising, opposition and rebellion of peoples all over the world against colonialism, States established the right of peoples to self-determination, which enabled colonial peoples to accede to independence and facilitated the process of decolonisation. When non-international armed conflicts became the leading type of conflicts, they adopted Additional Protocol II, which extends to these types of conflicts the elementary considerations of humanity.[41]

One only wonders how many more wars and humanitarian crisis this time the international society needs to go through before an equitable rules-based system is to resuscitate and apply evenly around the globe. In the meantime, it would be ideal, next to idealistic, if nation-states, peoples, minority groups and individuals, would go by the minimum common regulatory inter-cultural and inter-religious 'Golden Rule' denominator, expressing the importance for each one to 'love for his brother what he loves for himself'[42] or, in other words, whereby 'all things whatsoever ye would that men should do to you, do ye even so to them',[43] or 'hurt not others with what pains yourself'.[44] And if war were to be considered as an unavoidable evil on earth, International Humanitarian Law has been devised throughout the centuries by the international society to contain its horrors and protect civilians. It has been convincingly argued that, in order for confidence in international law to be re-established, those who invoke international humanitarian legal principles and wish wrongdoers to be held accountable must engage in some 'ethics of reciprocity' and show that they are prepared to hold their own military and those of their allies to the same standards they invoke.[45]

---

41 Ahmed Abdulqawi Yusuf, 'Engaging with International Law' (2020) 69 International and Comparative Law Quarterly 505, 518.

42 Hadith 13, 40 Hadith an-Nawawi (Islam) in Denys Johnson-Davies and Ezzeddin Ibrahim (eds), An-Nawawi's Forty Hadith (Islamic Texts Society 1997).

43 Matthew 7:12 (Christianity) in Robert Carroll and Stephen Prickett (eds), The Bible: Authorized King James Version (Clarendon Press 1997).

44 Udana-Varga 5.18 (Buddhism) in W Woodville Rockhill (ed), Udânavarga: A Collection of Verses from the Buddhist Canon, (Routledge, re-printed 2000). Hathaway (n 6).

45 Hathaway (n 6).

Proceedings of the 5th ILA Italy Biennial Conference (Ferrara, 16 November 2023) on Alternative Dispute Resolution in International and EU Law: Recent Trends

ADR Mechanisms for Trade Disputes in MERCOSUR

*Facundo Pérez-Aznar**

1 Introduction

The present contribution will analyze the alternative dispute resolution ('ADR') mechanisms available for trade disputes in MERCOSUR.[1] The MERCOSUR system has multiple, relatively highly institutionalized ADR mechanisms, although these have not necessarily been used by States Parties or other entities.

MERCOSUR was created in 1991 when Argentina, Brazil, Paraguay, and Uruguay signed the Treaty of Asunción, aiming to create the Common Market of the South (in Spanish Mercado Común del Sur or 'MERCOSUR').[2] In 1994 MERCOSUR was institutionally restructured by the Ouro Preto Protocol ('OPP') and became a subject of international law.[3] The current structure of MERCOSUR has remained almost the same since then.[4]

Concerning dispute settlement,[5] the Treaty of Asunción, in Annex III, established a non-coercive, diplomatic dispute settlement system.[6] Later, States

* Senior Researcher, Geneva Center for International Dispute Settlement; Adjunct Professor of International Economic Law, University of Buenos Aires.

1 For a general overview on MERCOSUR in English, see Jan Peter Schmidt, 'MERCOSUR', in Rüdiger Wolfrum (ed), *The Max Planck Encyclopedia of Public International Law* (OUP 2017). See also Marcilio Franca Filho, Lucas Lixinski, and Maria Olmos Giupponi (eds), *The Law of Mercosur* (Hart Publishing 2010).

2 Treaty for the Establishment of a Common Market between the Argentine Republic, the Federative Republic of Brazil, the Republic of Paraguay and the Eastern Republic of Uruguay (done 26 March 1991, entered into force 29 November 1991) 2140 UNTS 257 (Treaty of Asunción).

3 Additional Protocol to the Treaty of Asunción on the Institutional Structure of MERCOSUR (signed 17 December 1994, entered into force 15 December 1995) 2145 UNTS 298 (Ouro Preto Protocol).

4 The institutional structure of MERCOSUR comprises the following bodies: a) the Common Market Council ('CMC'); b) the Common Market Group ('CMG' or 'GMC' from its Spanish acronym); c) the MERCOSUR Trade Commission ('MTC' or 'CCM' from its Spanish acronym); d) the MERCOSUR Parliament (or 'PARLASUR'); e) the Economic-Social Consultative Forum ('ESC' or 'FCES' from its Spanish acronym); and f) the MERCOSUR Administrative Secretariat ('MAS' or 'SAM' from its Spanish acronym).

5 For a general overview of the MERCOSUR dispute settlement system in English, see Paula Wojcikiewicz Almeida, 'MERCOSUR Dispute Settlement System', in Hélène Ruiz Fabri (ed), *The Max Planck Encyclopedia of International Procedural Law* (OUP 2018).

6 Annex III of the Treaty of Asunción provided a three-stage, non-binding dispute settlement mechanism: first, disputes between States Parties would be resolved through direct negotiations;

 DOI:10.1163/9789004727663_005

Parties adopted the Brasília Protocol ('BP') for the Settlement of Disputes, which provided a three-step dispute resolution mechanism for disputes arising between the States Parties: direct negotiations, intervention of the Common Market Group ('CMG') (which could be invoked unilaterally by one of the disputing parties and could make recommendations) and a last step comprising arbitration between the litigant States Parties.[7]

In addition, other ADR mechanisms were further created in the MERCOSUR dispute settlement system. The Ouro Preto Protocol established in an Annex the 'General Procedure for Claims before the MERCOSUR Trade Commission' which consisted of two levels of official mediation, first before the MERCOSUR Trade Commission ('MTC') and second before the CMG (OPP, article 21 and Annex). On the other hand, an informal procedure, the 'Consultation Mechanism', was elaborated before the MTC by Directive No 13/95, replaced by Directive No 17/99 in 1999.[8]

Since the beginning of MERCOSUR, States Parties have preferred to try to find a solution by diplomatic means, even if, in practice, some of these methods of dispute settlement have seemed inefficient. No formal disputes have been solved by negotiations and the CMG has very rarely been successful in resolving a case.[9] As we will see, other mechanisms have been more successful.

In 2002 the MERCOSUR States Parties adopted the Olivos Protocol for the Settlement of Disputes in MERCOSUR ('OP'), which entered into force in 2004 and established the dispute settlement system of today.[10] The Olivos Protocol

---

second, if a solution was not achieved, the States Parties would submit the dispute to the consideration of the CMG, which would formulate recommendations; third, if a solution was not reached, the dispute would be referred to the CMC, which would adopt recommendations.

7 Brasilia Protocol for the Settlement of Disputes (signed 17 December 1991, entered into force 22 April 1993) 2145 UNTS 252.

8 MERCOSUR/CCM/DIR No 17/99 'Consultation Mechanism in the MERCOSUR Trade Commission, Text Updated According to Resolution CMG No 20/18'.

9 Nadine Susani, 'Dispute Settlement', in Marcilio Franca Filho, Lucas Lixinski, and Maria Olmos Giupponi (eds), *The Law of Mercosur* (Hart Publishing 2010), 76–77. Susani noted in 2010 that only two disputes had been solved by mediation under the Ouro Preto Protocol rules. The dispute concerning the *Marketing of Table Salt, between Argentina and Uruguay*, was submitted to the MTC on 20 September 1996 and stayed before MERCOSUR bodies for 23 months. Finally, a partial solution was reached. The second dispute related to the *Application of Minimum Specific Importation Duties (DIEM) to the Intra-Zonal Trade*, between Paraguay, on the one hand, and Brazil and Uruguay, on the other. The proceedings before MERCOSUR bodies lasted 18 months.

10 Olivos Protocol for the Settlement of Disputes in MERCOSUR (signed 18 February 2002, entered into force 1 January 2004) 2251 UNTS 243.

is complemented by the 'Implementing Regulations of the Olivos Protocol for the Settlement of Disputes in MERCOSUR', whose most recent version was adopted by MERCOSUR/CMC/DEC. No 05/22 ('CMC 05/22') in 2022.[11]

The Olivos Protocol provides for five dispute settlement mechanisms: (i) direct negotiations between States, (ii) optional intervention by the CMG, (iii) individual claims, (iv) *ad hoc* arbitration with the possibility to appeal before the Permanent Appeals Court ('PAC', in Spanish Tribunal Permanente de Revisión or 'TPR') and (v) possible direct recourse to the PAC with the agreement of the States party to the dispute.

In this sense, one of the most important achievements of the Olivos Protocol is the establishment of the PAC, a permanent judiciary body with its seat in Asunción, Paraguay.[12] The PAC has a dual jurisdiction: it decides disputes of a legal nature that are submitted to it by MERCOSUR States Parties and it delivers advisory opinions on legal questions in response to requests by the States Parties, their highest courts, or the MERCOSUR organs.[13]

It is important to have in mind the scope of the Olivos Protocol and how it regulates the choice of forum, because these provisions are applicable to most ADR mechanisms provided in that protocol. First, as regards the subject matter of the dispute covered by the Olivos Protocol, the protocol applies to disputes between the States Parties regarding the interpretation and application of the Treaty of Asunción, the Ouro Preto Protocol, the protocols and agreements concluded within the framework of the Treaty of Asunción, and the measures adopted by the CMC, the CMG and MTC (OP, article 2(1)).

Second, as regards the choice of forum, Olivos Protocol article 1(2) is an election of remedies clause similar to those in many other regional trade agreements. It provides that if a dispute falls within the scope of application of the Olivos Protocol, the WTO or another trade agreement, the claimant may raise it in any of those forums, but once 'a dispute resolution procedure has been initiated', neither party may take the dispute to any of the other forums (OP, article 1(2)). In a formal dispute where a complainant State has lost a claim brought in one forum (for instance MERCOSUR), this election of remedies clause prevents the claimant from re-litigating its unsuccessful claim in another forum. The choice of forum must be raised before the commencement of direct negotiations and individual claims, and it is understood that a State Party opted for

11 MERCOSUR/CMC/DEC No 05/22 ('CMC 05/22') 'Implementing Regulations of the Olivos Protocol for the Settlement of Disputes in MERCOSUR', adopted on 20 July 2022.

12 See Marianne Klumpp, 'MERCOSUR, Permanent Appeals Court', in Rüdiger Wolfrum (ed), *The Max Planck Encyclopedia of Public International Law* (OUP 2018).

13 Advisory opinions are regulated in Arts 3 to 14 of CMC 05/22.

the dispute settlement system of the Olivos Protocol when it requested the initiation of those procedures (CMC 05/22, Arts 1.2 and 1.3). Applied to ADR, the forum election clause means that if there is more than one forum that could be used to settle a dispute, initiating ADR in one of these forums locks in the disputants and precludes using ADR in any other forum.

The following sections will focus on the ADR mechanisms provided for in the Olivos Protocol (i.e. direct negotiations, intervention of the CMG, and individual claims) and in the other ADR options available for MERCOSUR States Parties outside the Olivos Protocol.

2 ADR Mechanisms in the Olivos Protocol

2.1 Direct Negotiations

In disputes between the States Parties, the Olivos Protocol provides for mandatory State-to-State negotiations (which, implies giving the parties an opportunity to settle the dispute before opening an arbitration process) as the first step in the formal dispute settlement mechanism (OP, Arts 4 and 5). These provisions replicate almost exactly those of the previous regime under the Brasília Protocol (BP, Arts 2 and 3). Direct negotiations are a political ADR mechanism available to the parties, with no third-party facilitator or neutral. The process can be commenced unilaterally by one of the disputing parties. In many cases, when disputes surface as formal matters under the Olivos Protocol, they are not new. The parties may have discussed these issues informally for years. In these cases, direct negotiations (or consultations) under the Olivos Protocol offer the complaining party and its stakeholders a platform to escalate negotiations and get more attention to the problem.

The Olivos Protocol provides that States Parties will seek to resolve their disputes, first of all, through direct negotiations (OP, article 4). Negotiations may not, unless agreed between the States party to the dispute, exceed a period of 15 days from the date on which one of them communicated to the other the decision to initiate the dispute settlement procedure (OP, article 5(1)). The communication must be sent in writing to the other party to the dispute, with a copy to the MERCOSUR Secretariat and to the other States Parties, and must contain a preliminary and basic statement of the issues that the party understands to be part of the object of the dispute, as well as the proposed date and place for direct negotiations (CMC 05/22, article 15(1)).

Direct negotiations are conducted by the National Coordinators of the CMG of the States party to the dispute or by the representatives designated by them (CMC 05/22, article 15(2)). The States party to the dispute must record the results of the direct negotiations in written minutes, and inform the CMG, through the MERCOSUR Secretariat, about the efforts carried out during the negotiations and their results (OP, article 5(2), and CMC 05/22, article 15(3)).

If an agreement is not reached through direct negotiations or if the dispute is only partially resolved, any of the States party to the dispute may directly initiate an *ad hoc* arbitral procedure under the Olivos Protocol (OP, article 6(1)).

Different MERCOSUR tribunals, both under the Brasília Protocol and the Olivos Protocol, applied and analyzed recourse to direct negotiations since it is a pre-requisite for recourse to arbitration. The 1999 tribunal in *Subsidies for the Production and Export of Pork* stated that '[i]f the object of the dispute has been established at the stage of diplomatic negotiations, from then on there can be no modification of the object of the litigation by the parties involved'.[14] Following a similar reasoning, the 2002 tribunal in *Prohibition on the Importation of Remolded Tires from Uruguay* considered that 'every arbitral tribunal within the MERCOSUR system must verify that the object of the dispute that is the subject of the arbitration procedure is included and directly related to the issues discussed in the previous stage of diplomatic negotiations'.[15] The 2005 tribunal in *Prohibition on the Importation of Remolded Tires* considered that, in line with article 14 of the Olivos Protocol, the object of the dispute is determined by the presentation of the request and its respective response to the arbitral tribunal, 'as well as the evidence of what was discussed in the negotiation stages prior to the beginning of the arbitral proceedings'.[16] In 2012 Paraguay alleged before the PAC that it was unable to comply with the requirement of direct negotiations since it had been suspended from MERCOSUR. The PAC considered that if Paraguay had requested negotiations and those negotiations had been rejected, the situation would be different, but 'there is no

14 Arbitral Tribunal *ad hoc* of MERCOSUR, *Case Concerning Subsidies for the Production and Export of Pork (Argentina v Brazil)* (27 September 1999) Award No 2 under the BP, para 44. This and the subsequent quoted awards are available at <www.tprmercosur.org/es/sol_contr_laudos.htm> accessed 23 September 2024.

15 Arbitral Tribunal *ad hoc* of MERCOSUR, *Case Concerning the Prohibition on the Importation of Remolded Tires (Uruguay v Brazil)* (9 January 2002) Award No 6 under the BP, 26.

16 Arbitral Tribunal *ad hoc* of MERCOSUR, *Case Concerning the Prohibition on the Importation of Remolded Tires (Uruguay v Argentina)* (25 October 2005) Award under the OPP, para 17.

demonstration, in the case, that Paraguay has sought to carry out the direct negotiations required by the rule'.[17]

2.2 *Intervention by the Common Market Group* (CMG)

Under the former mechanisms of the Brasília Protocol, the intervention of the CMG in disputes between States Parties was mandatory and did not require prior agreement of the parties, so a State Party could reach the CMG unilaterally.[18] The Brasília Protocol provided that if an agreement was not reached through direct negotiations any of the States party to the dispute may submit it to the CMG for consideration (BP, article 4(1)). When the dispute could not have been resolved by applying direct negotiations or through the intervention of the CMG, any of the States party to the dispute could resort to the arbitration procedure (BP, article 7(1)).

The Olivos Protocol also provides that if the States party to an inter-State dispute agree, the CMG may intervene. However, unlike the Brasília Protocol, the mechanism under the Olivos Protocol is optional and requires the agreement of the States party to the dispute. This is a political (and potentially technical) ADR mechanism. Unlike direct negotiations, here there is a third entity, the CMG, which acts as a sort of 'mediator'[19] even though the CMG includes representatives of States party to the dispute. The CMG is composed of four regular members and four alternate members per country, designated by their governments; they must include representatives of the ministries of foreign affairs, economy (or equivalent) and the central bank (OPP, article 11).

The Olivos Protocol provides that 'without prejudice' to direct negotiations and the arbitration proceedings, the States party to the dispute may, by mutual agreement, submit it to the consideration of the CMG (OP, article 6(2)). If such an agreement is reached, the States party to the dispute must notify the CMG 10 days in advance of a regular meeting of that body, but if there are more than 45 days before that meeting, they may request the CMG to meet extraordinarily (CMC 05/22, article 16(1)).

Each of the States party to the dispute must present to the MERCOSUR President Pro Tempore, 10 days prior to the date of the meeting, a document

---

17 Permanent Tribunal of Revision, *Case Concerning Exceptional Urgency Procedure requested by the Republic of Paraguay in relation to the suspension of its participation in the Organs of MERCOSUR* (21 July 2012) PAC Award No 01/2012, para 60.

18 For an application of the intervention of the CMG under the BP see, eg *Case Concerning the Prohibition on the Importation of Remolded Tires* (*Uruguay v Brazil*) (n 15) 4.

19 The intervention by the CMG is qualified as 'mediation' according to the PAC web page. See <https://www.tprmercosur.org/es/sol_contr_ini_proc_gral.htm> accessed 23 September 2024.

providing a basis for the CMG to evaluate the dispute, and must also transmit a copy to the other States Parties. The document must include, at least: a. indication of the State or States party to the dispute; b. preliminary statement of the matter in dispute; c. description of the background; d. legal foundations of the claim, with a precise indication of the MERCOSUR regulations involved, without prejudice to later supplemental claims; and e. evidence, also subject to later supplemental submissions. The President Pro Tempore then includes the dispute on the CMG agenda (CMC 05/22, article 16(3)).

The CMG then evaluates the situation, giving the States party to the dispute the opportunity to present their respective positions (OP, article 6(2)(i)). The CMG may request, when it considers necessary, the advice of experts selected from a list of experts provided for in the Olivos Protocol (OP, article 6(2)(i)). In that case, the CMG designates the experts, and defines their mandate and the deadline for their report (CMC 05/22, article 16(6)). The opinion of the group of experts and its effects will be governed by the provisions of article 44(1) of the Olivos Protocol (CMC 05/22, article 16(7)). Expenses and costs of expert advice are shared equally by the States party to the dispute, or divided as determined by the CMG (OP, article 6(2)(ii)). The CMG meeting minutes must include a summary of the arguments of the disputing parties and the CMG's conclusions if any. The CMG meeting minutes must also attach the recommendations formulated by the CMG and the written submissions of the parties (CMC 05/22, article 16(8)).

A MERCOSUR State Party that is *not* a party to the dispute can also bring the dispute to the attention of the CMG after conclusion of the direct negotiations phase (OP, article 6(3)). The non-disputant can even request CMG intervention while a formal arbitration is pending before a tribunal; it must submit a written request to the other States Parties through the MERCOSUR President Pro Tempore, and the arbitral proceeding will continue uninterrupted unless the parties to the dispute agree otherwise (OP, article 6(3), CMC 05/22, article 17).

The CMG may make recommendations or comments. If a dispute is submitted to the CMG by the disputing parties, the CMG is to formulate recommendations aimed at solving the dispute (OP, article 7(1)), and to this end, the disputing parties must submit proposals to resolve the dispute (CMC 05/22, article 18(1)). If a non-disputant State requests CMG intervention, the CMG may optionally make comments or recommendations (OP, article 7(2)) and in that case the disputing parties must cooperate in their preparation (CMC 05/22, article 18(2)).

The Olivos Protocol sets a time limit of 30 days for proceedings before the CMG, starting from the date of the meeting when the dispute was submitted for CMG consideration (OP, article 8).

The legal framework for CMG intervention in the Olivos Protocol establishes such intervention as an option available only when the disputing parties all agree. Moreover, if the CMG makes a recommendation, all MERCOSUR States Parties must agree to it by consensus – even States that are not involved in that dispute. The obvious potential for blockage explains the fact that no State Party has ever yet asked for CMG intervention in a MERCOSUR dispute under the Olivos Protocol.

As for parallel proceedings in overlapping forums: while the choice of forum clause in Olivos Protocol article 1(2) requires a complaining party to choose whether to seek dispute settlement under MERCOSUR or a different dispute settlement system, a request for CMG intervention does not lock a party into choosing MERCOSUR as a forum, since it is not listed among the ADR mechanisms that would have that effect (CMC 05/22, Arts 1.2 and 1.3).

2.3 *Individual Claims*

The Brasília Protocol already provided a forum for claims by individuals (BP, Arts 25–32). This mechanism was maintained and updated under the Olivos Protocol (OP, Arts 39–44), in particular by broadening the measures that can be challenged and reinforcing the analysis of admissibility.

The Olivos Protocol provides the (very limited) possibility for individuals to submit claims through a non-adjudicatory mechanism. It is a three-stage mechanism before, first, the National Section of the CMG involved in the dispute, second, through the CMG and, third, through the intervention of a group of experts.

Concerning the subject matter of the claims, under the Olivos Protocol individual claims cover disputes between individuals (physical and legal entities) 'due to the enactment or application, by any of the States Parties, of legal or administrative measures of restrictive, discriminatory or unfair competition effect, in breach of' the Treaty of Asunción, the Ouro Preto Protocol, the protocols and agreements entered into within the framework of the Treaty of Asunción, the Decisions of the CMC, the Resolutions of the CMG and the Directives of the MTC (OP, article 39).

An affected individual formally submits its claim before the National Section of the CMG of the State Party where it has its habitual residence or business headquarters (OP, article 40(1)). The claim must provide elements permitting determination of the 'plausibility of the violation and existence or threat of harm' (OP, article 40(2)). Individuals' claims must be submitted in writing in clear and precise terms, including in particular: a. the identification of the particular claimant, whether a natural or legal person, and the claimant's domicile; b. indication of the legal or administrative measures at issue in the alleged violation; c. allegation of existence or threat of injury; d. causal relationship between the challenged measure and the existence or threat of injury; e. legal grounds on which they are based; and f. indication of evidence presented (CMC 05/22, article 46).

If the National Section of the CMG considers the claim admissible, it must enter into consultations with the National Section of the CMG of the State Party to which the violation is alleged, in order to seek a mutually agreed solution withing 15 days (OP, article 41(1)). Consultations will be conducted by the National Coordinators of the CMG of the State Parties involved, or by the representatives designated by them. For the purposes of initiating consultations, the State Party of the nationality of the individual who filed the claim must send a communication to the other State Party stating the elements on which the claim is based and proposing the place and date for carrying out the consultations (CMC 05/22, article 47).

In the event that consultations end without a solution within 15 days, the National Section of the CMG must submit the claim to the CMG (OP, article 41(2)), at least 10 days before the next meeting of the CMG; if the next CMG meeting will take place more than 45 days later, an extraordinary meeting may be requested (CMC 05/22, article 48(1)). The State Party will submit to the President Pro Tempore, with a copy to the other States Parties, a document that allows the CMG to evaluate the claim (CMC 05/22, article 48(2)). If the respondent State decides to submit a reply to the CMG, it shall also send it to the President Pro Tempore, with a copy to the other States Parties, before the CMG meeting (CMC 05/22, article 48(3)).

Once the claim has been received, the CMG will evaluate (also) the admissibility requirements of article 40(2) of the Olivos Protocol. If it concludes that these requirements are not met, it will reject the claim in a decision by consensus (OP, article 42(1)). If the claim is not rejected, it will be considered accepted, and the CMG will immediately proceed to convene a group of three experts, which must issue an opinion within 30 days from its appointment (OP, article 42(2)). The CMG will appoint the experts by agreement or, failing agreement, it will choose one or more of the experts by vote from an experts roster (OP, articles 43(1) and 43(2), and CMC 05/22, articles 49–51).[20] The experts group will give the individual concerned and the States involved in the dispute

20 The MERCOSUR Administrative Secretariat will notify the CMG of the name of the expert or experts who received the greatest number of votes. In the latter case, and unless the CMG decides otherwise, one of the designated experts may not be a national of the State against which the claim was made, nor of the State in which the individual formalized his or her claim, under the terms of art 40 (OP, art 43(1)).

the opportunity to be heard and to present their arguments in a joint hearing (OP, article 42(2)).

The experts group meets as many times as it deems necessary and may do so virtually (CMC 05/22, article 52(1)). The experts group may set a hearing to hear the States Parties involved in the claim and the interested individuals from said States, respecting the 30-day deadline (CMC 05/22, article 52(2)). The experts group submits its reasoned opinion to the CMG (OP, article 44(1); CMC 05/22, article 54(1)). The CMG must consider this opinion at the ordinary meeting following its receipt (CMC 05/22, article 54(3)).

If the claim against a State Party is affirmed unanimously, any other State Party may require the adoption of corrective measures or the annulment of the questioned measures. If the request for corrective measures is unsuccessful within a period of 15 days, the State Party that made it may resort directly to arbitration (OP, article 44(1)(i)). If the experts group does not reach a unanimous opinion, it must submit its conclusions to the CMG, which immediately ends this proceeding (OP, articles 44(1)(ii) and (iii). The CMG's conclusion of an individual claims proceeding is without prejudice to the claimant State Party initiating a State-to-State dispute proceeding through direct negotiations, intervention by the CMG and arbitration (OP, article 44(2)).

One of the particularities of individual claims, unlike the other ADR mechanisms in MERCOSUR, is that the 2011 'Code of Conduct for arbitrators, experts and officials acting within the framework of the Olivos Protocol' applies also to experts in individual claims proceedings.[21] The Code includes provisions on duties and obligations for the persons covered by it and procedures to follow in cases of alleged violation of that duties and obligations. The same applies for the 2004 'Fees of Arbitrators and Experts in the Framework of the Dispute Resolution System in MERCOSUR' which applies also to experts.[22] Concerning the costs of the proceedings, the expenses of the group of experts will be borne in the proportion determined by the CMG or, in the absence of an agreement, in equal amounts by the States Parties directly involved in the claim (OP, article 43(3)). The expenses can be financed through the Special Fund for Disputes (CMC 05/22, article 53).

The procedure of individual claims has only been applied once (and under the former regulation in the Brasília Protocol, not under the Olivos Protocol),

21 MERCOSUR/CMC/DEC No 31/11 'Code of Conduct for MERCOSUR arbitrators, experts and officials acting within the framework of the Olivos Protocol for the Settlement of Disputes in MERCOSUR'.

22 MERCOSUR/GMC/RES No 40/04 'Fees of Arbitrators and Experts in the Framework of the Dispute Resolution System in MERCOSUR'.

in a case concerning measures on trade of tobacco and tobacco products adopted by Brazil, which resulted later in an arbitral award between Uruguay and Brazil in 2005.[23] The dispute originated from an application filed by a company domiciled in Uruguay. The complaint was judged admissible by the group of experts. Uruguay considered that Brazil had failed to comply with the experts group's opinion within the prescribed period, and Uruguay resorted to arbitral proceedings.[24]

The overall mechanism of individual claims depends upon the political decisions of the States Parties directly concerned. The decision of the CMG not to reject the claim requires the unanimous consensus of States Parties, including that of the State allegedly responsible for the violation. These characteristics can explain the low use of the mechanism.

Apart from the individual claims mechanism just analyzed, currently the MERCOSUR dispute resolution system leaves no room for access to justice in the case of individuals, although the PAC Secretariat has the human resources and well-defined structure to provide mediation and arbitration services with certainty and security for individuals in their commercial relationships.[25] The only additional option for individuals is to pursue claims through proceedings before national courts and national courts may apply MERCOSUR law and resort to the PAC through the mechanism of advisory opinions.[26]

3 ADR Mechanisms Outside the Olivos Protocol

3.1 *Consultation Mechanism within the MERCOSUR Trade Commission (MTC)*

As already mentioned, the Ouro Preto Protocol established in an Annex the 'General Procedure for Claims before the MERCOSUR Trade Commission' which consisted in two levels of official mediation, first before the MTC and in a second step before the CMG.[27] On the other hand, an informal procedure,

23 Arbitral Tribunal *ad hoc* of MERCOSUR, *Dispute Concerning Discriminatory and Restrictive Measures on Trade of Tobacco and Tobacco Products* (*Uruguay v Brazil*) (5 August 2005) Award No 10 under the BP.

24 Wojcikiewicz Almeida (n 5).

25 Juan Manuel Rivero Godoy, 'Servicios de arbitraje y mediación: desafíos y posibilidades en el Mercosur', in Secretaría del Tribunal Permanente de Revisión del MERCOSUR (ed), *Aportes Académicos* (2022), 15–23.

26 Wojcikiewicz Almeida (n 5).

27 Art 21 of the Ouro Preto Protocol provides that the MTC will consider claims presented by the National Sections of the MTC, originated by the States Parties or by individuals. The

the 'Consultation Mechanism', was elaborated before the MTC by Directive No 13/95, replaced by Directive No 17/99 ('CCM 17/99') in 1999.[28]

The MTC is composed of four regular members and four alternate members per State Party and is coordinated by the Ministries of Foreign Affairs (OPP, article 17). It meets at least once a month (OPP, article 18).

The Consultation Mechanism in the MTC can be commenced unilaterally by one of the disputing parties. States Parties may submit Consultations to the MTC to one or more States Parties 'on matters within its competence' (CCM 17/99, article 1). Those competences are very broad. The functions of the MTC include ensuring the application of the instruments of common trade policy and considering and ruling on the requests presented by the States Parties with respect to the application of and compliance with the common external tariff and the other instruments of the common trade policy (OPP, article 18).

A request for consultations may be presented in an ordinary meeting of the MTC or in an extraordinary meeting where it has been agreed to include them in the agenda. The agenda of ordinary meetings includes a permanent item called 'Consultations', which includes 'New Consultations' and 'Consultations in Plenary' (CCM 17/99, article 2).

A consultation request must be submitted in writing and in digital form in accordance with model forms ('New Consultations', 'Response' and 'Technical Note'), annexed to Directive CCM 17/99. A State Party may send a 'New Consultations', 'Responses' or 'Technical Notes' request between meetings of the MTC, in order to facilitate the States Parties expressing their position on them, for the meeting following the date of receipt. Such documents must be addressed to the President Pro Tempore, with a copy to the other National Coordinations of the MTC (CCM 17/99, article 3).

When more than one State Party submits a consultation request to another State Party on the same topic, the consulting countries will coordinate the filing

Annex to the Ouro Preto Protocol establishes the 'General Procedure for Claims before the MERCOSUR Trade Commission'. Under this mechanism the complaining State Party presents its claim to the Pro-Tempore Presidency of the MTC, which will take the necessary steps to incorporate the issue in the agenda of the next meeting of the MTC (Annex, art 2). If a decision is not adopted at said meeting, the MTC will forward the information, without further processing, to a technical committee (ibid). The technical committee will prepare and submit to the MTC an opinion on the matter, which would be taken into consideration by the MTC when deciding on the claim (Annex, art 3). If the MTC is unable to decide on the matter, it will submit the dispute to the CMG so that it can take a decision on the dispute (Annex, art 5). If there is consensus on the claim the responding State Party shall adopt the measures approved by the MTC or the CMG (Annex, art 6).

28 MERCOSUR/CCM/DIR No 17/99 'Consultation Mechanism in the MERCOSUR Trade Commission', Text Updated According to Resolution CMG No 20/18 ('CCM 17/99').

of a single consultation request (CCM 17/99, article 5). Consultations must be answered in writing using the Response form, within a period not exceeding the second ordinary meeting after the one in which it was presented (CCM 17/99, article 6), i.e. within two months.

The consulting State Party will consider a consultation 'Concluded' when the response is considered satisfactory, or the issue that generated the consultation has been resolved. Likewise, a consultation may be deemed 'Unsatisfactorily Concluded' if its object has not been resolved and the possibilities of solution within the scope of the MTC have been exhausted (CCM 17/99, article 7). After four consecutive MTC meetings starting when a consultation was listed in the category of 'Consultation in Plenary', the consultations will be treated as 'Concluded by Expiration of the Term', unless the consulting and the consulted States Parties decide otherwise by mutual agreement (CCM 17/99, article 8).

The minutes of the MTC meetings will record a list of 'New Consultations' and a list of 'Consultations in Plenary' with their evolution. The forms of the 'New Consultations, 'Responses' and 'Technical Notes' must appear as an Annex to said minutes (CCM 17/99, article 9). The MERCOSUR Administrative Secretariat distributes a document with the chronological list of the consultations that have not been concluded and their respective progress at each ordinary meeting of the MTC (CCM 17/99, article 10).

The application of the consultation mechanism does not prevent a State Party from resorting the other dispute settlement mechanisms in MERCOSUR and the initiation of such proceedings will conclude the consultation before the MTC (CCM 17/99, article 11).

Besides being established prior to Olivos Protocol, this mechanism still functions and appears to be the most utilized ADR mechanism inside MERCOSUR. By 2010 more than 500 consultations had been presented since 1995.[29] The high amount of consultation submitted appears to be maintained.[30]

3.2 *Bilateral Consultations*

Besides the mechanisms already mentioned in the previous section, it is common for MERCOSUR States Parties to resort to other ADR mechanism outside MERCOSUR to try to solve their trade disputes. This is the case for Argentina

29 Susani (n 9), 76–77.

30 The minutes of the MTC meetings are available at <https://documentos.mercosur.int> accessed 23 September 2024. Some examples of minutes where numerous consultations were listed are the following MERCOSUR/CCM/ACTA No 05/2019, MERCOSUR/CCM/ACTA No 06/2020, and MERCOSUR/CCM/ACTA No 03/21.

and Brazil, which very often resort to a bilateral safety valve, the 'Bilateral Production and Trade Commission' ('BPTC', in Spanish 'Comisión Bilateral de Producción y Comercio').[31]

The BPTC was created in 2003 by a bilateral agreement between Argentina and Brazil.[32] It is chaired by the ministries of both countries that deal with trade matters and it counts also with the participation of ministries of foreign affairs. BPTC's main function is the treatment of bilateral trade issues and for this purpose it can invite other parties interested in the topics to be examined to participate in its meetings. Meetings are held at the request of any of the governments. At the request of any of them, the BPTC can consider specific cases. The Commission can also promote meetings between representatives of entities or companies in the private sector of the two countries, to stimulate the understanding among them and to overcome the reasons that led to the presentation of the case. The BPTC can submit joint executive recommendations and has among its functions also to monitor compliance with the understandings reached and the decisions adopted.

The BPTC, which is supposed to meet regularly, seeks to provide effective impetus for resolving outstanding issues that affect bilateral trade.[33] During the BPTC meetings, topics relevant to the commercial relationship between the two countries are generally discussed, including issues affecting MERCOSUR, in addition to discussing the bloc's external trade agenda. The topics have included productive integration, trade facilitation, removal of non-tariff barriers and regulatory convergence. As for MERCOSUR, Brazil and Argentina discussed alternatives to speed up the decision-making process within the bloc, in addition to agreeing to boost negotiations on government purchases and investment facilitation.[34] Although the subject matter covered by this body is quite broad in terms of trade matters, there are some issues that are not covered, such as energy, agriculture, livestock, fishing and agroindustry.

The activity of the BPTC depends on the momentum of the trade relations between the two countries.[35] For instance, the BPTC met in March 2023, after 4

31 See 'Argentina y Brasil acordaron fortalecer la relación bilateral' *Portal oficial del Estado argentino* (31 January 2017) <www.argentina.gob.ar/noticias/argentina-y-brasil-acordaron-fortalecer-la-relacion-bilateral> accessed 23 September 2024.

32 Memorandum of Understanding for the Creation of the Trade Monitoring Commission Between Argentina and Brazil (signed 16 October 2003, entered into force 16 October 2003).

33 See 'Comissão bilateral de produção e comércio define agenda' *ApexBrasil* <https://portal.apexbrasil.com.br/noticia/COMISSAO-BILATERAL-DE-PRODUCAO-E-COMERCIO-DEFINE-AGENDA/> accessed 23 September 2024.

34 Ibid.

35 See 'Décima reunião da Comissão de Produção e Comércio Brasil-Argentina marca retorno de relação bilateral' *Seviços e Informaçõnes do Brasil* (10 March 2023) <www.gov.br

years of inactivity, and after a commitment made by the presidents of the two countries.[36]

4 Conclusion

The challenges that MERCOSUR faces as an integration project are many. This applies also to the settlement of disputes in the integration bloc. There are numerous challenges within the MERCOSUR dispute settlement mechanism and States Parties prefer diplomatic procedures without interference from an external authority.[37] There has been a low use of adjudicatory mechanism under MERCOSUR dispute settlement system: ten arbitral awards by *ad hoc* tribunals under the former mechanisms of the Brasília Protocol, two arbitral awards by *ad hoc* tribunals under the current mechanism of the Olivos Protocol, and five awards of the PAC (derived from the two cases under the Olivos Protocol).[38]

The low use of the adjudicatory mechanism shows that in most instances, the many issues arising between the States Parties to MERCOSUR are actually settled or analysed through ADR mechanisms. However, the preferred ADR mechanism are those outside the Olivos Protocol, i.e. the consultation mechanism within the MTC or bilateral consultations outside MERCOSUR.

A reason that could explain the dynamics in the use of ADR mechanisms in MERCOSUR, is that according to the Olivos Protocol, once a dispute resolution procedure has been initiated in accordance with the Olivos Protocol, neither party may resort to the dispute settlement mechanisms established in the WTO or other 'preferential trade schemes' (OP, article 1(2)). Other characteristic of MERCOSUR that perhaps goes in that direction is that only national regulation can be challenged before MERCOSUR dispute settlement mechanisms, not MERCOSUR rules. Yet, another reason could be the mistrust in the MERCOSUR dispute settlement mechanism as a whole by the States Parties.

/mdic/pt-br/assuntos/noticias/2023/marco/decima-reuniao-da-comissao-de-producao-e-comercio-brasil-argentina-marca-retorno-de-relacao-bilateral> accessed 23 September 2024.

36 See 'Queja de la Argentina a Brasil por el Comercio' *El Cronista* (16 March 2023).

37 Wojcikiewicz Almeida (n 5).

38 The awards of the MECOSUR dispute settlement mechanisms are available at <www.tprmercosur.org/es/sol_contr_laudos.htm> accessed 23 September 2024.

ADR in International Investment Law: Recent Trends (a Specific Focus on Mediation)

*Maria Chiara Malaguti**

1 Introduction

In the international *fora* where alternative dispute resolution (ADR) in investor-state dispute settlement (ISDS) is discussed, the recent achievements on mediation are amongst the most tangible. They come at the end of a slow trend that somehow started with the 2012 *IBA Rules for Investor-State Mediation* (a few times used under the International Centre for Settlement of Investment Disputes - ICSID), and consist, firstly, of the 2022 *ICSID Rules and Regulations on Mediation relating to an Investment*, and, secondly, of the 2023 *UNCITRAL Guidelines* and *UNCITRAL Model Provisions on Mediation for International Investment Disputes*.

Considering their recent adoption, the ICSID and United Nations Commission on International Trade Law (UNCITRAL) instruments have not yet been tested against any concrete case. On the other hand, many authors are still quite skeptical that mediation could be possible in a context where one of the parties is a sovereign State. Beyond some criticisms leveled at mediation in general, it is often stated that the issues addressed in investor-State disputes can touch on issues of such general scope for States, and with effects on so many stakeholders, that they cannot be resolved through bilateral negotiation as mediation is; or that the imbalance of powers between the two parties would jeopardize the essence of the exercise. State representatives might be bound by public accountability or transparency principles limiting their freedom to negotiate a compromise.

All these issues bear some relevance but can be individually addressed. Moreover, the fact that ICSID members agreed to adopt rules on mediation shows at least some openness in principle to such an alternative mechanism. Similarly, States convened at UNCITRAL to discuss and converge on some general principles, and finally shared a common understanding of the role and features of such a mechanism at least at a high level.

* Full Professor of International Law, Catholic University of the Sacred Heart, Rome; President, International Institute for the Unification of Private Law (UNIDROIT).

 | DOI:10.1163/9789004727663_006

In addition to such declarations of commitment towards mediation as a possible mechanism for the resolution of international investment disputes, which may be considered a novelty *per se*, what emerges from these most recent trends is above all the apparent prevalence of the belief that mediation could be successfully used in combination with other remedies, and in particular with arbitration, either beforehand (as is the case in some countries that have passed legislation to negotiate possible settlements before the dispute is taken to arbitration, or because of a multi-tier clause in a treaty or an investment agreement), or at a point when arbitration shows that positions could be at least partially reconciled. It is not rare that a dispute concludes with a settlement. In fact, the use of a more structured mechanism for mediation would permit a better organization of such a process and thus strength its possible use within a more flexible set of tools for addressing investment disputes, which may indeed benefit of such flexibility according to circumstances and help preserving economic relationships between the investor and the host State besides the individual dispute.

The ICSID Mediation Rules have indeed been conceived that way: they may be used as a stand-alone process or may be combined with others. Mediation may be conducted prior to or in parallel with (ICSID) arbitration. If a full settlement is reached during the mediation, the parties may agree to discontinue arbitration, or resume arbitration and request the arbitral tribunal to incorporate the mediated settlement agreement into the arbitral award. If a partial settlement is reached, the parties may continue to arbitrate the remaining issues in dispute.

Moreover, the flexibility of mediation may allow for the participation of non-disputing parties in the process, helping to address one of the most compelling issues of the current debate: the need to account for new (general) interests and stakeholders, also linked to sustainability principles. This is recognized by the 2023 UNCITRAL Guidelines, stating that involvement of such stakeholders would be a way to consider the public interest in investment disputes. Examples of non-disputing parties mentioned in the Guidelines include States Parties to the underlying investment treaty not party to the individual dispute, local communities affected by the investment, the dispute, or any negotiated solution, and the civil society at large.

These last elements may in fact highlight another aspect of mediation that merits to be explored in the context of ISDS: the flexibility of mediation, together with the due process guarantees that organized/institutionalized procedures may grant, could indeed play as the framework for management of disputes in investments taking into account a wider set of interests (of other stakeholders) and offering more articulated solutions to changes in the legal and regulatory context or other general circumstances.

2 Mediation in Investor-State Disputes: Do the Latest International Instruments Represent a Change?

2.1 *Mediation versus Conciliation*

To describe and draw some conclusions from the new instruments by ICSID and UNCITRAL, a premise is needed in terms of definitions and scope of the instruments: as well known, the Washington Convention covers arbitration and conciliation,[1] and ICSID recent rules on mediation have been drafted under the understanding that these differ from conciliation and thus require separate proceedings. UNCITRAL over the years has instead taken the stance that the two terms must be considered as interchangeable, and consequently provides a single set of rules under the unitary label of mediation.[2]

Within ICSID, a definition of conciliation can be drawn directly from the Convention as a cooperative, non-adversarial dispute resolution process, where the conciliator (a Conciliation Commission) is to clarify the issues in dispute between the parties and to endeavor to bring about agreement on mutually acceptable terms.[3] Rule 17 of the Mediation Rules in turn qualifies the features of mediation as a voluntary process in which an independent and

1 Convention on the Settlement of Investment Disputes Between States and Nationals of Other States (done at Washington on 18 March 1965, and entered into force on 14 October 1966) ICSID/15 (Washington Convention).

2 In 1980, UNCITRAL Conciliation Rules were adopted, which yet presented already features that would make the boundaries between the two legal concepts blurring. See infra, n 5. The text of the UNCITRAL Conciliation Rules can be found at <https://uncitral.un.org/sites/uncitral.un.org/files/media-documents/uncitral/en/conc-rules-e.pdf> accessed 23 September 2024. Such a stance has been equally taken by the Permanent Court of Arbitration (PCA), which, whilst adopting the 1996 PCA Optional Rules for Conciliation, stated therein that in modern international practice, 'the word mediation is sometimes used to designate a process that is very similar to the procedures for conciliation'. See PCA, Optional Conciliation Rules (1996), <https://docs.pca-cpa.org/2016/01/Permanent-Court-of-Arbitration-Optional-Conciliation-Rules.pdf> accessed 23 September 2024, 152.

3 Art 34: (1) It shall be the duty of the Commission to clarify the issues in dispute between the parties and to endeavour to bring about agreement between them upon mutually acceptable terms. To that end, the Commission may at any stage of the proceedings and from time to time recommend terms of settlement to the parties. The parties shall cooperate in good faith with the Commission in order to enable the Commission to carry out its functions, and shall give their most serious consideration to its recommendations. (2) If the parties reach agreement, the Commission shall draw up a report noting the issues in dispute and recording that the parties have reached agreement. If, at any stage of the proceedings, it appears to the Commission that there is no likelihood of agreement between the parties, it shall close the proceedings and shall draw up a report noting the submission of the dispute and recording the failure of the parties to reach agreement. [...].

impartial third party assists disputing parties to amicably resolve all or parts of their dispute.[4]

The UN Convention on International Settlement Agreements Resulting from Mediation (also known as the Singapore Convention) provides instead a wider definition of mediation, as 'a process, irrespective of the expression used or the basis upon which the process is carried out, whereby parties attempt to reach an amicable settlement of their dispute with the assistance of a third person or persons ('the mediator') lacking the authority to impose a solution upon the parties to the dispute' (Article 2). This is indeed repeated in the 2023 UNCITRAL Model Provisions (Provision 1(1)). Despite UNCITRAL had in the past adopted instruments on conciliation, it declares that these are superseded by the new instruments on mediation.[5]

It is true that conciliation and mediation are often used interchangeably, especially when conciliation is declined as 'facilitative conciliation' (where reduced powers are granted to the conciliator) and mediation as 'evaluative mediation' (where instead the mediator has a wider role in helping to define the issues at stake), as especially in these cases there are considerable

4 'The mediator shall assist the parties in reaching a mutually acceptable resolution of all or part of the issues in dispute. The mediator has no authority to impose a resolution of the dispute on the parties'. A definition is also given in the ICSID Background Paper on Investment Mediation of July 2021: 'Mediation is a consensual process in which parties negotiate their dispute directly with one another, with the help of a third party (the mediator). The mediator's role is to assist the disputing parties with their negotiations. Therefore, mediation is often called 'facilitated negotiation' or 'facilitated dialogue'. These terms are used interchangeably in this document. The consensual nature of mediation and the principle of party autonomy are reflected not only at the outset of a mediation in the agreement to mediate, but throughout the facilitated negotiation process', see <https://icsid.worldbank.org/sites/default/files/publications/Background_Paper_on_Investment_Mediation_Oct.2021.pdf> accessed 23 September 2024.

5 'UNCITRAL recognized the value of conciliation or mediation, an interchangeable term used to adapt to the actual and practical use, as a method of amicably settling disputes arising in the context of international commercial relations and responded by adopting the UNCITRAL Conciliation Rules (1980), which offer an internationally harmonized set of procedural rules for the conduct of conciliation proceedings, and which were amended by the UNCITRAL Mediation Rules (2021). Further, in the context of recognition of the increasing use of conciliation as a method for settling commercial disputes, the UNCITRAL Model Law on International Commercial Conciliation (2002) was initially developed and later amended by the UNCITRAL Model Law on International Commercial Mediation and International Settlement Agreements Resulting from Mediation (2018). It complements the United Nations Convention on International Settlement Agreements Resulting from Mediation, which opened for signature in Singapore on 7 August 2019 and entered into force on 12 September 2020. The Convention will further enhance the use of mediation and foster access to justice', see <https://uncitral.un.org/en/texts/mediation> accessed 23 September 2024.

overlaps between the two. The flexibility and thus possible articulations of such methods of settlement of disputes may indeed make boundaries blur. However, when focusing specifically on ADR in international investment law, it cannot be ignored that in international law a difference does exist. As stated by J. Crawford:

> [C]onciliation is distinct from mediation and emerged from the commissions of inquiry provided for in the Hague Conventions for the Pacific Settlement of International Disputes of 1899 and 1907 and the commissions which figured in the series of arbitration treaties concluded by the US in 1913 and 1914 (the Bryan treaties). Conciliation has a semi-judicial aspect, since the commission of persons empowered has to elucidate the facts, may hear the parties and must make proposals for a settlement, which is normally non-binding.[6]

One should also remember the focus on the use of conciliation as an alternative to arbitration in the first place, in cases where arbitration would be considered unacceptable. Going back to the negotiations leading to the 1969 Vienna Convention on the Law of Treaties and the insertion of conciliation as a 'last-minute compromise' because of the tensions on the use of arbitration, would possibly suffice to reinforce this awareness.[7]

In the context of ISDS, the distinction might be less significant than in State-to-State disputes or have blurred in practice and in the understanding of scholars (as it might have blurred indeed also in State-to-State disputes).[8] R. Weeramantry, B. Chang and J. Sherard-Chow, in an empirical study on treaty clauses on conciliation and mediation introduce an historical assessment of the ICSID Convention and further international instruments showing all ambiguities in the use of such terms.[9] Besides, and irrespective of the terminology,

---

6 James Crawford, Brownlie's Principles of Public International Law (9th edn OUP 2019) 693.

7 As well known, some States had favored the inclusion of arbitration as a 'comprehensive binding settlement procedure', while others strongly opposed the recourse to binding adjudication by third parties in State-to-State disputes. This led indeed to the acceptance of binding conciliation as a 'last minute compromise'. See Sven Koopmans, Diplomatic Dispute Settlement: The Use of Inter-State Conciliation (TMC Asser Press 2008) 158.

8 John Merrills, International Dispute Settlement (5th edn CUP 2012); Ian Brownlie, 'The Wang Tieya Lecture in Public International Law: The Peaceful Settlement of International Disputes' (2009) 8 Chinese Journal of International Law 267.

9 Romesh Weeramantry, Brian Chang and Joel Sherard Chow, 'Conciliation and Mediation, in Investor State Dispute Settlement Provisions: A Quantitative and Qualitative Analysis', (2023) 38 *ICSID Review – Foreign Investment Law Journal* 201.

the instruments recently adopted by ICSID and UNCITRAL clearly exclude any method of a judicial or semi-judicial nature. Indeed, what is under scrutiny at present is rather the possibility to spur facilitated settlement by way of institutionalized procedures that would combine flexibility and due process. This might be indiscriminately achieved though a range of solutions and combinations that feature an independent third-party facilitating the exercise but abiding parties' autonomy.

To say it differently, one can now witness pleading for 'mediation' what has been pleaded by someone for 'conciliation': J. Cot described conciliation as a 'half-breed method for the settlement of disputes' that would stand 'some way between diplomatic methods for the settlement of disputes … and arbitral or judicial settlement'.[10] This would qualify it as a hybrid method to overcome differences (and thus possibly shortcomings) of other ADR methods: 'while mediation, inquiry and arbitration are fairly distinct from one another, conciliation is a combination of all three methods. One of its strengths might very well lie in its hybrid nature – by blending features from various methods of dispute settlement, conciliation might avoid the shortfalls of each individual method'.[11]

This qualification may now apply – under different terms – to mediation.

2.2 *Main Features of Mediation According to the New Instruments*

The ICSID mediation rules apply to disputes that relate to an investment, involve a State or a regional economic integration organization (REIO), and to which the parties consent in writing. There is no nationality requirement for parties, nor a requirement for either party to be linked to an ICSID Member. This permits a wide use of the established procedure, well beyond the use of arbitration (and conciliation) procedures, to the point that also nationals can resort to mediation against their own State. Moreover, the written agreement to mediate can be inserted in a contract or an *ad hoc* agreement, as well as based on mediation provisions contained in a bilateral or multilateral treaty or a domestic investment law.

Mediation under ICSID can be used whenever negotiations between the parties are deemed suitable, throughout the investment life cycle, during consultations, and alongside arbitration.

---

10 Jean-Pierre Cot, 'Conciliation', in Rüdiger Wolfrum (ed), *Max Planck Encyclopedia of Public International Law* (OUP 2006), para. 3.

11 Center for International Law (CIL), 'Background Paper for the 2027 Conference on *Conciliation, What is it and when to use it* (under Chatham House Rules)' <https://cil.nus.edu.sg/research/international-dispute-resolution/alternative-dispute-resolution-for-disputes-involving-states/> accessed 23 September 2024, 3.

Unlike ICSID conciliation proceedings, there is no jurisdictional determination by the mediator: the role of the conciliation commission to clarify the issues in dispute is not contemplated in mediation, where the role of the mediator is solely to assist the parties to reach a mutually agreeable solution. Equally, the mediator may not issue any recommendations absent agreement of the parties. Finally, a party to mediation may withdraw from the process at any time, as consent is required throughout the mediation process.

Moreover, a party individually or the parties jointly may appoint independent experts to provide with expert advice on legal, financial, or other matters. The scope of the expert's input and its terms are decided by the parties and the mediator. Furthermore, parties can consider whether to allow non-disputing parties to intervene and determine the scope and procedural framework for such participation, which can range from consultation on specific points, providing written statements, or having a more active role.

Mediation as regulated by ICSID is a structured process and consists of three main phases. In the initial phase, the parties provide the mediator with initial written statements, and the mediator works with the parties to develop a mediation protocol to regulate the mediation. Second, a phase of exploration and negotiation permits the parties to present their opening statements. The mediator then works with them to explore their expectations and constraints, and further develops a general framework where to input aspects important to the disputing parties for the settlement. It then assists the parties to develop options for settlement, and the exchange of offers and counteroffers. As a final stage, the parties develop and fix detailed terms of settlement. If no agreement is reached, the mediation gets to an end.

In this context, the role of the mediator is to assist the parties in reaching a mutually acceptable resolution of all or part of the issues in dispute, and in so doing, it has a duty to maintain impartiality and independence. It does not have the authority to impose a resolution on the parties and may make recommendations only upon the joint request of the parties.

One of the fundamental elements of facilitated negotiations is that parties must feel able to engage without concern that information exchanged could be used by the other party in another proceeding, either as evidence or otherwise.[12] Parties thus typically agree that the so-called 'without prejudice' principle applies, that is to say: a party may not rely on any document, statement, admission, or offer of settlement made by the other party, or anything said

12 The mediator may meet with the parties jointly or separately. When the mediator meets a party in caucus, the information shared by that party with the mediator must stay confidential unless such party expressly authorizes disclosure.

by the mediator, in any other proceeding, unless the parties jointly agree to waive this privilege.[13] Confidentiality becomes a central feature of mediation, although this is also one of the most controversial points of concern in the discussion of its use in ISDS (see *infra*).

The UNCITRAL Model Provisions do not establish an institutionalized mechanism such as ICSID, but rather list some high-level principles of general application.

Indeed, in the very first place they encourage parties to always consider mediation when in need of settling an international investment dispute and then advise to refer to either the 2021 UNCITRAL Mediation Rules, the ICSID Mediation Rules, the IBA Rules for Investor-State Mediation, or any other (institutionalized) rules.

The Model Provisions then establish the relationship between mediation and other procedures: mediation can be started at any point in time, before or during arbitration. However, upon the commencement of the mediation, a party cannot initiate or continue any other proceeding to resolve the dispute until the mediation is terminated. If the mediation commences while another proceeding is in progress, the parties must request the suspension of that proceeding pursuant to the rules applicable to that proceeding. Further, a party cannot rely in other proceedings on any positions taken, admissions or offers of settlement made or views expressed by the other party or the mediator during the mediation.

Finally, the Model Provisions recommend a time frame for proceedings by suggesting a maximum duration for some of the main stages of mediation and list some minimum requirements regarding the invitation to engage in mediation.

Despite the limited number and high-level nature of the UNCITRAL Model Provisions, these confirm the principle already expressed in ICSID that mediation could take various shapes according to the selection of the parties and be complementary to arbitration (or any other adjudicatory mechanism). The new instruments thus do seem to propose flexible schemes for negotiations whose main feature is that of being supported by an independent third party and a framework for reaching settlement in the respect of some due process principles: flexibility is combined with safeguards that such mechanism can ensure by offering a structured context and by involving in the process an

13 The ICSID Mediation Rules provide that information relating to the mediation, including documents generated in or obtained during the mediation shall be confidential unless the parties agree otherwise, the information or document is independently available, or disclosure is required by law. A complete description of the procedure can be found in ICSID Background Paper on Investment Mediation (n 4).

independent third party as a facilitator. Moreover, against such background mediation can indeed be represented as a form of facilitated negotiations where other amicable methods to solve disputes can be triggered and combined (as for instance the use of experts can under some circumstances recall fact finding procedures). To that end, one should notice how the rules of the new instruments differ from the 2012 IBA Rules for Investor-State Mediation, which contain many details on appointment of mediators and their conduct, seat of the proceedings, and costs and fees, as well as one should compare ICSID mediation rules with the arbitration-like rules established by the same institution for conciliation to perceive such difference and possibly glimpse on future concrete applications of this method.[14]

If this is the overall picture that emerges from the content of the new instruments on mediation in ISDS as representative of a possible trend with positive effects on management of disputes, some points of concern are still there and unresolved.

3 Mediation Faced with the Peculiarities of Investment Disputes

The newly adopted rules addressing investor-State disputes do not seem to depart relevantly from those applicable in commercial disputes. In fact, UNCITRAL, in advising how to address mediation, refers *inter alia* to its own 2021 Mediation Rules, that apply indiscriminately to commercial and investor-State proceedings and were elaborated having purely commercial disputes in mind.

However, many critical voices have been raised against the use of mediation in such disputes, for many reasons, including the difference in negotiating powers between the parties and the specific constraints of a state to achieve settlement.[15]

14 Nurick Lester, Stephen Schnably, 'The First ICSID Conciliation: Tesoro Petroleum Corporation v. Trinidad and Tobago', (1986) 1 *ICSID Review – Foreign Investment Law Journal* 340. The authors describe the conciliation procedure as occurring *de facto* like an arbitration: 'The conciliation procedures are similar in many respects to those governing arbitration – particularly in the procedural flexibility the parties enjoy – but with two key differences. First, while the arbitral procedures are intended to be flexible, the conciliation procedures are even more informal and so less expensive and, potentially, less time-consuming. Second, no binding award is rendered; instead, the conciliator's role is to help the parties reach a negotiated settlement'. See ibid., 346.

15 For a synthesis see Ignacio de la Rasilla, 'The Greatest Victory'? Challenges and Opportunities for Mediation in Investor-State Dispute Settlement', (2023) 38 *ICSID Review – Foreign Investment Law Journal* 169.

The UNCITRAL Guidelines have attempted a synthesis of perceived constraints for mediation in investment disputes, together with the potential benefits of the method.

As part of the obstacles to mediation, the UNCITRAL Working Group on ISDS mentioned primarily the difficulties regarding coordination among the relevant government agencies when negotiating an amicable settlement, the legal certainty necessary for officials to be involved in such settlements to be protected against personal liability, and the need to ensure that the necessary approval process be set up, including that those negotiating the settlements had the necessary authority to agree to a settlement. It was then said that policies as well as the legal framework for encouraging mediation would need to be developed or strengthened. Furthermore, it was noticed that very few treaties offer mediation and fewer regulate the mediation procedure. Unless the investment treaty does refer to mediation or include a provision requiring the disputing parties to undertake mediation, an *ad hoc* agreement to mediate is required to conduct mediation. However, concluding such an agreement is an additional procedural step, requires efforts and time and for government officials the necessary authority to engage in a voluntary mediation.[16]

Beyond those mentioned in the UNCITRAL papers, more constraints have yet been identified, getting to the core of the mechanism. In particular, and as mentioned, confidentiality is a basic feature of mediation. However, disclosure may be imposed when public interests are concerned.[17] The Mauritius Convention has made transparency the rule in investment arbitration.[18] Applying the same philosophy to mediation might deprive it of one of its essential features for working properly, since negotiations for settlement require that a candid approach is taken to reach a genuine settlement, and this is also the reason why information received in the course of a mediation cannot then be used in other proceedings. However, it is equally undeniable that some interests

16 UNCITRAL, 'Possible Reform of Investor-State Dispute Settlement (ISDS). Draft Provision on Mediation' (12 July 2022) A/CN.9/WG.III/WP.217, paras 11–12. See also Seraphina Chew, Lucy Reed, Christopher Thomas, 'Report: Survey on Obstacles to Settlement of Investor-State Disputes' NUS – Centre for International Law Working Paper 18/01 (September 2018) <https://cil.nus.edu.sg/wp-content/uploads/2018/09/NUS-CIL-Working-Paper-1801-Report-Survey-on-Obstacles-to-Settlement-of-Investor-State-Disputes.pdf> accessed 23 September 2024.

17 ICSID Rule 10 (1): 'All information relating to the mediation, and all documents generated in or obtained during the mediation, shall be confidential, unless: […] (c) disclosure is required by law'.

18 Convention on Transparency in Treaty-based Investor-State Arbitration (adopted on 10 December 2014 and entered into force on 18 October 2017) 3208 UNTS 54749 (Mauritius Convention on Transparency).

of a general nature, or touching upon many stakeholders outside the dispute, would justify transparency to the same extent than transparency is called for in arbitration.

This would be especially true since settlement usually consists in a change of contractual terms, the withdrawal of some regulatory measure, or the obtainment of benefits previously refused. These measures might result discriminatory against other stakeholders, or might be taken without having other stakeholders' interests in mind. This might also imply accountability of the officials taking these decisions with no transparency.[19]

Finally, although less explored, investors might also have some concerns. This is usually linked to the fear of not having the same bargaining powers against a State, although investors have also usually the compelling need to maintain the investment in the country and thus preserve good relationships with the host state.

Such concerns are indeed acknowledged and addressed as much as possible in the new sets of principles and rules that the various institutions have produced over the years – also beyond ICSID and UNCITRAL, since many other institutions had in any event proceeded to issue rules or guidelines to cope with the needs of mediation since the first Guidelines by IBA.[20] These did not prove to solve all concerns, as the reports of discussions within UNCITRAL WG III show. However, the international debate has at least permitted to conclude that in some fields or under some circumstances, mediation does indeed have merits that overcome any identified shortcomings. It is indeed that conviction that led to the new instruments that were adopted by ICSID and UNCITRAL between 2022 and 2023.

To that end, the UNCITRAL Guidelines list benefits that should guide the concrete decision whether to start mediation: (a) desirability of maintaining the parties' relationship also in light of retaining the current investments as well as the possibility of attracting future investments; (b) willingness of the parties to enter into a dialogue or negotiations and understand the other

---

19 Esmé Shirlow, *Investor-State Arbitration Meets Mediation: Potential Problems?*, Kluwer Arbitration Blog (30 September 2020) <https://arbitrationblog.kluwerarbitration.com/2020/09/30/investor-state-arbitration-meets-mediation-potential-problems/> accessed 23 September 2024.

20 Far from any intent of exhaustiveness, mention can be made to the Singapore International Mediation Center (SIMC), which signed in 2015 with the Singapore International Arbitration Center (SIAC) the Arb-Med-Arb Protocol (AMA Protocol); to the Energy Charter Treaty Secretariat, which elaborated the ECT Guide on Investment Mediation in 2016; and to Vienna International Arbitration Center (VIAC), which adopted the VIAC Rules of Investment Arbitration and Mediation in 2021.

party's positions; (c) number of the parties involved, including those with potentially different interests; (d) desirability of resolving a dispute in a time- and cost-effective manner; (e) nature of the dispute and the underlying grievance; (f) complexity of the issues in dispute and urgency to address them; (g) usefulness for the parties to streamline the issues at stake; (h) desirability of involving a third party; (i) desirability of the parties having control over the resolution process and the outcome; (j) desirability of the parties developing tailored and creative solutions; (k) any implication of complying with any settlement agreement, including any political, economic, social and financial implication.[21]

This list is heterogeneous and contains elements specifically pertaining to the working of the mechanism, others relating to the concrete needs of parties under the circumstances, and others relevant for procedural strategy.[22] However, they point to one major element, i.e., the need for parties to solve a specific dispute in a situation where relationships want to be preserved and/or where interests at stake would not fit into the typically adversarial scheme of adjudication.

This logic is very well known in contracts, especially for infrastructures or large projects, that is to say: in investment contracts. While we started our considerations from conciliation and its features as alternative to those of arbitration to then move to mediation as a catch-all definition of methods to solve disputes aside from arbitration, we now reverse the exercise: in fact, mediation as emerging from the new trends and the current debate takes stock of the results of dispute resolution in big investment deals based on contracts, where by definition parties' autonomy favors the elaboration of autonomous pre- and post-dispute mechanisms to align the terms of the commercial relationship

---

21 UNCITRAL Guidelines on Mediation for International Investment Disputes, 2023, available at <https://uncitral.un.org/sites/uncitral.un.org/files/media-documents/uncitral/en/2401497e_mediation_guidelines_-ebook_eng.pdf> accessed 23 September 2024, para 3.

22 Strategic choices seem to qualify the list of questions that ICSID proposes for parties to choose mediation in its Background Paper (n. 4), which yet offer a confirmation of the main issues at stake: '1) Is there a desire to continue the relationship of the parties? 2) Do the parties wish to manage (or terminate) their relationship amicably? 3) Is there a willingness to enter into negotiations or have a dialogue? 4) Is there hostility or distrust between the disputing parties? 5) Do the parties want a rapid resolution of the dispute or a more rapid resolution than might be achieved through other available processes? 6) Do the parties prefer to keep control over the outcome? 7) Do the parties seek tailored solutions other than the relief available in accordance with the applicable provision (usually monetary relief)? 8) Are there multiple conflicts or issues in dispute between the parties, some of which could be negotiated/mediated? and 9) Are there multiple parties involved with differing interests?' See *ibid*, 5.

to the renewed circumstances. This approach transforms the pathology of a dispute into in fact one of the possible accidents that occur in a long-term relationship requiring redefinition of terms and conditions as part of physiology of the relationship.

Against this background, we strength the 'private' dimension of such method of solution of the dispute, which is extremely interesting but also extremely challenging, and can clash not only with the inherent qualities of a sovereign, but also with the need of protecting also interests outside of the perimeter of the dispute. However, this is exactly what scholars and practitioners are struggling with in relation to commercial contracts, where sustainability goals and social responsibility of enterprises oblige to reconsider the methods of solving disputes and protecting diversified interests. It is thus necessary to move a step further and see how this new instrument can indeed address the new constraints and challenges that we face today.

4 Will Facilitated Settlement Have a Fresh Chance in the Future of Investment Disputes Resolution?

The rise of support to mediation has been read as a reaction to the 'public legitimacy crisis' experienced by arbitration in ISDS. In fact, such crisis has different roots that cannot be simply solved by supporting mediation. Rather, mediation can address some of the possible issues at stake if it is modernized and made functionally appropriate for the needs it intends to address. However, mediation – if so modernized – may indeed be part of the solution.

In the first place, the new instruments testify to a use of mediation as a complement to arbitration (or litigation). This is not a novelty *per se*; however, what is a novelty is the widening of the practice of inserting multi-tier clauses for dispute resolution in investment treaties.

Amongst the most recent treaties, the Canada-Ukraine 2023 Free Trade Agreement (FTA)[23] regulates amicable solution of disputes in general and the recourse to mediation specifically through a multi-tiered system:

> Article 17.21: Request for Consultations
> 1. In the event of an investment dispute under this Agreement, an investor of a Party shall seek to resolve the dispute through consultations,

23 Text of the 2023 Canada – Ukraine Free Trade Agreement, Ch 17, see <https://investmentpolicy.unctad.org/international-investment-agreements/treaty-files/8324/download> accessed 23 September 2024.

> which may include the use of non-binding, third party procedures, such as good offices, conciliation, or mediation […].
>
> Article 17.22: Mediation
> The disputing parties may at any time agree to have recourse to mediation. A respondent shall give sympathetic consideration to a request for mediation made by a micro, small, or medium-sized enterprise. Recourse to mediation is without prejudice to the legal position or rights of the disputing parties under this Section and is governed by the rules agreed to by the disputing parties, including any applicable rules for mediation adopted by the Joint Commission. If the disputing parties agree to have recourse to mediation, paragraphs 4, 5, and 8 of Article 17.21 (Request for Consultations) and all timelines pursuant to an arbitration under this section are suspended from the date on which the disputing parties agreed to have recourse to mediation, and shall resume on the date on which either disputing party decides to terminate the mediation. A decision by a disputing party to terminate the mediation shall be transmitted by way of letter to the mediator and the other disputing party.

In the same line, the 2023 Turkey-United Arab Emirates Bilateral Investment Treaty (BIT)[24], after having regulated investment-State disputes resolution by way of arbitration, at article 13 includes mediation:

> Mediation
> 7. Notwithstanding the provision of this Article, the disputing parties may at any time agree to have recourse to mediation.
> 8. Recourse to mediation is without prejudice to the legal position or rights of either disputing party under this Agreement and is governed by the rules agreed to by the disputing parties.
> 9. The mediator is appointed by agreement of the disputing parties. The disputing parties may also request that the Secretary-General of ICSID appoint the mediator.
> 10. The disputing parties shall endeavour to reach a resolution of the dispute within sixty (60) days from the appointment of the mediator.

24 Agreement between the Government of the Republic of Türkiye and the Government of the United Arab Emirates concerning the Reciprocal Promotion and Protection of Investments, see <https://investmentpolicy.unctad.org/international-investment-agreements/treaty-files/8396/download> accessed 23 September 2024.

> 11. A decision by a disputing party to terminate the mediation shall be transmitted by way of a letter to the mediator and the other disputing party.

On the other side, and just to randomly cover different parts of the world, the 2022 Pacific Alliance – Singapore FTA[25] includes mediation in combination with arbitration as in the other mentioned examples:

> Article 8.19: Mediation
> 1. The disputing parties may at any time agree to have recourse to mediation.
> 2. The mediator shall be appointed by agreement of the disputing parties.
> 3. Recourse to mediation is without prejudice to the legal position or rights of a disputing party under this Chapter and is governed by the rules agreed to by the disputing parties including, if available, the rules for mediation adopted by the Free Trade Commission.
> 4. If mediation resolves the dispute, a consent award should be issued by the tribunal, if one has been constituted.
> 5. For greater certainty, the initiation of mediation shall not be construed as recognition of the jurisdiction of the tribunal under this Section.

The widening of treaties and investment contracts' multi-tier clauses does not by itself ensure the use of ADR in ISDS. However, it grants the legal basis to permit parties to agree on more articulated and hybrid mechanisms to solve disputes.[26] Institutional rules as those adopted by ICSID in 2023 reinforce such patterns.

There is yet a different line of considerations to appreciate: in the second place, aside from its connection to, or complementarity with arbitration and/or litigation, the fact itself that mediation is an hybrid mechanism where flexibility can be coped with due process, and where stakeholders whose interests are traditionally placed outside of the perimeter of the dispute settlement can take their voice, should indeed be explored as a possible tool for resolution of disputes where interests are multiple and articulated, and often general

25 Pacific Alliance – Singapore FTA (2022), Ch 8, see <https://investmentpolicy.unctad.org/international-investment-agreements/treaty-files/6439/download> accessed 23 September 2024.

26 For an assessment of the kinds of clauses found in treaties and the reference therein to the different ADR mechanisms, as well as various other considerations on the use of mediation in ISDS, see Catherine Kassedjian et al., 'Mediation in Future Investor-State Dispute Settlement', (2023) 14 *Journal of International Dispute Settlement* 192.

in kind or pertaining a category of people (not individually pertaining to an individual or an entity that can defend them directly). Furthermore, as said, mediation can work as a method to *prevent* disputes, in the sense that it can permit changes in terms and conditions or adjustments affecting future behaviors, that can equally be the result of negotiations or confrontation with third parties or taking charge of some general interests.

Confidentiality is an issue in this context which is difficult to overcome. As it was discussed, confidentiality is an inherent feature of the mechanism. However, the possibility to consider (to what extent will depend on the level of openness of parties and on the concrete circumstances) non-disputing third-parties' interests, or the point of view of other stakeholders, might constitute a relevant improvement to cope with the issue of how to integrate the protection of such interests within the situation under dispute, which is an issue that sovereign States must consider and that constitutes one of the challenges of present times. Somehow, structured mechanisms for mediation should by themselves guarantee against the risks that transparency would otherwise mitigate. Even if parties are left free to come up with original solutions or accommodate their different perceptions by ensuring confidentiality and no prejudice to any further defense of own rights in case mediation fails – once experts can be called upon and third parties permitted to intervene – transparency might be of more limited use.

Protection of human rights may also be an issue, in the sense that protection of human rights might not fit into the logics of mediation. However, the example of the 2019 Hague Rules on Business and Human Rights Arbitration[27] seems to tell the opposite: these rules, resulted from a private initiative by a diverse team of international practitioners and academics for the promotion of the use of arbitration as a remedy in the important field of business and human rights inspired by the UN Guiding Principles on Business and Human Rights, also include mediation at article 56. Its commentary reads to that end:

> [A]rticle 56 is a new article as compared to the 2013 UNCITRAL Arbitration Rules, which emphasizes the importance of collaborative and dialogue-based settlement mechanisms in business and human rights disputes. Article 56 establishes a framework for mediation that takes place in parallel to or in conjunction with arbitration under these Rules, in keeping

27 Center for International Legal Cooperation, 'The Hague Rules on Business and Human Rights Arbitration', <https://www.cilc.nl/cms/wp-content/uploads/2019/12/The-Hague-Rules-on-Business-and-Human-Rights-Arbitration_CILC-digital-version.pdf> accessed 23 September 2024.

> with other provisions in the Rules concerning the facilitation of settlement through collaborative settlement mechanisms, such as Article 18(3), Article 47 (Settlement or other grounds for termination) and paragraph 4 of the Preamble.

On the other side, examples already exist of collective disputes resolutions through mediation, for instance in labor law. Some of their mechanisms could be assessed as to whether they could be implemented generally and fit ISDS.[28]

Even more significantly, the procedures in front of the National Points of Contact (NPCs) for implementation of the OECD *Guidelines for Multinational Enterprises on Responsible Business Conduct*[29] provide for mediation procedures where behaviors of enterprises are challenged against the principles of the Guidelines.[30] Indeed, as part of making available good offices, and where relevant to the issues at hand, NPCs do offer, or facilitate access to, consensual and non-adversarial processes, such as mediation or conciliation, to assist the parties in resolving issues at hand. In common with accepted practices on conciliation and mediation, these processes would be used only upon agreement of the parties concerned and their commitment to participate in good faith during the procedure. If mediation is the option chosen, NPCs may choose to carry out the mediation themselves or engage external mediators in consultation with the parties to conduct or support mediation.

Among the many interesting aspects of this kind of mediation, pronouncing on human rights and international standards on sustainability (including protection of the environment and interests of local communities), is the level of transparency achieved. Procedures are confidential and parties are subject to a duty of confidentiality. However, the results of mediation may be made partially public, as the results of the whole procedure within the NPCs. As an example, in 2019 the Belgian NPC, when dealing with a case concerning an alleged non-observance of the Guidelines in relation to principles on human rights, employment and industrial relations by the Belgian company AB-InBev in India, resorted to mediation. It then published an intermediary mediation

---

28 International Labor Organization (ILO), 'Collective Dispute Resolution through Conciliation, Mediation and Arbitration: European and ILO Perspectives (2017)' <https://www.ilo.org/resource/conference-paper/collective-dispute-resolution-through-conciliation-mediation-and> accessed 23 September 2024.

29 OECD, *OECD Guidelines for Multinational Enterprises on Responsible Business Conduct* (OECD Publishing Paris).

30 The NCPs are agencies established by governments whose mandate is twofold: to promote the OECD Guidelines and related due diligence guidance, and to handle cases (referred to as 'specific instances') as a non-judicial grievance mechanism.

statement in 2020, where stock was given of the main steps conducted by the Belgian NPC since the publication of its Initial Assessment, the challenges and achievements of the mediation and the conclusion reached at that stage (since settlement was not achieved but claims reduced to a few issues), and consequent decision from the Belgian NPC on how to proceed.[31]

---

31 Belgian National Contact Point for the OECD Guidelines for Multinational Enterprises, 'Statement from the Belgian National Contact Point on the Specific Instance IUF/AB-InBev – 2nd March 2020', <https://economie.fgov.be/sites/default/files/Files/Entreprises/Mediation-Statement-NCP-IUF-ABInbev-EN.pdf> accessed 23 September 2024.

The EU and the Energy Charter Treaty: A Future of ADR in the Energy Sector?

Nikos Lavranos *

1 Introduction

On 27 June 2024, the European Union (EU) adopted the decision to formal withdraw from the Energy Charter Treaty (ECT).[1] This follows in the footsteps of a proposal to modernise the ECT, which did not gather the required majority among Member States. Modernising the ECT was aimed at bringing it in line with *Achmea*[2] and *Komstroy*[3] judgments as well as with the Comprehensive Economic and Trade Agreement (CETA). In addition, the intention was to green the ECT by incorporating the Paris Agreement targets.

After 3 years of negotiations, an agreement in principle was reached in June 2022.[4] Effectively, the EU and its Member States reached all of its aims. Thus, a disconnection clause for intra-EU Bilateral Investment Treaties (BITS) was explicitly included, meaning intra-EU ECT disputes would not be possible any longer. Moreover, the Paris Agreement targets were included, the protection of fossil fuels was reduced from 20 to 10 years, and all the new CETA substantive protection standards, in particular the closed fair and equitable treatment and the indirect expropriation without compensation except in rare circumstances provisions were all incorporated.

---

* Guest Professor, Leiden University; Secretary General, European Federation for Investment Law and Arbitration; Founder, NL-investmentconsulting.

1 Council of the EU, Press release, EU notifies its withdrawal from ECT (27 June 2024) <https://www.consilium.europa.eu/en/press/press-releases/2024/06/27/energy-charter-treaty-eu-notifies-its-withdrawal/> accessed 3 February 2025; Nikos Lavranos, 'Comment: Leaving the Energy Charter Treaty Also Means Leaving a Legal Mess Behind' (Borderlex, 10 July 2023) <https://borderlex.net/2023/07/10/comment-leaving-the-energy-charter-treat-also-means-leaving-a-legal-mess-behind/> accessed 13 September 2024; European Parliamentary Research Service, 'EU Withdrawal From the Energy Charter Treaty', <https://www.europarl.europa.eu/RegData/etudes/BRIE/2023/754632/EPRS_BRI(2023)754632_EN.pdf> accessed 13 September 2024.

2 CJEU, Case C284/16 Slovak Republic v Achmea [2018] ECLI:EU:C:2018:158.

3 CJEU, Case C-741/19 République de Moldavie v Komstroy *LLC* [2021] ECLI:EU:C:2021:655.

4 Nikos Lavranos, 'Comment: How the EU Disconnected itself From the Energy Charter Treaty' (Borderlex, 27 June 2022) <https://borderlex.net/2022/06/27/comment-how-the-eu-disconnected-itself-from-the-energy-charter-treaty/> accessed 10 July 2023. The modernized ECT text of June 2022 is available at <https://www.bilaterals.org/IMG/pdf/reformed_ect_text.pdf> accessed 13 September 2024.

 | DOI:10.1163/9789004727663_007

Nonetheless, several EU Member States announced that they would withdraw from the ECT rather than sign the modernized version because they considered it to be not green enough. At this moment, France, Poland, Germany and Luxembourg have withdrawn from the ECT.[5]

Meanwhile, in December 2024, the remaining 20 plus Contracting Parties have adopted the modernized ECT text, which shall provisionally apply as of September 2025.[6] Given this chaos,[7] the question arises what will be the purpose of the modernized ECT without the EU and its Member States?

More specifically, this also raises questions regarding investors in the energy sector and any available dispute resolution mechanisms, now that the ECT and also the intra-EU BITs are effectively gone. Interestingly, the modernized ECT text does not contain anything on mediation, only on conciliation. Consequently, domestic courts of the EU Member States remain the only option, including as a final recourse possibly the European Court of Human Rights in Strasbourg.[8]

Therefore, flexible, non-treaty based, dispute settlement tools, such as mediation and conciliation and perhaps even dispute prevention mechanisms could become even more relevant and therefore should be developed further.[9] This will be indeed the focus of this contribution.

2 Role of Mediation in Energy Disputes

The ECT encourages amicable resolution of investment disputes and allows parties to an investment dispute to resort to mediation at any point in time. Article 26(1) of the ECT states that investment disputes related to breaches of obligations under Part III of the treaty 'shall, if possible, be settled amicably.' There is no specification within the ECT as to which mechanisms must be used

5 Damien Charlotin, 'ECT Secretariat Confirms That Luxembourg Has Notified the Treaty's Depository of its Withdrawal' (Investment Arbitration Reporter, 30 August 2023) <https://www.iareporter.com/articles/ect-secretariat-confirms-that-luxembourg-has-notified-the-treatys-depository-of-its-withdrawal/> accessed 13 September 2024.

6 ECT, Press release, The Energy Charter Conference Adopts Decisions on the Modernisation of the Energy Charter Treaty (3 December 2024) <https://www.energycharter.org/media/news/article/the-energy-charter-conference-adopts-decisions-on-the-modernisation-of-the-energy-charter-treaty/> accessed 3 February 2025.

7 See for a detailed analysis: Nikos Lavranos and Adhiraj Lath, 'The Paralysis of the Energy Charter Treaty' (2023) 33 Rivista dell'arbitrato 273.

8 Robert Spano, 'Intra-EU BITs and Achmea: On a Collision Course with Strasbourg?' (2024) 9 European Investment Law and Arbitration Review 161.

9 Fahira Brodlija, 'Dispute Prevention Mechanisms in Investment Treaties: A Solution Fit for the Future of ISDS', in Nikos Lavranos and Stefano Castagna (eds), International Arbitration and *EU* Law, 2nd edn (Elgar 2024) 462.

under such 'amicable settlement' process within the three months cooling-off period. Therefore, parties have the freedom and flexibility to agree to use good offices, structured negotiation, mediation or conciliation using existing mechanisms or even have the option to agree on a tailor-made mechanism.

While available arbitral awards under the ECT have not confirmed the existence of a duty to mediate in article 26(1) of the ECT, they confirmed that parties need to seriously attempt to reach an amicable settlement.[10]

Already in 2016, the ECT Contracting Parties adopted the Guide on Investment Mediation.[11] In this guide, it was also stated that there has been a settlement agreement in eight investment cases: *ČEZ v Albania* (2013), *Slovak Gas Holding BV et al v Slovak Republic* (2012), *Türkiye Petrolleri Anonim Ortaklığı v Kazakhstan* (2011), *EVN AG v The Former Yugoslav Republic of Macedonia* (2010), *Vattenfall v Germany* (2011), *Barmek Holding A.S. v Azerbaijan* (2006), *Alstom Power Italia SpA, Alstom SpA v Mongolia* (2004), and *AES Summit Generation Ltd. v Hungary* (2002). In these cases, the arbitration proceedings were discontinued due to the later settlement entered into by the parties. Out of these eight cases, at least three settlements were embodied in an award and are publicly available.[12]

In late 2023 upon requesting some statistics from the ECT Secretariat, I received the following response which I quote:

> Procedural records in cases, as reflected in publicly available arbitral and judicial decisions, as well as media reports, have not allowed us to come up with any statistical data on mediation thus far – there is normally no meaningful information on attempts to settle the disputes amicably. Anecdotally, investors prefer direct negotiations.
>
> As of today, we are aware of 11 cases under the ECT which were settled through negotiations after the arbitral proceedings had been initiated. In four cases, settlement agreements were reflected in the awards.

Considering the total number of more than 160 ECT cases,[13] the available statistics illustrate that mediation does not seem to be an often-used dispute settlement tool.

---

10 *Petrobart Limited v The Kyrgyz Republic*, SCC Case No 126/2003, Award (29 March 2005) 73; *Limited Liability Company Amto v Ukraine*, SCC Case No 080/2005, Award (26 March 2008) para 50; *Anatolie Stati, Gabriel Stati, Ascom Group SA and Terra Raf Trans Traiding Ltd v Kazakhstan*, SCC Case No 116/2010, Award (19 December 2013) paras 828–830.

11 Available at <https://www.energycharter.org/fileadmin/DocumentsMedia/CCDECS/2016/CCDEC201612.pdf> accessed 13 September 2009.

12 Ibid.

13 See the ECT website: <https://www.energychartertreaty.org/cases/statistics/> accessed 13 September 2024.

- The hesitation to resort to mediation arises from several factors that include:
- a lack of familiarity with mediation among small and medium-sized businesses;
- confidentiality of such procedures and outcomes;
- and skepticism over the effectiveness of mediation – seen as a delaying tactic or a 'waste' of time and energy due to the non-binding nature of its outcome;
- lack of political and legal authority or mandate to resolve conflicts;
- lack of political will of the host country's government to proceed in good faith;
- reluctance of authorities of the host country to respond to problems on time.

Similar conclusions have been reached by a recent, very detailed study on mediation in Investor-State Dispute Settlement (ISDS) disputes by Catherine Kessedjian, Anne van Aken, Loukas Mistelis and others.[14] The following conclusions are particularly interesting and relevant.

- The potential of the cooling-off periods, which are often included in investment treaties and usually range between 3-6 months, are not used as a meaningful option to negotiate a solution. However, studies have found that this timeframe is rather short to allow for a meaningful attempt at resolving the dispute. States and governments will require a considerable amount of time to identify the breach and responsible institutions among a myriad of government agencies.
- This study also runs into the problem of lack of publicly available data regarding actual use of mediation and any results of it. Little information is available in the public domain regarding the usage of mediation in investor state disputes.
- The authors also point out to the results of the Queen Mary University of London study[15] which interviews investors and their preferences for dispute resolution. While 30% of investors are strongly in favour of mandatory mediation, and 34% are somewhat in favour, 22% are strongly opposed, while 11% are somewhat opposed.

---

14 Catherine Kessedjian, Anne van Aaken, Runar Lie, Loukas Mistelis and José Maria Reis, 'Mediation in Future Investor – State Dispute Settlement' (2023) 14 *Journal of International Dispute Settlement* 192.

15 'Queen Mary University of London and White & Case 2021 International Arbitration Survey: Adapting arbitration to a changing world', available at <https://arbitration.qmul.ac.uk/media/arbitration/docs/LON0320037-QMUL-International-Arbitration-Survey-2021_19_WEB.pdf> accessed 13 September 2024.

- One concern that was highlighted by investors was the perception that mandatory mediation would increase the costs and duration of the proceedings.
- The authors flag very similar reasons as the ECT Secretariat as to why mediation is not used more frequently, but they mention some other reasons too, i.e., such as the concerns of civil society and the fact that mediation is conducted in confidentiality, which raises concerns of 'secret deals' that are made between investors and host States. The enforcement issue comes up too as well as the link between mediation and Third-Party Funder and the confidentiality that exists between the funder and the investor as regards their deal.

The Energy Community, which comprises Westen Balkan countries, which are also EU candidate countries, has successfully used mediation in several cases for resolving disputes between energy companies and national energy authorities.[16]

3 Efforts to Promote Mediation

Despite the underuse of mediation in investor-State disputes, States continue and even enhance their efforts to promote mediation as an alternative to arbitration.

For example, the EU has integrated mediation as part of the toolbox of resolving disputes between investors and the CETA parties. In 2021, the EU and Canada have adopted Decision No 002/2021, which contains further specific mediation rules for investor-State disputes under CETA.[17]

Also, in 2022, the International Centre for Settlement of Investment Disputes (ICSID) has adopted new Mediation Rules, marking the first institutional mediation rules designed specifically for investment disputes.[18]

16 Energy Community website: <https://www.energy-community.org/aboutus/disputeresolution.html> accessed 13 September 2024.

17 Rafal Morek, 'The EU and Canada adopt mediation rules for the CETA investment court system' (Kluwer Arbitration Blog, 18 February 2021) <https://mediationblog.kluwerarbitration.com/2021/02/18/the-eu-and-canada-adopt-mediation-rules-for-the-ceta-investment-court-system/> accessed 13 September 2024.

18 ICSID Mediation Rules (2022), available at <https://icsid.worldbank.org/rules-regulations/mediation> accessed 13 September 2024.

In addition, the Singapore Convention[19] for enforcing mediation settlements has been adopted but has only been ratified by 13 States so far, most recently by Nigeria, but none of the EU Member States or the EU itself has signed or ratified yet. Interestingly, several Western Balkan countries have actually signed but not yet ratified the Singapore Convention, i.e., North Macedonia, Montenegro, Serbia.

Most recently, in July 2023, after six years of discussions, the Working Group III (WGIII) of the United Nations Commission on International Trade Law (UNCITRAL) delivered several significant documents, including the Draft Provisions on Mediation[20] and the Draft UNCITRAL Guidelines on Investment Mediation.[21]

4 Benefits of Mediation

Prima facie, mediation offers an appealing alternative to arbitration for several obvious reasons:
- mediation is faster and cheaper;
- mediation can restore the relationship between investor and host State;
- mediation can offer other solutions rather than only monetary satisfaction.
- Nonetheless, despite these advantages, it is also clear that mediation can only be a viable alternative to arbitration in particular circumstances, namely:
- the problem has not yet escalated into a full-blown dispute, so mediation must be used in the very early pre-arbitration stages;
- both parties (investor and host State) have a genuine interest in continuing their relationship, so both parties are interested in finding a mutually acceptable solution;
- the dispute is relatively small in terms of the invested amount of money and relatively uncomplicated;
- both parties have given the participants in the mediation all the necessary powers and authorities to agree on a mediated settlement.

19 Singapore Convention on Mediation, https://www.singaporeconvention.org/; see: Nadja Alexander, Shouyu Chong and Vakhtang Giorgadze, *The Singapore Convention on Mediation: A Commentary*, 2nd edn (Kluwer 2022).

20 UNCITRAL 'Draft Provisions on Mediation' (2023) UN Doc A/CN.9/WG.III/WP.226.

21 UNCITRAL 'Draft Guidelines on Investment Mediation' (2023) UN Doc A/CN.9/WG.III/WP.227.

In short, it seems to me that mediation for investor-State disputes is a viable option only for certain particular situations and – at least as it stands now – is not a suitable alternative for arbitration. At the same time, however, States seem to attach increasing importance to mediation as is evidenced by their investment treaty practice and the new mediation rules they recently have agreed upon. Consequently, a lot still needs to be done to make mediation a more effective and generally accepted tool for dispute resolution.

5 The Way Forward

Turning back to European investors in the energy sector, what needs to be done, now that the ECT and also the intra-EU BIT s are gone?

Obviously, domestic courts of the EU Member States remain an option, including, ultimately, the European Court of Human Rights. However, as the former President of the European Court of Human Rights made clear in his recent EFILA Lecture, it is going to be an uphill battle for European investors to proof a breach of the ECHR.[22]

Thus, from this perspective, flexible, non-treaty based, dispute settlement tools, such as mediation and conciliation and even dispute prevention mechanisms inevitably will become more relevant for European investors, and therefore should be developed further.

The following suggestions could be made in this regard.

- Timing of the mediation. Mediation should take place at a very early stage. If mediation takes place at an early stage, the dispute is not yet full crystalized and there are good reasons to believe that it may be easier to mediate the entire problem and not only the financial aspects. This is key to a long-term solution. But there are also strong arguments to give mediation opportunities (windows) during the arbitration process as well.
- A clear line of authority will have to be established within the State. All participants in the mediation must have full decision-making authority in order to enter into a mediated settlement. Such authority must come from the highest level since otherwise the risk exists that the settlement will not be executed.
- Transparency and adaptation of the confidential parts of the process are needed (drawing for example on (parts of) the Mauritius Convention[23] or

22 Spano (n 8).

23 United Nations Convention on Transparency in Treaty-Based Investor-State Arbitration (New York, 2014) (the 'Mauritius Convention on Transparency'), available at <https://uncitral.un.org/en/texts/arbitration/conventions/transparency> accessed 13 September 2024.

the Hague Rules on Business and Human Rights Arbitration[24]). Guidelines as to what happens with the documents and arguments used during the mediation, if it is unsuccessful and the case proceeds to arbitration/ litigation, must be established. In civil and commercial matters, these documents and arguments are strictly confidential and nothing said or done during the mediation can be used in arbitration. It may be appropriate to maintain confidentiality of (some) documents and arguments even if investor – State mediation has a degree of transparency.

- Capacity building is important. Training new mediators for investor-State disputes is essential. Currently, there is no sufficient large pool of mediators for investment disputes and neither is there a mediator community for this specific area.
- Universities play an important role. Mock mediation competitions for young students and lawyers should be established as part of the standard curriculum. Also, mediation trainings should be offered by universities and the professional educational bodies of lawyers and arbitrators.
- The UNCITRAL WG III Advisory Centre could play an important role for training government officials in how to deal with mediations.
- A much wider ratification of the Singapore Convention is needed.
- Hence, in conclusion, it is certainly a good development that many States and the arbitration community are talking more and more about mediation and ADR, but as has been highlighted in this contribution a lot more needs to be done to make mediation a really useful tool for investors to solve problems with host States.

24 The Hague Rules on Business and Human Rights Arbitration (2019), available at <www.cilc.nl/cms/wp-content/uploads/2019/12/The-Hague-Rules-on-Business-and-Human-Rights-Arbitration_CILC-digital-version.pdf> accessed 13 September 2024.

The Role of ADR in Favoring Completion of International Energy Infrastructure Projects

Michael McIlwrath and Chiara Tondini***

1 Introduction

A sizeable portion of the global economy is devoted to delivering energy in various forms to those who need it. Keeping up with the needs of an expanding population requires a continuous massive investment in, and creation of, new infrastructure. In addition, the need for entirely new infrastructure to replace the use of fossil fuels requires a staggering amount of capital investment. According to the Bloomberg NEF (BNEF) annual reports, the global investment in the energy transition in 2020 amounted to $501.3 billion and more than doubled, to $1.1 trillion, in 2022.[1]

Unfortunately, a significant percentage of the capital needed to build new infrastructure is trapped in disputes that arise even before energy projects can get underway. While it is difficult to quantify the total amount of energy-related disputes, the available statistics suggest that significant numbers are pending before the courts and arbitration institutions around the world. For example, in referring to engineering and construction projects – of which energy infrastructure projects are a considerable portion – the expert company HKA's sixth CRUX annual report[2] highlights that the sums in dispute related to the 1,801 projects examined – for a cumulative capital expenditure value of $2.247 trillion – exceeded $91.3 billion. As a similar data point, the International Chamber of Commerce (ICC), the leading institution for resolving international commercial disputes through arbitration, currently manages over $100 billion of disputes

* Academic Fellow, Bocconi University, Milan; Former President of the Governing Body for Dispute Resolution Services of the International Chamber of Commerce (ICC).

** International Disputes Counsel; COO at MDisputes.

1 Oktavia Catsaros, 'Global Low-Carbon Energy Technology Investment Surges Past $1 Trillion for the First Time' (BlombergNEF, 26 January 2023) <https://about.bnef.com/blog/global-low-carbon-energy-technology-investment-surges-past-1-trillion-for-the-first-time/> accessed 28 January 2024.

2 CRUX Insight, 'Sixth Annual Report. Forewarned is Forearmed. Anticipating challenges, mitigating risks. A regional and sector analysis of claims and disputes causation' (*HKA*, 23 October 2023) <www.hka.com/crux-insight-sixth-annual-report-forewarned-is-forearmed/> accessed 28 January 2024.

 | DOI:10.1163/9789004727663_008

related to energy and energy projects.[3] Importantly, these numbers refer to the amounts in dispute only, and do not include the costs of the lawyers, experts, or the operational distraction that these disputes can create.

When it comes to green energy projects, the delay in putting them into operation has not only an impact on financial investments but also obvious implications in achieving the climate objectives of the Paris Agreement, with consequences for the environment, public health, human rights and – ultimately – economic growth.[4]

If these disputes could be prevented or, if not prevented, resolved earlier, then projects could be concluded faster, energy infrastructure could be put into operation sooner, and more would be available to achieve energy transition goals sooner.

This article aims to examine the causes of the breakdowns that lead or may lead to disputes in energy infrastructure projects, and how different uses of ADR can help achieve the goals of the energy transition.

2 Key Features and Actors in Energy Infrastructure Projects

Typical large energy projects have a structure of mega collaborations that stem from an initial relationship among a few key contracting parties and financing institutions with a supporting complex contractual structure involving heterogeneous categories of stakeholders, normally from different countries and regulated by different jurisdictions. Among these:

Project owner (or, as often qualified, the 'Employer'): Entities initiating and overseeing the development of the energy infrastructure project. They may be companies whose core business is the construction of energy infrastructure, or investors whose objective is to complete the project and place it on the market in order to make a profit. The prevalent scenario is a project owner constituted by a consortium of companies with the form of a joint venture. The paramount distinction is between unincorporated joint ventures, *i.e.* a contractual agreement among all investors under the name of Joint Operating Agreement (JOA) which regulates the construction and operation of the project, and

3 The ICC currently handles over 1,800 pending arbitrations with a total aggregate value of over $250 billion. The average size of these cases at the time they are filed with the ICC is over $40 million, and then this average grows to over $170 million as cases progress. Approximately a quarter of these cases are energy-related, and they rank among the highest claim amounts.

4 International Monetary Fund, *2022 World Economic Outlook: Countering the Cost-of-Living Crisis* (Washington, October), Chapter 3.

incorporated joint ventures, with the setup of a new legal entity with limited liability (the Joint Venture Company – JVC). Counterintuitively, the substantial financial outlay required for the implementation of such projects is not the ultimate reason why investors endeavor in such partnerships. As it will be more extensively elaborated later, it is instead the need to share and mitigate the many categories of risks associated with this type of investments.

Buyers: Entities purchasing the energy generated by the project, typically through power purchase agreements.

Government authorities: Regulatory bodies and government agencies overseeing permits, approvals, and compliance.

Contractors and EPC firms: Responsible for the engineering, procurement, and construction of the project.

Equipment suppliers: Companies providing key equipment and components for the energy infrastructure.

Investors and financiers: Provide the necessary capital to fund the project, including equity, loans, and guarantees.

Operation and maintenance ('O&M') service providers: Entities responsible for the operation and maintenance of the infrastructure.

Grid operators: Entities managing the transmission and distribution infrastructure to which the project connects.

Technology providers: Companies supplying innovative technologies for energy generation and storage.

Local communities: Communities near the project site that may be impacted by the project or benefit from it.

The types of contracts constituting major energy infrastructure projects include:

Project agreements: overarching agreements that outline the fundamental terms and conditions of the project. These contracts include the agreed project scope, objectives, timelines, and financial arrangements.

Power purchase agreements (PPA s): PPA s govern the sale of the energy generated by the infrastructure project to a buyer or utility. They include pricing mechanisms, delivery terms, and the duration of the power purchase.

Grid connection agreements: Outline the terms for connecting the energy infrastructure to the grid. Address technical requirements, connection fees, and grid access conditions.

Government agreements: Include agreements with host governments addressing regulatory approvals, permits, fiscal treatment and compliance with local laws. They also may involve stability agreements to protect the investor against adverse regulatory changes.

Engineering, procurement, and construction (EPC) *contracts*: EPCs are the core contractual instrument in energy infrastructure projects. They are signed between the Project Owner and the Contractors and define the responsibilities of the contractor for designing, procuring materials, and building the energy infrastructure. They include provisions regulating technical specifications, quality standards, and performance requirements.

Supply contracts: They govern the procurement of key materials, such as turbines, solar panels, or fuel. SCs specify delivery schedules, quality standards, and pricing mechanisms.

Operation and maintenance (O&M) agreements: These agreements detail the responsibilities and obligations for the operation and maintenance of the infrastructure.

Financing agreements: Detail the financial arrangements for the project, including loans, guarantees, and equity contributions. They specify repayment terms, interest rates and financial covenants.

Insurance contracts: Provide coverage for various risks such as construction delays, equipment breakdowns, and natural disasters. They ensure financial protection for project stakeholders.

In an ideal world, this framework would distribute the project risks to those in the best situation to efficiently mitigate or manage them. In reality, a number of factors can inject unexpected risks and costs over the course of long project implementation timelines (typically years).

Fairness in treatment, proactive collaboration, and effective communication among these stakeholders, along with contracts with clear scopes and obligations, are critical for the success of international energy infrastructure projects.

3 Predominant Causes of Disputes in Energy Projects

According to the analysis presented in HKA's report, the primary catalysts for disputes within the domain of energy projects are identified as changes in project scope and contract-associated issues. Changes in project scope account for 29.32% of disputes, with a notable increase to 45% in offshore wind energy initiatives, surpassing other categories of infrastructure projects. Contract-associated issues, encompassing 20% of disputes, predominantly revolve around challenges in contract interpretation, deficiencies in contract management and administration, and inadequate maintenance of professional relationships with contractors and subcontractors.

Such phenomena can be attributed to several factors, notably:

Poor preliminary assessment: Frequently, projects receive approval before the comprehensive assessment of contract components is finalized. Often, political and business strategies, rather than technical evaluations, dictate the initiation timeline of projects. Consequently, imminent electoral events, ministerial obligations, or corporate promotional activities may supersede thorough consideration of the project's execution framework. This oversight typically results in unforeseen design immaturities necessitating renegotiations of timelines and financial terms, and unrealistic delivery schedules devoid of alignment with project execution requirements. The HKA report notes instances where contractors sought extensions exceeding 876 cumulative years.[5]

Procurement strategies focused solely on cost reduction: The procurement phase often becomes a race to the lowest bid, regardless of the presence of financial constraints. The primary focus remains on cost reduction rather than project design, timelines, or the project itself. Furthermore, a disconnect between the tendering and project delivery teams frequently occurs, where pricing strategies fail to incorporate the delivery team's perspective.

Absence of a shared objective among contract parties: Rather than viewing the project as a mutual goal, the prevailing dynamic between the employer and the contractor is often adversarial. The employer's primary concern becomes ensuring the project's completion within the stipulated timeframe and budget, whereas the contractor focuses on maximizing profit and minimizing liabilities.

These challenges are common across both conventional (hydrocarbon-based) and transitional energy projects. However, the latter, given their relative novelty, also introduce unique conflict catalysts, including:

Governmental actions or inactions: The viability and stability of projects, especially those initially dependent on state subsidies, are jeopardized by governmental failures to deliver or threats of subsidy withdrawal.

Market demand fluctuations: The potential for market demand collapse prior to project completion poses a significant risk to the project's feasibility.

Innovation and emerging technologies: The use of new technologies introduces the risks associated with all pioneering advancements.

The 'Future of International Energy Arbitration. Survey Report 2022' by Queen Mary University of London[6] highlights regulatory changes (influenced

5 CRUX Insight (n 2)

6 Pinsent Masons, Queen Mary University London, 'Future of International Energy Arbitration. Survey Report 2022' (20 January 2023) <www.qmul.ac.uk/arbitration/media/arbitration/docs/Future-of-International-Energy-Arbitration-Survey-Report.pdf> accessed 28 January 2024.

by States' enactment of international agreements, notably the Paris Agreement, with a significance of 60%), infrastructure construction (51%), and price volatility (39%) as probable dispute catalysts amidst the energy transition.

In response to the European energy security crisis triggered by geopolitical events in early 2022, in May of the same year a closed-door summit among industry leaders and governmental representatives was organized in Florence with the contribution of the then-acting United States Ambassador to Italy. The aim was to identify strategies to expedite the construction of new energy infrastructure.[7] The discourse validated known hurdles to swift project realization and converged on the necessity for enhanced collaboration, improved communication, and the implementation of proactive dispute resolution methodologies to mitigate project delays.

4 Mechanisms for the Resolution of Energy Infrastructure Disputes

In the context of energy infrastructure implementation, maintaining alignment between the parties' interests is paramount and – at the same time – represents the major challenge to project completion. Disparities in these interests, when not reconciled, can lead to disputes that, if unresolved, might disrupt the execution of projects. The design of a dispute resolution mechanism tailored to effectively face these misalignments is therefore essential.

When it comes to renewable energy projects, the selected dispute resolution mechanism should at the same time bridge the gap between divergent parties' interests and address the unique challenges presented by this innovative field.

This section provides an overview of the potential of each available mechanism in this regard.

4.1 *Arbitration and Court Proceedings*

The role of arbitration in resolving disputes pertaining energy projects is hereby exemplified through the lens of Michael McIlwrath's case studies.

A wind farm construction dispute: the project's viability was compromised following the withdrawal of governmental subsidies post-construction commencement, leading the owner to renege on payments for ordered equipment and file a request for arbitration.

---

7 The work of the summit was summarized in the paper 'Energy Independence: principle for fast-tracking infrastructure projects' (*MDisputes*, 19 May 2022) <www.mdisputes.com/wp-content/uploads/2022/06/Energy-Independence_Key-principles-to-fast_track-infrastructure-projects-4.pdf> accessed 29 January 2024.

An LNG plant construction dispute: significant investments were made by the project owner based on the expectation of servicing a nearby power plant, a project later abandoned by the local government. The resulting loss of anticipated revenue prompted the owner to initiate disputes with its equipment suppliers in an attempt to recover or reduce investment costs.

These scenarios underscore the substantial financial and time resources consumed in arbitration processes, not to mention the broader socio-economic implications, such as the stand-by of energy projects and missed business opportunities. Non-adversarial dispute resolution mechanisms might have avoided these outcomes, differently from litigation and arbitration, which often exacerbate rather than reconcile parties' divergences.

The 2022 Queen Mary's Survey Report reveals a preference for litigation in addressing disputes of public interest, such as those related to climate change, nuclear safety, and energy supply, while recognizes arbitration's advantages in terms of reliability and enforceability of the award. However, a notable inclination towards dispute avoidance was observed particularly among end-users, who favored negotiation exactly for its potential to more directly reconcile parties' interests.[8]

Arbitration and Court litigation for renewable energy disputes: Renewable energy projects, in contrast to traditional energy projects, face an augmented level of uncertainty in arbitration or court litigation, largely due to the absence of established jurisprudence. Traditional energy disputes benefit from a body of jurisprudence that lends a degree of predictability to their resolution. In contrast, renewable energy disputes lack a comparable corpus of industry customs or practices, leading to greater unpredictability in dispute outcomes. This distinction underscores the nascent state of renewable energy jurisprudence, as articulated by Timothy Martin, John Gilbert, and Peter Roberts in their book *Joint Venture Disputes in the Energy and Natural Resource Sectors* noting the absence of a 'lex ventus' or 'lex solis' akin to the established 'lex petroleo'.[9]

The same authors also denounce a still undefined jurisprudence when it comes to disputes in the matter of unincorporated Joint Ventures (JOAs) related to Oil and Gas projects. In their article 'Joint Operating Agreements in the International Oil & Gas Industry: ICC Arbitral Awards', Martin, Gilbert and Roberts provide a valuable analysis of arbitral decision arising from ICC administered procedures on the five main causes of conflict between JVA

8 Pinsent Masons, Queen Mary University London (n 6) 34.

9 Timothy Martin, John Gilbert, Peter Roberts, *Joint Venture Disputes in the Energy and Natural Resource Sectors* (OUP 2023).

partners, which serves as useful guidance for legal practitioners to navigate the uncertainties of energy dispute resolution.[10]

4.2 *Proactive and Early Resolution Methods*

In the domain of legal dispute resolution, a spectrum of mechanisms exists, designed to preclude or mitigate the effects of divergent interests between parties engaged in contractual or project-based collaborations. These mechanisms, which encompass both adjudicative and non-adjudicative processes, aim primarily to foster the alignment of interests among the parties towards the successful completion of the project, rather than focusing solely on the adjudication of disputes.

The essence of these mechanisms lies in their innovative and adaptable nature, allowing for implementation across varied contexts and disciplines with distinct characteristics.

4.2.1 Adjudication and Expert Determination

Predominantly utilized within the sectors of construction and engineering projects, adjudication and expert determination serve as critical tools for the early resolution of disputes. Despite their proven efficacy in these fields, their application within energy project disputes remains notably limited.

Adjudication involves the intervention of an independent third party, referred to as the adjudicator, who, upon examination of evidence and arguments presented by the parties, issues a binding resolution on the matter in dispute. Typically, an adjudicator possesses specialized knowledge pertinent to the disputed subject matter and may be appointed either by the parties or by an external authority, depending on the terms of the adjudication agreement.

The resolution issued by the adjudicator, known as the 'adjudication award' provides a binding interim settlement of the dispute. The adjudication award remains effective unless subsequently revised through arbitration or litigation, adhering to the principle of 'pay now, argue later'. The adjudicative process is characterized by its reliance on documentary evidence, with oral hearings being rare or significantly limited.

One of the hallmarks of adjudication is its expeditious nature. The leading adjudication rules typically provide for a duration of the process of two

10 Timothy Martin, John Gilbert, Peter Roberts, 'Joint Operating Agreements in the International Oil & Gas Industry: ICC Arbitral Awards' (2019) 35 *ICC Dispute Resolution Bulletin* 35.

months from initiation.[11] This period may be extended by mutual consent of the parties or due to specific circumstances set forth by the rules.

Failure of the losing party to comply with the adjudicator's decision enables the prevailing party to seek enforcement before the competent court. The rapidity, cost-efficiency, and deferment of conventional litigation post-project completion are attributes that render adjudication a viable option for continuing project execution with minimal disruption.

The applicability and regulation of adjudication vary across jurisdictions and are influenced by the contractual terms agreed upon by the parties. In certain jurisdictions, such as the United Kingdom, statutory provisions for adjudication are in place,[12] accompanied by a developed body of case law applicable to specific contract types, predominantly within the construction sector.

Incorporating an adjudication mechanism within the dispute resolution clause of a contract necessitates a thorough consideration of the contract's nature and scope, its value, and the governing law. This approach aids in delineating the process, identifying procedural requirements, and anticipating potential challenges to the enforceability of the adjudication award.

Critics of adjudication argue that challenges to the adjudication award, or subsequent initiation of arbitration or litigation post-project completion, undermine the benefits of adjudication by escalating time and costs. Contrary to this viewpoint, the 2022 'Construction Adjudication in the United Kingdom: Tracing Trends and Guiding Reform' Report, published by the Centre of Construction Law & Dispute Resolution at King's College (London),[13] presents data affirming the value of adjudication as a dispute resolution mechanism within the context of large-scale energy infrastructure projects.

Particularly, 25% of respondents say they have never experienced a dispute decided by an adjudicator being referred to a court or arbitration tribunal, 42% of respondents answered that less than 5% of cases proceed to litigation or arbitration, 15% of the respondents stated that between 6% and 10% of

11 Art 58 of the Adjudication Rules elaborated by the Hong Kong International Arbitration Centre (HKIAC) requires the adjudicator to reach a decision within 56 days from the referral submission. See HKIAC, 'Adjudication Rules' (2009) <www.hkiac.org/sites/default/files/ck_filebrowser/PDF/Adjudication/HKIAC_Adjudication_Rules_2009.pdf> accessed 28 January 2024. Art 108, paragraph 2, letter c), of the UK Housing Grants, Construction and Regeneration Act of 1996 requires the adjudicator to reach a decision within 28 days from the referral.

12 UK Housing Grants, Construction and Regeneration Act (n 11).

13 Renato Nazzini, Aleksander Kalisz, *2022 Construction Adjudication in the United Kingdom: Tracing trends and guiding reform* (Centre of Construction Law & Dispute Resolution, King's College London, 2022).

the adjudicated disputes are referred to litigation or arbitration. Only 12% of respondents answered that their adjudication disputes are referred to litigation or arbitration in 11% or more of cases.

4.2.2 Dispute Review/Adjudication Boards

In the realm of large-scale construction and infrastructure projects, Dispute Boards (DBs) have emerged as a pivotal mechanism for the preclusion and resolution of disputes. These entities serve not only as a means to deter disputes from advancing to arbitration or court litigation, but also as a forum for the issuance of expedited decisions or recommendations. DBs are distinguished by their capacity to offer expert insights and adjudicative determinations, thereby facilitating the continuous progress of projects without the impediments of protracted legal disputes.

Dispute Boards are categorized based on their operational dynamics and the nature of their resolutions:

Dispute Review Boards (*DRBs*): Typically constituted by a sole expert or a panel of three experts, DRBs are composed of professionals with extensive knowledge in construction, engineering, law, or accounting. Their primary function is to deliver non-binding recommendations on disputes submitted by contracting parties. The influence of DRBs lies in the persuasive authority of their recommendations, which, despite being non-compulsory, command respect due to the expertise of the board members and the contractual commitment of the parties to the DRB process.

Dispute Adjudication Boards (*DABs*): Analogous to DRBs in composition, DABs differ for the binding nature of their decisions as opposed to DRBs mere recommendations. The decisions rendered by DABs carry an interim binding effect, necessitating immediate compliance, albeit subject to subsequent challenge in arbitration or litigation. DABs are predominantly utilized in international projects, particularly those governed by the International Federation of Consulting Engineers (FIDIC)[14] contracts.

Combined Dispute Boards (*CDBs*): Representing a hybrid model, CDBs operate as either a DRB or a DAB depending on the dispute's escalation or the mutual agreements of the contracting parties. Initially, CDBs may offer non-binding recommendations transitioning to binding decisions if the dispute remains unresolved.[15]

---

14 FIDIC, *Conditions of Contract for Construction*, 2nd ed (2017).

15 These three categories of DBs are reflected in the Dispute Board Rules of the International Chamber of Commerce (ICC). See ICC, 'Dispute Board Rules' (2022) <https://iccwbo.org/wp-content/uploads/sites/3/2015/09/icc-dispute-board-rules-english-version.pdf>

Enforceability of DB Decisions: The legal enforceability of DB decisions depends on the specific type of DB, the contractual terms agreed upon by the parties, and the jurisdictions involved.

It is fundamental for contractual agreements to delineate explicitly the role, authority, and procedural framework of the DB, including the binding nature of its decisions and the mechanisms for their challenge. To ensure enforceability and operational efficacy of DB resolutions, clarity is of the essence.

DBs significantly contribute to a smooth execution of energy infrastructure projects by leveraging their members' specialized knowledge to promptly address and resolve disputes, thereby preserving the working relationships among parties. Nevertheless, the success of DBs in achieving these outcomes is largely dependent on the parties' adherence to and respect for the DB's determinations.

Despite the widespread adoption of DBs in engineering and construction contracts, their utilization within the energy sector, except the nuclear sub-sector,[16] remains limited. This may be attributed to the unique complexities and the anticipated inevitability of disputes in such projects, underscoring the need for bespoke and specialized dispute resolution mechanisms.

4.2.3 Emergency Arbitration

Emergency arbitration permits parties to seek provisional relief expeditiously prior to the establishment of the formal arbitral tribunal. This procedural

accessed 30 January 2024. The Dispute Resolution Board Rules of the Milan Chamber of Arbitration (CAM), instead, conceive DB as a Dispute Resolution Board, which can issue an informal opinion or a recommendation depending on the parties' request. Recommendation become binding if not rejected by the losing party within 30 days of its issuance. See MCA, 'Dispute Resolution Board Rules' (2016) <www.camera-arbitrale.it/upload/documenti/Dispute%20Resolution%20Board/dispute-resolution-board-rules%20(3)-edited%20(1).pdf> accessed 30 January 2024.

16 Interestingly, respondents to The Queen Mary's Survey confirmed the unpopularity of dispute board, excepted for disputes relating to 'energy infrastructure' (11%) and 'nuclear' disputes (12%), where respondents selected dispute boards as the most effective forum for resolving disputes. The reasons are the size and cost of nuclear projects, the inevitability that disputes will arise, and the complexity of the design and construction process, along with the very lengthy project construction phase, which may help explain why respondents were more comfortable using dispute boards for nuclear disputes. The survey clarifies that 'Contractors (entities building / delivering energy assets) generally like dispute boards. This may be due to the fact that certain standard forms of construction contract (e.g., FIDIC) contain a dispute adjudication board mechanism and they are commonly deployed on World Bank funded projects. One such respondent stressed that he would first seek to refer any claim to a dispute board before arbitration. He stated that every time he has used a dispute board, they have avoided unfairness, even where the contract at issue heavily weighted risks in favor of the employer'. See Pinsent Masons, Queen Mary University London (n 6) 35.

avenue is of paramount importance in scenarios necessitating immediate judicial intervention to avert potential irreparable damage or to maintain the prevailing conditions pending the resolution of the dispute via standard arbitral proceedings. The significance of emergency arbitration is notably pronounced within the energy infrastructure sector, wherein delays or operational interruptions can exert profound financial and operational repercussions.

Upon the submission of a request for emergency arbitration, an emergency arbitrator is designated promptly, often within a matter of days and an award is issued in a few weeks.[17] These expedited proceedings preserve due process while entailing abbreviated schedules for the submission of documents and the conduct of hearings, should such hearings be convened.

The decision rendered by an emergency arbitrator takes the form of an order, encompassing provisional measures such as injunctions, preservation orders, or alternative forms of interim relief. These orders are of a provisional nature, pending the subsequent review or amendment by the arbitral tribunal in the main proceedings.

The recourse to emergency arbitration necessitates a thorough assessment of the potential risks and implications associated with the accelerated adjudicative process. Decisions emanating from emergency arbitration are, in general, enforceable across jurisdictions that acknowledge and effectuate international arbitral awards, albeit with variances.

Particularly in jurisdictions less acquainted with emergency arbitration, challenges may arise concerning the emergency arbitrator's jurisdictional authority or the enforceability of their decisions. Furthermore, due process concerns may emerge due to the constrained examination of evidence and arguments, potentially impacting the decision-making process.

In essence, emergency arbitration serves as an indispensable instrument for the expedient addressal of critical issues within complex projects, especially within the energy sector, where project delays may entail extensive ramifications.

4.2.4 Expedited Arbitration

The recourse to expedited arbitration emerges as a viable alternative to circumvent or mitigate disruptions to energy projects. Expedited arbitration is particularly suited to circumstances where the amount in dispute and financial

---

17 Art. 6(4) of Appendix V (Emergency Arbitrator Rules) of the ICC Arbitration Rules provide that the emergency arbitration order must be issued "no later than 15 days" from the transmission of the file to the arbitrator; Art. 9b of the London Court of International Arbitration (LCIA) Arbitration Rules 2020 provide that the claim must be decided "as soon as possible, but no later than 14 days following the Emergency Arbitrator's appointment".

implications do not justify the expenditure and duration associated with conventional arbitration proceedings.

Expedited arbitration is delineated by its efficiency and streamlined nature, characterized by a compressed schedule and the simplification of procedural norms. This mechanism is optimally applied to disputes necessitating prompt resolution, those of low monetary relevance, or those that are inherently less complex.

The salient features of expedited arbitration comprise:

Financial thresholds: Procedural rules and arbitration agreements usually foresee a monetary threshold for the amount in dispute for expedited arbitration to validly take place, albeit such a threshold may be adjusted subject to mutual consent among the disputing parties.

Shortened deadlines: The procedural stages of expedited arbitration, encompassing the submission of documentary evidence, the convening of hearings, and the issuance of the arbitral award, are subject to significantly reduced deadlines.

Discovery limitations: Expedited arbitration may impose constraints on the scope of discovery, including but not limited to the breadth of document requisitions, depositions, and witness examinations, aiming to streamline the evidentiary phase.

Procedural simplification: The arbitration process under expedited conditions is often made more efficient through the reduction of formalities concerning submissions and the facilitation of a more direct tribunal appointment process.

Sole arbitrator as the rule: Expedited arbitration usually involves the appointment of a sole arbitrator, thereby economizing both time and financial resources.

Finality of the award: The arbitral award, rendered in an expedited manner, is generally final and binding, with minimal provisions for appeal, ensuring a swift resolution to the dispute.

The majority of international arbitration regulations incorporate clauses that govern the conduct of expedited arbitration. For parties recurring to expedited arbitration, it is required and sufficient at the same time that the relevant arbitration clause explicitly states that arbitration proceedings shall be conducted in accordance with the rules of an arbitral institution that offers such service.

Recent revisions to international arbitration rules have introduced expedited arbitration as the default procedure once specific criteria are fulfilled, albeit preserving the option for parties to opt-out.[18]

---

18 For example, Art 30 of the ICC Arbitration Rules on expedited procedure reads: '1) By agreeing to arbitration under the Rules, the parties agree that this Art 30 and the Expedited

4.2.5 Mediation

Mediation stands as an invariably accessible mechanism for the expedient resolution of disputes within the realm of energy infrastructure projects. Notably, its implementation does not necessitate a pre-existing mediation clause, offering a significant degree of procedural autonomy.

This process is quintessentially aimed at facilitating collaborative problem-solving, thereby serving as an instrumental means of either re-establishing or enhancing the interests balance among the parties involved. The inherent procedural flexibility of mediation—ranging from process design to scheduling and outcome—permits customization in alignment with the specific exigencies and operational dynamics of the project at hand, which are distinctively absent in the mechanisms previously delineated.

The expeditious organization and execution of mediation proceedings underscore its pertinence to the energy sector, characterized by its dense operational timeline. The ability of mediation to yield resolutions within a condensed timeframe is thus of paramount importance.

Furthermore, the confidential nature of mediation processes offers a protective veil over commercially sensitive information, a feature particularly advantageous in the context of energy projects.

It is crucial to underscore that mediation does not impose any restrictive effects on the disputing parties' recourse to alternative dispute resolution mechanisms in the event of an unsuccessful mediation attempt, thereby preserving the full spectrum of judicial and arbitral remedies.

Nevertheless, the decision to employ mediation as a strategy to circumvent disruptions in energy infrastructure projects mandates a thorough assessment of various factors including the conflict's degree of escalation, its inherent nature, the identities of the disputing parties, the project's current phase, and the anticipated enforceability of any mediated settlement agreement.

Procedure Rules set forth in Appendix VI (collectively the 'Expedited Procedure Provisions') shall take precedence over any contrary terms of the arbitration agreement.' See ICC, 'Arbitration Rules' (2021) <https://iccwbo.org/dispute-resolution/dispute-resolution-services/arbitration/rules-procedure/2021-arbitration-rules/#block-accordion-30> accessed 25 September 2024. In addition, Art 1.1 of the Annex D of the Milan Chamber of Arbitration Rules states 'the Simplified Arbitration Procedure shall apply to arbitrations commenced after the date on which the Procedure entered into force, if the value of the claims filed by the Claimant does not exceed Eur. 250.000, and unless one of the parties opts-out in the request for arbitration or in the reply to the request for arbitration'. See CAM, 'Arbitration Rules' (2020) <www.camera-arbitrale.it/upload/documenti/arbitrato/cam%20arbitration%20rules%202020.pdf> accessed 25 September 2024.

In cases where the conflict has profoundly impacted the parties' relationship already at a nascent stage of the project with still a plethora of risks and uncertainties to be faced before its completion, the prospect of non-compliance with a mediated settlement agreement loom, potentially resulting in additional delays and financial burdens, especially in jurisdictions lacking streamlined enforcement protocols.

The strategic resolution of disputes in energy infrastructure projects represents a paradigm wherein the significance of the Singapore Convention on Mediation[19] is particularly pronounced. In fact, in cases when direct enforceability of mediated settlement agreements is available, mediation can surpass in efficacy all the previously discussed mechanisms.[20]

4.2.6 Negotiation

Implementing a negotiation strategy that encompasses a long-term perspective and effectively utilizes the full spectrum of dispute resolution mechanisms at the parties' disposal can significantly enhance the value derived from the resolution process.

As an example, the co-authors have direct experience of the facilitation of a profitable settlement concerning the construction and ownership of Italy's first small-scale LNG terminal, alongside the transaction of shares.

The contractual framework of the project was constituted by a Joint Venture Agreement (JVA), consolidating the project owner with two contractors. This collaboration was characterized by a robust commercial relationship and mutual confidence. Beyond the stipulations of the JVA, informal arrangements were in place between the employer and one contractor for the establishment of an Operation & Maintenance (O&M) Agreement subsequent to project finalization.

The trajectory of project execution encountered a pivotal shift due to a managerial transition at the employer's helm, with the departure of its CEO in bad terms. This event, coupled with the advent of the COVID-19 pandemic, resulted in a substantial misalignment of the parties' objectives. Consequentially, both the contractor and project owner initiated various claims against each other.

---

19 United Nations Convention on International Settlement Agreements Resulting from Mediation (adopted 20 December 2018, entered into force 12 September 2020) 3360 UNTS 56376(Singapore Convention on Mediation).

20 Pinsent Masons, Queen Mary University London (n 6) 35: 'Most of the time, we have been able to reach settlement with the other side once you have clarity. Everyone's trying to find a solution, sometimes you need a third party who knows what they are saying to say this is what I think is the problem, then parties sit down and try to find a workaround. This a difference between engineers and lawyers – lawyers want an outcome, who's right and who's wrong – engineers want to fix the problem'.

The advent of a new CEO led to decisions that the contractor interpreted as indicative of eroding trust. Notably, the assignment of the promised O&M contract to a third company. Concurrently, the pandemic induced project delays, which the employer attributed to the contractor's failure, raising claims for liquidated damages amounting to $6 million. Those claims were disputed by the contractor, which invoked force majeure as per the EPC contract, and lodged a counterclaim for approximately $4 million, encompassing the final payment installment, additional costs for spare parts and labor, and threatened the suspension of project activities.

The dispute resolution clause of the contract set forth to attempt negotiation through the issuance of a notice of dispute. Should the negotiation be unsuccessful, the clause provided for either expert determination or arbitration under the rules of the International Chamber of Commerce (ICC), with arbitration seat in London.

Additionally, the contract provided that, unless otherwise agreed, both parties were to continue fulfilling their respective contractual obligations amidst the dispute.

The resolution strategy unfolded as follows.

Issuance of a notice of dispute to the employer, reproducing in structure and substance the essence of a request for Arbitration. This offered the dual benefits of time and cost efficiency in the event of unsuccessful negotiations and conveying the message of the contractor's lawyers readiness to the subsequent arbitration.

Concurrently, arbitration counsel was appointed, and a budget for potential arbitration proceedings was established.

Following four months of negotiations, the dispute reached an amicable settlement, enabling the project's completion without disruption. The contractor, initially facing a demand for $6 million in liquidated damages, obtained $4 million covering the contract price, additional expenses, and an additional $1.1 million for its equity share upon exiting the joint venture.

5 Conclusions

Embedding ADR mechanisms for resolving disputes promptly and effectively is not merely a tactical decision but also indispensable for the successful fulfillment of energy infrastructure investments.

Utilizing various approaches under assorted conditions, mechanisms such as adjudication, Dispute Boards, emergency and expedited arbitration, alongside mediation and negotiation, serve as the pathway for liberating financial resources and assets that could otherwise be ensnared in extended legal battles. This liberation of resources facilitates the progression and realization of energy initiatives, contributing positively to environmental sustainability and economic development.

The landscape of dispute resolution in the energy sector is marked by a dynamic interplay between traditional and innovative mechanisms, each with its strengths and limitations. The choice of an appropriate dispute resolution method must be informed by a comprehensive understanding of the project's specific challenges and the broader objectives of maintaining alignment between parties. As the energy sector continues to evolve, so too will the strategies for managing and resolving disputes, with a growing emphasis on proactive and collaborative approaches that prioritize the timely and efficient completion of projects.

The role of judicial entities and dispute resolution organizations in this transformative process is crucial. By implementing strategies that encourage the adoption of ADR, these institutions can significantly reduce their case burdens and, more crucially, foster a cooperative ethos in resolving disputes within the energy sector. The International Chamber of Commerce (ICC) Commission on Arbitration and ADR, through its report 'Resolving Climate Change Related Disputes through Arbitration and ADR,[21] offers invaluable insights into the facilitation of early dispute resolution concerning energy and climate change conflicts through ADR mechanisms.

This advocacy for ADR can be further reinforced by industry practices that promote collaborative engagement and effective communication amongst stakeholders. Implementing contractual frameworks that incentivize shared objectives and align interests, in conjunction with targeted training and educational initiatives, can cultivate a culture that emphasizes consensual solutions and the efficient management of the inevitable challenges encountered in the execution of large-scale projects.

Finally, governmental actions substantially contribute to this transformative shift. The establishment of a regulatory and policy framework that promotes transparent interaction and the seamless dissemination of information to investors, alongside the facilitation of ADR techniques, can foster a *milieu* in which energy projects are perceived as more feasible and carry reduced investment risk. In this regard, the legislation of the United Kingdom concerning adjudication exemplifies the effective implementation of such instruments.

---

21 ICC, 'Resolving Climate Change Related Disputes through Arbitration and ADR' (2019) <https://iccwbo.org/wp-content/uploads/sites/3/2019/11/icc-arbitration-adr-commission-report-on-resolving-climate-change-related-disputes-english-version.pdf> accessed 31 January 2024.

La Mediation En Matiere Civile Et Commerciale

Quelle Place Pour La Convention De Singapour Dans Les Litiges Transfrontaliers Intracommunautaires?

*Roberta Clerici**

1 La Convention de Singapour sur la médiation

Il est bien connu que l'internationalisation de la vie économique conduit à une augmentation inévitable des litiges transnationaux en matière civile et commerciale,[1] dans une sorte de globalisation des conflits[2] qui a retenu l'attention de la communauté internationale et de l'Union européenne. Dans ce contexte, outre la prolifération de Cours (ou Chambres) commerciales spécialisés dans de nombreuses régions du monde,[3] les 'Alternative Dispute Resolutions' (ADR) sont également au centre du débat. Il s'agit de modes de résolution des conflits alternatifs au système judiciaire, réglementés au niveau des systèmes juridiques nationaux et supranationaux, principalement en raison des avantages considérables que leur utilisation comporte : par exemple, des coûts peu élevés et la brièveté des délais nécessaires pour parvenir à une solution.

Parmi ces instruments, le plus connu est la médiation,[4] une procédure de règlement extrajudiciaire des différends de nature 'auto-réglée', dans laquelle le principe de l'autonomie des parties trouve sa pleine expression : cette

---

* Professeure retraitée de Droit international privé, Université de Milan. Merci à Federica Sartori, Doctorante de l'Université de Pavie, pour son aide efficace.

1 Voir Renate Dendorfer-Ditges and Philipp Wilhelm, 'Mediation in a Global Village: Legal Complexity of Cross-Border Mediation in Europe' (2017) 5 *YB International Arbitration* 235.

2 En ce sens Maria João Mimoso, 'The Singapore Convention and the European Reality', in Yilmaz Bayar (ed.) *Proceedings of 15th SCF International Conference on Economic, Social, and Environmental Sustainability in the Post Covid-19 World, Istanbul, 2–3rd December 2022* (Bandirma Onyedi University 2022) 181.

3 Singapour a également créé la Singapore International Commercial Court (SICC), une division de la Haute Cour de Singapour, en 2015. Pour une étude approfondie sur le sujet, voir Salvatore Domenico Zannino, 'The new frontier of international commercial courts, is Milan on the march too?', *NT+Diritto*, 16 janvier 2023, au site internet ntplusdiritto.ilsole24ore.com ; et plus largement Albert Henke, Marco Torsello, Elena Zucconi Galli Fonseca (eds.), *International Commercial Courts. A Paradigm for the Future of Adjudication?* (Edizioni Scientifiche Italiane 2024).

4 Voir Christina G Hioureas, 'The Singapore Convention on International Settlement Agreements Resulting from Mediation: A New Way Forward', (2019) 37 Berkeley J Intl L 216, également pour une comparaison avec le droit international public, notamment avec les moyens de règlement pacifique des différends prévus par l'article 33 de la Charte des Nations Unies.

 | DOI:10.1163/9789004727663_009

autonomie s'exprime, par exemple, dans la possibilité de choisir le médiateur et la procédure. La médiation se caractérise principalement comme un instrument flexible, informel, rapide, peu coûteux, qui non seulement facilite le dialogue, mais surtout vise à maintenir des relations amicales entre les parties elles-mêmes:[5] ces dernières s'efforcent ainsi de trouver un compromis entre leurs intérêts opposés, de sorte qu'il n'est pas possible d'identifier clairement des gagnants ou des perdants.[6] De plus, le recours massif au règlement extrajudiciaire des litiges conduit également à un allègement de la charge de travail des juridictions nationales, ce qui rend les systèmes judiciaires en général plus efficaces.

On comprend alors l'immense écho suscité par la signature, provenant de 46 Etats, le 7 août 2019 à Singapour, de la Convention des Nations Unies sur les accords de règlement internationaux issus de la médiation ; élaborée au sein de la CNUDCI[7] (qui avait déjà préparé une Loi type en la matière), elle avait d'abord été adoptée par une résolution de l'Assemblée générale le 20 décembre 2018 avec une nouvelle Loi type sur la médiation mise à jour.[8]

Le succès immédiat de cette Convention est également attesté par son entrée en vigueur rapide, qui a eu lieu le 12 septembre 2020, en pleine pandémie de Covid-19, soit trois mois après les trois ratifications prévues à cet effet par l'article 14, alinéa 1.[9] A ce jour, les Etats signataires sont au nombre de 56 et le nombre d'Etats parties s'élève à 15 :[10] l'évaluation globale d'une situation

---

5 Mimoso, 'The Singapore Convention' (n 2) 182; Hioureas, 'The Singapore Convention' (n 4) 224.

6 En ce sens Michal Malacka, 'The relations between the Singapore Mediation Convention and the European Mediation Directive' (2022) 9 *European Studies – the Review of European Law, Economics and Politics* 243.

7 Commission de Nations Unies pour le droit commercial international (plus connue comme UNCITRAL).

8 Le nom 'Convention de Singapour' provient du fait que Singapour était le Pays hôte de la cérémonie de signature de ce Traité. Depuis que Singapour a également créé la Singapore International Commercial Court (n 3), l'intention claire de cet Etat de jouer un rôle central dans la résolution des litiges commerciaux, judiciaires et extrajudiciaires, dans le monde émerge : v. Joséphine Hage Chahine, Ettore M Lombardi, David Lutran, Catherine Peulvé, 'The Acceleration of the Development of International Business Mediation after the Singapore Convention' (2021) 32 Eur Business L Rev 782.

9 Ibid 773, les auteurs mettent l'accent sur l'utilité de l'entrée en vigueur de la Convention dans la période pandémique où les litiges commerciaux transnationaux ont augmenté principalement en raison de l'inexécution de contrats internationaux, de sorte que la Convention de Singapour a contribué à enrichir le cadre juridique de la résolution extrajudiciaire des litiges au moment le plus opportun.

10 Données remontant au 8 janvier 2025 : voir singaporeconvention.org.

'prometteuse'[11] est donc confirmée, même si – à l'exception de la récente ratification du Japon à la fin de 2023 – aucun des Etats signataires les plus importants sur le plan économique (par exemple, les Etats-Unis, la Chine, l'Inde ou le Brésil) n'a encore exprimé son consentement à être lié par ce Traité.

Cette Convention (qui est plutôt synthétique, puisqu'elle ne comporte que 16 articles) vise à concilier sécurité juridique et souplesse.[12] Selon son article 1 elle s'applique à tout accord issu de la médiation et conclu par écrit – ou par voie électronique – par des parties pour régler un litige commercial ('accord de règlement') qui, au moment de sa conclusion, est international en donnant en même temps une définition de ce dernier critère. Cet article exclut du champ d'application de ce Traité les litiges avec le consommateurs ou relatifs au droit de la famille, des successions et de travail ou les accords déjà insérés dans une procédure judiciaire ou arbitrale ou encore déjà exécutoires.

Il s'agit ici d'un processus, quels que soient sa dénomination ou son fondement, par lequel les parties cherchent à parvenir à un règlement amiable de leur différend avec l'aide d'un ou de plusieurs tiers ('le médiateur') qui n'ont pas le pouvoir de leur imposer une solution (médiation facilitatrice : article 2).

La disposition centrale est contenue dans l'article 3, qui engage les Etats contractants à accorder l'exécution, sans contrôle judiciaire, aux accords résultant de la médiation. Cela implique que la partie à un accord issu d'une médiation qui n'obtient pas l'exécution spontanée des obligations qu'il contient peut demander à l'autorité 'compétente' (c'est-à-dire, pas seulement judiciaire) d'un Etat contractant à la Convention l'exécution de ces obligations, sans aucune procédure ultérieure ; donc, sous une forme similaire à celle prévue par l'article 39 du règlement Bruxelles I bis.[13] Mais ici, on vise un accord de droit privé, et le contexte de cette disposition est mondial. D'autre part, le même article

11 En ce sens Javier Fernández-Samaniego, 'The Effects on Cross-Border Disputes One Year after the Entry into Force of the Singapore Mediation Convention' (2022) 40 *Alternatives to the High Cost of Litigation* 4.

12 Pour un aperçu général de cette Convention voir Nadja Alexander, Shouyu Chong, Vakhtang Giorgadze, *The Singapore Convention on Mediation. A Commentary* (2nd edn, Kluwer Law International 2022); Guillermo Palao (ed.), *The Singapore Convention. A Commentary on the United Nations Convention on International Settlement Agreements Resulting from Mediation* (Elgar 2022); Caroline Asfar-Cazenave, 'The Singapore Mediation Convention' (2020) 8 *Int Business* LJ 47.

13 Règlement (UE) no 1215/2012 du Parlement européen et du Conseil du 12 décembre 2012 concernant la compétence judiciaire, la reconnaissance et l'exécution des décisions en matière civile et commerciale (refonte) [2012] JO L351/1. L'art 39 dispose en effet qu'une décision rendue dans un Etat membre et qui est exécutoire dans cet Etat membre jouit de la force exécutoire dans les autres Etats membres sans qu'une déclaration constatant la force exécutoire soit nécessaire.

prévoit aussi qu'une partie peut être autorisée par son Etat à se prévaloir d'un tel accord résultant d'une médiation devant un for ou un tribunal arbitral dans la même mesure que dans le cadre d'une procédure d'exécution, 'afin de prouver que la question a déjà été réglée' (article 3, alinéa 2), ce qui a pour effet de paralyser les litiges devant le juge ou devant les arbitres.

La force exécutoire prévue pour l'accord et pour ce moyen de défense sont régis par la Convention pour ce qui est des conditions requises et par les règles de chaque Etat pour ce qui est de la procédure. En effet, l'article 4 prévoit et réglemente comme condition fondamentale la signature, également par voie électronique, de l'accord par les parties et la preuve que l'accord est vraiment issu de la médiation, apportée par exemple par la signature du médiateur ou bien par d'autres éléments de preuve indiqués ou tout-de-même acceptés par l'autorité compétente.

L'article 5 contient quant à lui certains motifs de refus d'admettre la demande ou le moyen introduits qui sont également réduits au minimum, à savoir l'incapacité d'une partie, les éventuels défauts ou vices de l'accord ou les éventuelles fautes du médiateur, l'incompatibilité avec l'ordre public et l'interdiction de soumettre l'objet du différend à la médiation selon la loi de la Partie requise. Le système de Singapour fait alors preuve d'une souplesse dans son application, puisque l'article 8, consacré aux réserves, permet aux Etats contractants de déclarer qu'ils appliqueront la Convention uniquement dans la mesure où les parties au litige auront consenti à son application.

Des règles encore plus importantes aux fins de notre analyse sont contenues dans l'article 12 qui ouvre explicitement la signature, la ratification ou l'adhésion aux 'organisations régionales d'intégration économique' tout en donnant leurs définition.[14]

De plus, on a introduit une clause de déconnexion ou *give-away clause*,[15] puisque cet article établit que la Convention ne prévaut pas sur les règles contraires d'une organisation régionale d'intégration économique, soit en vigueur soit futures, lorsque une demande ou un moyen de défense sont introduits dans un Etat qui est membre d'une telle organisation et si tous les Etats concernés

---

14 La définition contenue dans l'art 12, alinéa 1er, correspond parfaitement au caractère de l'Union européenne : voir Paolo Fois, 'L'Unione europea è ancora un'organizzazione internazionale?', (2016) 99 *Rivista di diritto internazionale* 371. Egalement dans l'alinéa 2 cette organisation est invitée à effectuer auprès du dépositaire une déclaration indiquant les matières régies par la Convention pour lesquelles ses Etats membres lui ont transféré leur compétence.

15 Palao, 'The Singapore Convention' (n 12) 265; Norel Rosner, 'The Singapore Convention: Reflections on Articles 1.3 on Scope, 8.1(b) on Reservations, and 12 on Regional Economic Integration Organizations' (2019) 20 *Cardozo J Conflict Resolution* 1259.

sont membres de cette organisation ;[16] ou encore en ce qui concerne la reconnaissance ou l'exécution de jugements entre les Etats membres.

La Convention de Singapour est unanimement perçue comme une grande opportunité pour la promotion de la médiation, à l'instar de ce qui s'est passé, dans le domaine de l'arbitrage, pour la Convention pour la reconnaissance et l'exécution des sentences arbitrales étrangères, signée à New York le 10 juin 1958,[17] dont l'entrée en vigueur a largement contribué à la diffusion de cet instrument. Cependant, malgré l'enthousiasme général suscité par l'entrée en vigueur de la nouvelle discipline et la mise en place d'une règle spéciale qui lui est dédiée,[18] l'Union européenne n'a pas encore adhéré à la Convention.

2 La directive 2008/52/CE

L'attitude négative qui vient d'être soulignée ne découle cependant pas d'un sentiment général de fermeture à l'égard du sujet de la médiation. En effet, dix ans avant la rédaction de la Convention de Singapour, la Communauté européenne avait déjà arrêté la directive 2008/52/CE du 28 mai 2008 sur certains aspects de la médiation civile et commerciale.[19]

Même à cette occasion précédente, une attitude de souplesse transparaît : l'utilisation de l'instrument de la directive au lieu du règlement indique sans doute un certain *self-restraint*, avant tout de la part de la Commission, à édicter des règles particulièrement strictes en la matière. En effet, la directive contient des règles *de minimis* sur la médiation dans les litiges transfrontaliers. Ces derniers sont définis comme des litiges entre deux ou plusieurs parties dont 'au moins une des parties a son domicile ou sa résidence habituelle dans un

16 Sur ce point Palao, 'The Singapore Convention' (n 12) 303.

17 En ce sens Eunice Chua, 'The Singapore Convention on Mediation. A Brighter Future for Asian Dispute Resolution' (2019) 9 *Asian J Intl L* 195; en conséquence, mais avec l'observation critique qu'un tel effet prendra beaucoup de temps, Clemens Treichl, 'The Singapore Convention: Towards a Universal Standard for the Recognition and Enforcement of International Settlement Agreements ?' (2020) 11 *J Intl Dispute Settlement* 409. Pour une comparaison entre la Convention de Singapour et la Convention de New York voir Suraj Sajnani, 'The Singapore Convention: Is This the New York Convention for Mediation ?' (2020) 50 *Hong Kong LJL* 863.

18 En ce sens Treichl, 'The Singapore Convention' (n 17) 426.

19 Pour un aperçu général voir Sylvaine Poillot Peruzzetto, 'Médiation', Répertoire de droit européen, 2014, au site internet dalloz.fr; et plus récemment Guillaume Payan, 'Directive 2008/52/CE du Parlement européen et du Conseil du 21 mai 2008 sur certains aspects de la médiation en matière civile et commerciale', in Guillaume Payan (dir.), *Espace judiciaire civil européen : arrêts de la C.J.U.E. et commentaires* (Bruylant 2020) 1041.

Etat membre autre que celui de toute autre partie' au moment où la médiation commence.

La directive établit donc des règles de base auxquelles les Etats membres doivent conformer leur législation. En particulier, selon l'article 4, ils doivent assurer la qualité de la médiation en mettant en place des systèmes de contrôle dont le choix est entièrement laissé aux Etats eux-mêmes. En outre, ils doivent veiller à ce que les juridictions saisies d'un litige puissent, 'si elles l'estiment approprié' (article 5), inviter les parties à recourir à la médiation pour régler le litige. Il convient toutefois de souligner que cela ne porte pas atteinte au droit de chaque Etat membre de rendre le recours à la médiation obligatoire ou soumis à des incitations ou à des sanctions.[20]

Les deux règles essentielles de cet instrument sont contenues dans les articles 6 et 8. L'article 6 régit la force exécutoire des accords résultant de la médiation, qui sont généralement considérés comme étant de nature contractuelle. Cette règle prévoit que les Etats membres veillent à ce que les parties, ou l'une d'entre elles avec le consentement explicite des autres, aient la possibilité de demander que le contenu d'un accord écrit résultant de la médiation soit rendu exécutoire. Il est clair que la force exécutoire n'est pas automatique, mais résulte d'un accord précis entre les parties, qui peut – bien sûr – être conclu au début de la médiation, mais qui peut aussi faire défaut.

Des motifs de refus d'exequatur sont prévus si le contenu de l'accord 'est contraire à la loi de l'Etat membre' dans lequel la demande est introduite ou même si la loi de l'Etat membre requis ne prévoit pas la force exécutoire de tels accords.

L'article 6 établit ensuite que chaque Etat membre peut prévoir que la force exécutoire d'un accord peut être accordée par un jugement, par une 'décision' (décret, dirait-on en Italie) d'un tribunal ou par un acte authentique d'une autre autorité compétente en vertu du droit de l'Etat membre dans lequel la demande est introduite, telle qu'un officier public (le greffier, l'huissier ou le notaire). De son côté, l'article 8 dispose que les Etats membres veillent à ce que le recours à la médiation ne porte pas atteinte au droit des parties de saisir une juridiction au-delà du délai de prescription.

Cette directive a été mise en œuvre à des degrés divers dans les Etats membres, mais surtout par rapport aux procédures nationales de médiation. L'attitude de l'Italie, qui a introduit une procédure de médiation obligatoire (décret législatif n° 28/2010, modifié par le décret législatif n° 149/2022), est citée en exemple dans de nombreux documents de l'UE, en particulier du Parlement

20 Comme il est prévu au considérant 14.

européen. Dans l'un de ces actes, la question du sort des accords de médiation conclus dans un Etat non membre de l'UE a été soulevée, notamment sous les pressions des acteurs du commerce international.

Aujourd'hui, donc – comme indiqué – presque dix ans après la publication de la directive, la Convention de Singapour serait l'instrument international prêt à agir sur cette question.

3 La non-adhésion de l'Union européenne à la Convention de Singapour

L'importance croissante prise par l'instrument de médiation au sein de l'Union européenne est attestée par l'inclusion par le Traité de Lisbonne en 2007 de ce mode de résolution des litiges dans le domaine de la coopération judiciaire en matière civile, notamment à l'article 81, alinéa 2, lettre g) du TFUE ; et plus récemment par l'envoi de son propre délégué, Norel Rosner, tant au sein du groupe de travail chargé de la rédaction de la Convention que par la suite à la conférence diplomatique convoquée en vue de la signature de ce Traité.

Lors de la première phase des travaux préparatoires, Rosner avait soutenu qu'il était nécessaire de rédiger, au lieu d'une convention, une loi type, à savoir un instrument de *soft law*. Cependant au cours de la cérémonie d'ouverture à la signature de ce Traité il a utilisé des termes très positifs, déclarant qu' 'il existe désormais des instruments internationaux clairs, distincts et complémentaires pour la médiation, le contentieux et l'arbitrage'. Il a de plus souligné que la Convention de Singapour jouerait le même rôle que la Convention de New York sur l'arbitrage de 1958 et, plus tard, des deux nouvelles conventions élaborées dans le cadre de la Conférence de La Haye de droit international privé : la Convention de La Haye du 30 juin 2005 sur les accords d'élection de for et la Convention de la Haye du 2 juillet 2019 sur la reconnaissance et l'exécution des jugements étrangers en matière civile ou commerciale, toutes les deux signées et ratifiées par l'Union européenne.[21]

Toutefois, l'Union reste prudente ou insensible à cette ouverture pour le moment. Parmi les nombreux arguments avancés explicitement ou

21 Il est bien connu que ces deux Conventions ont été ratifiées par l'Union européenne sur la base de ses nouveaux pouvoirs en tant que nouvel membre de la Conférence de la Haye de droit international privé, v. Peter McEleavy and Andrea Schulz, 'The Accession of the European Community to the Hague Conference on Private International Law' (2007) 56 *ICLQ* 939. L'ouverture montrée à ce propos par l'art 12 de la Convention de Singapour semble justement envisager ce nouveau rôle.

simplement supposés pour justifier cette attitude de réticence, certains sont désormais anachroniques, autres sont peu convaincants.

On avait indiqué, par exemple, le manque de compétence de l'Union en la matière. Cependant on a déjà rappelé le texte de l'article 81 du TFUE,[22] auquel on peut ajouter l'article 3, alinéa 2, qui donne à l'Union européenne une compétence exclusive pour conclure des traités.[23]

Des doutes ont étés également soulevés sur l'application de l'article 5, alinéa 1, lettre a), de la Convention déjà évoqué, concernant le motif de refus de la force exécutoire de l'accord relatif à l'incapacité d'une partie. Ici, l'obstacle présumé à la ratification européenne dépendrait du manque de clarification de la loi applicable à cette incapacité. Cependant, il devrait être communément admis que, dans tout instrument international ou supranational de droit international privé, cet aspect – s'il n'est pas expressément réglementé – est laissé soumis à la loi de la nationalité ou de la résidence de l'individu, ou à d'autres lois s'il s'agit de sociétés, sans aucun problème.

D'autres objections, en revanche, sont plus compliquées à surmonter. En ce qui concerne la proposition, déjà mentionnée, du délégué Rosner relative à l'adoption d'un instrument non contraignant pour réglementer la médiation internationale, tel qu'une loi type qui pourrait inspirer la législation des différents Etats, craignant l'absence d'une approche harmonisée en la matière, il a déjà été constaté que dans la version finale des travaux préparatoires on a opté pour un régime à 'double voie', c'est-à-dire pour l'élaboration d'une convention et d'une loi type, également sous l'influence des Etats-Unis d'Amérique, promoteurs et partisans de l'ensemble du projet depuis son début.[24]

Ce résultat n'a cependant pas été jugé satisfaisant dans le contexte européen en raison de la diversité des réglementations des Etats membres déjà présentes dans leurs systèmes juridiques. D'où l'approche prudente des Institutions européennes consistant à déclarer l'intention d'évaluer l'instrument de manière plus approfondie, même en impliquant l'exigence d'avoir l'opinion des entreprises ; mais la raison sous-jacente réside dans le manque de volonté politique.[25]

---

22 Voir aussi Palao, 'The Singapore Convention' (n 12) 19, 270; Laura Carpaneto, 'International and EU Perspective on Mediation: The 2008/52 Directive on Mediation on Civil and Commercial Matters', in Francesco Pesce and Dana Rone (eds.), *Mediation in Civil and Criminal Cases to Foster European Wide Settlement of Disputes* (Aracne 2016) 169.

23 En ce sens Alexander, Chong, Giorgadze, 'The Singapore Convention' (n 12) 307.

24 Sur l'attitude du délégué Rosner voir aussi H. Brink, 'The Singapore Convention on Mediation – Where's Europe?», 26 mars 2021, au site internet https://mediate.com/the-singapore-convention-on-mediation-wheres-europe; Chua (n 17).

25 Sur ce point voir Giovanni Matteucci, 'The Singapore Convention on Mediation, challenges and opportunities', The 2nd KIMC International Seminar, Seoul, December 3, 2021,

En effet, on a douté d'un intérêt réel pour l'Union européenne d'adhérer à la Convention de Singapour, puisque la matière, comme on l'a vu, est déjà réglée par le droit européen, même si on a choisi de promulguer une directive minimaliste et généraliste qui laissait aux Etats membres une grande marge de manœuvre dans sa mise en œuvre. Il s'agissait justement de répondre, comme d'ailleurs la Convention de Singapour, à des exigences d'harmonisation et non d'uniformité, que l'on craignait à l'époque (et peut-être aujourd'hui aussi) irréalisable.

De plus, il a été avancé que l'Union dispose d'un cadre complet et approprié pour réglementer la médiation dans l'espace juridique européen, de sorte qu'il n'est nullement nécessaire de compléter la discipline en la matière, et encore moins par une convention internationale.

En effet, le système européen réglemente déjà plusieurs aspects de la médiation, tels que la reconnaissance et l'exécution de l'accord, bien que de manière médiatisée, par son incorporation dans un jugement ou dans une décision ou un acte d'une autorité compétente, comme prévoit la directive européenne 2008/52/CE. On a évoqué aussi le règlement Rome I sur la loi applicable aux contrats internationaux pour la règlementation des accords de médiation.[26]

En outre, la médiation est également prévue (bien qu'à différents niveaux, à notre avis) dans divers règlements européens concernant différentes matières : par exemple, dans le règlement Bruxelles II ter en ce qui concerne la responsabilité parentale,[27] le règlement (CE) n° 4/2009 sur les obligations alimentaires,[28]

(2022) 1 *ADRITALIA* 80; Hage Chahine, Lombardi, Lutran, Peulvé, 'The Acceleration of the Development' (n 8) 772; Timothy Schnabel, 'The Singapore Convention on Mediation: A Framework for the Cross-Border Recognition and Enforcement of Mediated Settlements' (2019) 19 *Pepperdine Dispute Resolution LJ* 1; Elisabetta Silvestri, 'The Singapore Convention on Mediated Settlement Agreements: A New String to the Bow of International Mediation ?' (2019) 2 *Access to Justice in Eastern Europe* 5.

26 Règlement (CE) n° 593/2008 du Parlement européen et du Conseil du 17 juin 2008 sur la loi applicable aux obligations contractuelles JO L 177/6. Plus largement à cet égard voir Carlos Esplugues, José Iglesias, 'Mediation and private international law: improving free circulation of mediation agreements across the EU', Analysis included in European Parliament, Directorate-General for Internal Policies. Policy Department C, Citizens' Rights and Constitutional Affairs, The Implementation of the Mediation Directive, 29 November 2016, 70.

27 Arts 25 et 79, lettre g), du règlement (UE) 2019/1111 du Conseil du 25 juin 2019 relatif à la compétence, la reconnaissance et l'exécution des décisions en matière matrimoniale et en matière de responsabilité parentale, ainsi qu'à l'enlèvement international d'enfants (refonte) JO L 178/1.

28 Arts 45, lettre a) et 51, alinéa 2, lettre b), du règlement (CE) no 4/2009 du Conseil du 18 décembre 2008 relatif à la compétence, la loi applicable, la reconnaissance et l'exécution des décisions et la coopération en matière d'obligations alimentaires JO L7/1.

le règlement (CE) n° 207/2009 sur la marque communautaire,[29] le règlement (UE) n° 650/2012 sur les successions.[30]

En tout cas, c'est la diversité du régime de la force exécutoire de la médiation entre les systèmes de *Civil Law* et de *Common Law* une des raisons peut-être parmi les plus fortes invoquées pour justifier la réticence de l'Union européenne à ratifier la Convention.[31] En effet, alors que dans le premier, la force exécutoire de l'accord de médiation nécessite l'intervention d'une autorité *super partes* autre que le médiateur, à savoir le juge ou le notaire, dans le second, la force exécutoire est automatique. La directive a choisi la première solution, la Convention la seconde, toujours dans le sillage des aspirations des Etats-Unis d'Amérique.

Certes, l'Union a privilégié un mécanisme de reconnaissance et d'exécution uniquement pour les décisions émanant d'une autorité, de sorte que les actes émanant de parties privées, tels que l'accord de médiation, ne peuvent bénéficier de ce régime que s'ils sont incorporés dans une décision. Il convient toutefois de souligner à cet égard que le système restrictif de la directive en ce qui concerne spécifiquement la circulation intracommunautaire a également été critiqué au sein des Institutions européennes il y a une dizaine d'années.[32] L'inertie qui persiste en la matière ne serait pas donc un bon signe pour l'avenir.

4 Les voix favorables à une telle adhésion

En dépit de ce qui précède, on peut aussi remarquer des points de vue différents à ce sujet. Il convient de distinguer les positions de la doctrine en faveur

29 Art 42, alinéa 4, du règlement (CE) no 207/2009 du Conseil du 26 février 2009 sur la marque communautaire JO L78/1. Voir également le règlement (UE) 2017/1001 du Parlement européen et du Conseil du 14 juin 2017 sur la marque de l'Union européenne (texte codifié).

30 Art 8 du règlement (UE) no 650/2012 du Parlement européen et du Conseil du 4 juillet 2012 relatif à la compétence, la loi applicable, la reconnaissance et l'exécution des décisions, et l'acceptation et l'exécution des actes authentiques en matière de successions et à la création d'un certificat successoral européen JO L 201/107.

31 Malacka, 'The relations' (n 6) 244, souligne que l'un des problèmes concernant l'adhésion de l'Union européenne à la Convention de Singapour découle justement de l'origine anglo-américaine de son approche, notamment en ce qui concerne la force exécutoire automatique de l'accord de médiation. De même, Matteucci, 'The Singapore Convention on Mediation' (n 25) 80 précise que les différences culturelles constituent un obstacle majeur. Voir aussi Chua, 'The Singapore Convention on Mediation' (n 17) 195.

32 Esplugues, Iglesias, 'Mediation and private international law' (n 26).

d'une modification de la directive sur la médiation de celles en faveur de la ratification de la Convention.

En ce qui concerne les premières, la thèse critique que nous venons de mentionner a également conduit à la perspective d'une sorte d'alignement – à l'époque inconscient – entre les deux systèmes de Singapour et de Bruxelles en faisant du caractère exécutoire une règle générale en la matière, par exemple en incluant une référence explicite à la force exécutoire immédiate des accords issus d'une médiation internationale dans le règlement Bruxelles I bis,[33] ou en instaurant une sorte de 'certificat européen d'accord de médiation' délivré par les autorités compétentes de l'Etat d'origine, peut-être étendu également aux accords de médiation de nature purement privée, à l'instar du certificat successoral européen introduit à titre facultatif par le règlement (UE) n° 650/2012.[34]

Une option encore plus forte pour l'Union découlait de la proposition de modifier le cadre juridique européen actuel afin de l'aligner sur la Convention de Singapour, notamment en ce qui concerne le régime de la force exécutoire automatique de ces accords. Pour le monde des affaires, il serait en effet très utile que les régimes intra-européen et extra-européen coïncident afin de garantir une libre circulation mondiale de ces accords.[35] Cela pourrait se faire par une sorte de transposition de la Convention de Singapour dans un acte juridique typique de l'UE ou par l'adhésion de cette dernière à ce Traité, éventuellement en exerçant la possibilité de formuler des réserves, comme le prévoit l'article 8 de la Convention.[36]

Enfin, une autre proposition contient une thèse opposée à cette dernière qu'on vient d'illustrer puisque, au lieu de suggérer l'adhésion de l'Union à la Convention de Singapour, elle propose la possibilité que l'Union s'abstienne complètement de réglementer cette matière, comme cela s'est produit pour

---

33 En ce sens Esplugues, Iglesias, 'Mediation and private international law' (n 26) 70. A ce jour, seul le Portugal a transposé la directive européenne en prévoyant un régime de force exécutoire directe de l'accord de médiation, sans qu'il soit nécessaire de l'incorporer dans un instrument judiciaire lorsque la médiation est exécutoire dans l'Etat d'origine, si le litige peut être soumis à la médiation sans qu'il soit nécessaire de recourir à l'instrument judiciaire : voir l'art 9, alinéa 4, Loi no 29 du 19 avril 2013, publiée au *Diário da República*, 1ère série, n° 77, 19 avril 2013.

34 Le certificat successoral européen est réglé par les articles 62–73 du règlement (UE) no 650/2012 (n 30).

35 Esplugues, Iglesias, 'Mediation and private international law' (n 26) 76.

36 En faveur d'une modification substantielle du cadre juridique européen actuel par le biais de la ratification de la Convention ou d'une révision complète de la directive, voir récemment Haris Meidanis, 'Enforcement of mediation settlement agreements in the EU and the need for reform' (2020) 16 *J Private Intl L* 275.

l'arbitrage, lorsque la Convention de New York de 1958 a été expressément exclue du champ d'application du règlement Bruxelles I bis.[37]

C'est précisément parce qu'elle suit ouvertement le paradigme de la Convention de New York que l'Union européenne pourrait, de la même manière, laisser la médiation transnationale être régie par la seule Convention de Singapour, même parmi les Etats membres qui souhaiteraient la ratifier.[38] Il a également été souligné que cette option serait la seule crédible, étant donné que l'existence de deux régimes pour la même matière pourrait affecter l'harmonie juridique dans le champ de la médiation transnationale.[39]

5 Remarques Finales

Dans l'état actuel des choses, l'Union européenne continue donc à se maintenir dans une position de simple observateur : elle semble évaluer l'impact de la directive sur la médiation en Europe et celui de la Convention de Singapour dans le monde.[40] Cette attitude montrerait que l'Union vise à privilégier l'élaboration d'une nouvelle directive sur la médiation en incluant sa (nouvelle) dimension transnationale : l'adhésion à la Convention annihilerait cette aspiration.[41] Cependant, la Convention répond effectivement aux besoins de sécurité juridique et, en facilitant la résolution pacifique des litiges transnationaux entre parties privées, vise à promouvoir – comme on l'a vu – ces mêmes principes universels de démocratie, de sécurité juridique et d'Etat de droit que l'Union européenne protège également en tant que 'valeurs' en vertu de l'article 2 du Traité de l'Union, tel que modifié par le Traité de Lisbonne.

En outre, la Convention de Singapour, bien que rédigée rapidement et certainement perfectible, a néanmoins comblé un vide juridique ;[42] elle est

37 Voir le considérant 12 du réglement no 1215/2012 (n 13). Récemment cependant on a plaidé pour un changement des rapports entre ces deux instruments : en ce sens Alberto Malatesta, 'Arbitrato e regolamento Bruxelles I-bis: una riforma necessaria', (2024) 60 Rivista di diritto internazionale privato e processuale 39.

38 Encore Haris Meidanis, *Singapore Convention Series: A Plea for The Adoption of the Singapore Convention by the EU*, Kluwer Mediation Blog, au site internet https://mediationblog.kluwerarbitration.com/2019/03/20/singapore-convention-series-a-plea-for-the-adoption-of-the-singapore-mediation-convention-by-the-eu.

39 En ce sens Mimoso, 'The Singapore Convention' (n 2) 189.

40 Pour une analyse approfondie sur ce sujet voir Malacka 'The relations' (n 6) 243.

41 Brink, 'The Singapore Convention on Mediation' (n 24).

42 A ce propos Piotre Wójtowics, Franco Gevaerd, 'How the Singapore Convention Will Enforce Mediated Settlement Agreements Across Borders' (2020) 38 *Alternatives to the High Cost Litigation* 11.

considérée comme *'the missing piece of the international dispute resolution jigsaw'*.[43]Bien que la position de l'Union européenne sur cette question soit pour l'instant fixe, il est possible d'émettre l'hypothèse d'un revirement en faveur de l'adhésion lorsque les Etats grands acteurs du commerce international auront également adhéré, afin de ne pas laisser l'ensemble de l'espace juridique européen à l'écart des règles internationales uniformes en matière de médiation transnationale. La récente ratification du Japon[44] pourrait être considérée comme un premier jalon dans cette direction.

43 En ce sens Hage Chahine, Lombardi, Lutran, Peulvé, 'The Acceleration of the Development' (n 8) 797.

44 (n 10).

ADR and EU Cross-Border Insolvency

Antonio Leandro *

1 Introduction

Interest in the interplay between cross-border insolvency and alternative dispute resolution (ADR) is increasingly growing among scholars and practitioners after the trend of handling business crises through non-judicial instruments has broken out. Confidentiality, time-and-cost efficiency, and flexibility are the main advantages ADR may ensure compared to in-court insolvency proceedings.

Interest in ADR is increasing in the European Union (EU) space, too. The EU Mediation Directive does not exclude insolvency from its scope.[1] Notably, the 2016 Report on the Directive stresses that 'one area where mediation remains underdeveloped is that of insolvency proceedings', adding that, by the 2014 Recommendation on a new approach to business failure and insolvency,[2] the Commission has encouraged the appointment of mediators by courts 'where they consider it necessary in order to assist the debtor and creditors in the successful running of negotiations on a restructuring plan'.[3] The 2019 Restructuring Directive has been adopted to prompt the use of out-of-court proceedings and achieve the outcomes that both the 2016 Report and the 2014 Recommendation hoped for.[4]

The European Insolvency Regulation (EIR)[5] expressly envisages the use of mediation in group insolvency. Furthermore, it implicitly permits the intervention of a third person to facilitate court-to-court and practitioner-to-practitioner

---

* Full Professor of International Law, Aldo Moro University of Bari.

1 Directive 2008/52/EC of the European Parliament and of the Council of 21 May 2008 on certain aspects of mediation in civil and commercial matters [2008] OJ L136/3.

2 Commission Recommendation of 12 March 2014 on a new approach to business failure and insolvency (2014/135/EU), para III.B.

3 Report from the Commission to the European Parliament, the Council and the European Economic and Social Committee on the application of Directive 2008/52/EC of the European Parliament and of the Council on certain aspects of mediation in civil and commercial matters (COM(2016) 542 final).

4 Directive (EU) 2019/1023 of 20 June 2019 on preventive restructurings frameworks, on discharge of debt and disqualifications, and on measures to increase the efficiency of procedures concerning restructuring, insolvency and discharge of debit and amending Directive (EU) 2017/1132 (Directive on restructuring and insolvency) [2019] OJ L172/18. See *infra*, para 4.

5 Regulation (EU) No 2015/848 of the European Parliament and of the Council of 20 May 2015 on insolvency proceedings (recast) [2015] OJ L 141/19.

 | DOI:10.1163/9789004727663_010

cooperation, even in the case of insolvency proceedings opened with respect to a single debtor.

The binomial ADR/insolvency is also under the spotlight of global arenas. Voluntary negotiation, mediation and informal dispute resolutions are strongly recommended by the World Bank's Principles for Effective Insolvency and Creditor/Debtor Regimes, especially vis-à-vis the insolvency of micro and small enterprises.[6] The 1997 UNCITRAL Model Law on Cross-border Insolvency envisages the appointment of a neutral person to implement the cooperation under articles 25 and 26,[7] including through the conclusion of protocols or other agreements. The UNCITRAL Law on Mediation[8] aims at fostering 'the non-judicial settlement of disputes in multiparty situations, especially those where interests and issues are complex and multilateral rather than bilateral'.[9] As 'notable examples', the Guide to Enactment gives 'disputes arising during insolvency proceedings or disputes whose resolution is essential to avoid the commencement of insolvency proceedings'.[10] Last but not least, the Singapore Convention on Mediation provides parties to commercial disputes with a way to enforce the settlement agreed upon either in out-of-court or in ordinary collective proceedings without sanctioning by courts.[11] There are no 'insolvency exceptions' to its scope.

Under such general premises, this paper will attempt to find key principles of coordination between ADR and EU cross-border insolvency from a private international law perspective.[12]

2 Why Dwell on Arbitration?

The expression 'ADR' does not properly fit arbitration. It mainly refers to instruments resulting in settlement agreements or non-binding third-party

6 See Recommendations B4 and D5.4.

7 UNCITRAL Model Law on Cross-Border Insolvency with Guide to Enactment (UNGA Resolution 52/158 of 15 December 1997).

8 UNCITRAL Model Law on International Commercial Mediation and International Settlement Agreements Resulting from Mediation (UNGA Resolution 73/99 of 20 December 2018).

9 Guide to Enactment and Use of the UNCITRAL Model Law on International Commercial Mediation and International Settlement Agreements Resulting from Mediation, para 48.

10 *Ibid.*

11 United Nations Convention of 20 December 2018 on International Settlement Agreements Resulting from Mediation. The Convention entered into force on 12 September 2020 and to date applies to 15 States. Neither the EU nor its Member States are parties. Further details are available at www.uncitral.com.

12 The paper focuses on corporate insolvency. However, it is worth noting that bank and financial resolution mechanisms are not barred to ADR, notwithstanding they usually fall under the supervision of public authorities.

acts. However, arbitration deserves attention in this study as it represents an alternative tool in terms of structure and purposes to in-court insolvency proceedings, which usually are public and collective, require judicial supervision with a *vis attractiva* over insolvency-related disputes, and are mandatory to creditors seeking satisfaction.

The interaction between cross-border insolvency and arbitration arises in many respects,[13] particularly in the case of international commercial arbitration.[14] This interaction is marked by well-known issues, such as i) the impact of the opening of the insolvency proceedings on the arbitration agreement, ii) the power of the insolvency practitioner to replace the debtor in previous arbitration agreements or to conclude new ones, iii) conversely, the ability of the debtor in possession to conclude arbitration agreements, iv) the arbitrability of 'ancillary actions', i.e. those generally lying with the *vis attractiva* of insolvency courts, v) the avoidance of arbitration agreements as acts detrimental to creditors, vi) the impact of insolvency proceedings on pending arbitrations, vii) the recognition and enforcement of awarded claims in the insolvency proceedings.

Some of the issues above are much debated. Others are well settled. For instance, no problems arise regarding the recognition of awarded claims for the purpose of their lodgment, provided that the arbitration starts before the

13 On the topic see particularly Fernando Mantilla-Serrano, 'International Arbitration and Insolvency Proceedings' (1995) 11 Arbitration Int'l 51; Philippe Fouchard, 'Arbitrage et faillite' (1998) Revue de l'arbitrage 471; Vesna Lazić, *Insolvency Proceedings and Commercial Arbitration* (Kluwer Law International 1998); Stefan M Kröll, 'Arbitration and Insolvency Proceedings: Selected Problems', in Loukas A Mistelis and Julian DM Lew (eds), *Pervasive Problems in International Arbitration* (Kluwer 2006) 374; Jason Chuah, 'Resolving Unresolved Relationships Problems – the Case of Cross Border Insolvency and Pending Arbitration' (2011) 8 European Company and Financial L. Rev. 423; Jay Lawrence Westbrook, 'International Arbitration and Multinational Insolvency' (2011) 29 Penn State Int'l L. Rev. 635; Massimo V Benedettelli, 'Cross-Border Insolvency and International Arbitration in the EU: a Playing Field for Regulated Forum Shopping' (2012) Cahiers de l'arbitrage 783; Neil Hannan, 'International Commercial Arbitration and Cross Border Insolvency' (2014) 17 Int'l Trade &. Business L. Rev. 454; Stefania Bariatti, 'The European Insolvency Regulation and Arbitration' (2016) 26 Rivista dell'arbitrato 267; Massimo V Benedettelli, 'Il (risolvibile) puzzle del rapporto tra arbitrato internazionale e insolvenze transfrontaliere nel diritto europeo', in Antonio Leandro, Giorgio Meo, Antonio Nuzzo (eds), *Crisi transfrontaliera di impresa: orizzonti internazionali ed Europei* (Cacucci 2018) 199; Reinhard Bork, 'Arbitration in Insolvency' (2022) 5 European Insolvency and Restructuring Journal accessed 24 January 2024; Ishaan Madaan and Christian Campbell (eds), *Crossroads of Insolvency and Arbitration* (Wolters Kluwer 2022); Richard Bamforth and Kushal Gandhi (eds), *Arbitration and Insolvency* (Edward Elgar 2024).

14 A different, not less interesting stimulus comes from investment arbitration. However, this paper is not the appropriate venue to address the topic.

opening of the insolvency proceedings, may continue notwithstanding the insolvency proceedings, and the award is recognized in the State of the insolvency proceedings with no annulment proceedings pending against it.[15] As a matter of fact, no mandatory rules, even in the EIR, prevent the claim from being assessed in foreign arbitrations and then verified in the insolvency proceedings through the recognition of the award.[16]

2.1 *Arbitrability and Insolvency*

Conversely, much debated is the arbitrability of disputes when one of the parties falls insolvent. This issue is linked to the general query of whether arbitration is an 'Appropriate Dispute Resolution' venue compared to in-court proceedings.

Actually, a distinction between 'pure insolvency matters' and 'claims disputed against or by the debtor' is needed to determine what problems arbitrability really raises.[17] Generally speaking, 'pure insolvency matters' include the insolvency proceedings themselves, the requirements for their opening, and the procedural profiles concerning rescue or liquidation. What prevents such profiles from being arbitrated is the lack of a genuine underlying dispute. Moreover, the demand to put rescue and liquidation under the supervision of courts for the collective satisfaction of creditors is commonplace and grounded on public policy concerns with which arbitration is said to be incompatible.

'Claims disputed against or by the debtor' account for intrinsically arbitrable disputes instead, which may lose 'arbitrability' due to insolvency or the opening of insolvency proceedings. While non-arbitrability is generally associated with 'pure insolvency matters' according to mainstream thought and practice,[18] 'claims disputed against or by the debtor' are treated differently depending on the law that governs arbitrability. Non-arbitrability may impair arbitration at the outset (basically as a limit to party autonomy in entering into

15 It does not properly fit the theme of the interaction between ADR and insolvency proceedings that an awarded debt may be relied upon by the creditor to request the opening of the insolvency proceedings. Irrespective of the requirements needed for the request to be approved, no insolvency proceedings are yet 'competing' with arbitration in that case.

16 With respect to the verification through foreign judgments see Corte di cassazione (Section I), 15 April 2019 no 10540 <www.italgiure.giustizia.it/sncass> accessed 24 January 2024. Given that judgments and awards are put on equal footing in the requested State after the recognition, the findings of the Italian Supreme Court may also extend to the verification through foreign awards.

17 Julian D.M. Lew, Loukas A. Mistelis, Stefan M. Kröll, *Comparative International Commercial Arbitration* (Kluwer Law International 2003) 205.

18 See the IBA Toolkit on Insolvency and Arbitration <www.ibanet.org> accessed 24 January 2024.

the arbitration agreement) or in the end (i.e. when the award is to be enforced, and non-arbitrability is claimed as a ground to set aside the award or refuse its enforcement).

In the pre-award stage, the court ruling on the validity of the arbitration agreement usually rules also on arbitrability. In the post-award phase, the question is for the court of the seat (presumably seized to set aside the award) or the courts of the State in which the award's enforcement is sought. Arbitrability in the pre-award stage is governed by the law that courts apply to decide on the arbitration agreement's validity (this point is evidently connected to the question of which law governs the arbitration agreement). The post-award phase is almost worldwide governed under article v(2)(a) of the New York Convention,[19] which implies the application of the law of the State in whichenforcement is sought. We might take for granted that the law of seat applies when non-arbitrability is claimed as a ground to set aside the award.

In light of the foregoing, the impact of insolvency proceedings on arbitrability will undergo a different treatment depending on which law governs arbitrability in the pre or post award stage. The law of the State in which the insolvency proceedings have been opened applies insofar as it governs arbitrability in the pre-award stage or when the recognition of the award is sought, or the annulment of the award demanded, in that State.

From the arbitral tribunal's perspective, the impact of insolvency on arbitrability intertwines with that of insolvency proceedings on pending arbitration. We will return to this point shortly.[20] Be that as it may, arbitrators should carefully determine these impacts under their duty to render an enforceable award.

2.2 *Insolvency Proceedings and Arbitration Agreements*

Insolvency is usually deemed to adversely affect an arbitration agreement concluded before the opening of the insolvency proceedings, even more so when the agreement is concluded in the so-called 'suspect period' relied upon by avoidance actions.

This impact is appreciated either from a purely legal perspective – e.g. because debtors lose their capacity to arbitrate – or from a factual perspective – e.g. because the arbitration agreement becomes inoperative due to the debtor's inability to allocate financial resources to arbitration. From a different perspective, the arbitration's costs may impinge heavily on the insolvency estate bookkeeping. After the opening of the insolvency proceedings,

19 New York Convention of 10 June 1958 on the Recognition and Enforcement of Foreign Arbitral Awards.

20 See para 2.4.

arbitration agreements may be also trumped by ii) the supervening non-arbitrability of the dispute, ii) their detrimental nature vis-à-vis unsecured creditors, iii) the replacement of the debtor by an insolvency practitioner who does not want to trigger or undergo the arbitration.

Under the EIR, all these topics are settled by the *lex concursus* according to article 7, whatever the impact of the insolvency proceedings under the law governing the validity of the arbitration agreement. In particular, the *lex concursus* applies i) under letter (c) to the mentioned issues that come across the powers of the insolvency practitioner, i) under letter (e) because the arbitration agreement qualifies as a contract (or contractual clause) to which the debtor is a party and the effects of the insolvency proceedings on pending contracts are determined by that law (unless the EIR refers to different laws or provides for uniform rules); iii) under letter (m) if the insolvency practitioner challenges the arbitration agreement as an act detrimental to creditors claiming for its 'voidness, voidability or unenforceability' according to the *lex concursus* (incidentally, it is debatable whether the avoidance of an arbitration agreement might be processed under article 16).

2.3 *Insolvency-Related Disputes, Non-Insolvency-Related Disputes, and Arbitration*

Insolvency-related disputes are those that meet the *Gourdain* requirements,[21] i.e., direct link to, and derivation from, the insolvency proceedings. In other words, it is the disputes falling under the *vis attractiva concursus* according to article 6(1) EIR.[22] Should the *lex concursus* hypothetically allow for arbitration, no obstacles arise from article 6 to trigger the arbitration. Although article 6(1) establishes the exclusive jurisdiction of the State of the insolvency proceedings, such exclusiveness compels judicial bodies and is restricted to the jurisdictional framework of the EIR also for the latter to be well coordinated with the Brussels Ibis Regulation.[23] Apart from article 18, the EIR does not deal with arbitration. Consequently, arbitration may commence if the *lex concursus* so permits, notwithstanding the *vis attractiva* established by article 6.

As noted above, the insolvency practitioner (or the debtor in possession) can enter into – or remain bound by – an arbitration agreement in the exercise of

---

21 Case C-133/78 *Henri Gourdain v Franz Nadler* [1979] ECLI:EU:C:1979:49.

22 See extensively Antonio Leandro, 'Article 6' in Gilles Cuniberti, Antonio Leandro (eds), *The European Insolvency Regulation and Implementing Legislation* (Edward Elgar 2024), also for further references.

23 Regulation (EU) No 1215/2012 of the European Parliament and of the Council of 12 December 2012 on jurisdiction and the recognition and enforcement of judgments in civil and commercial matters (recast) [2012] OJ L 351/1.

a 'power' stemming from the *lex concursus*. This law could earlier clarify if the insolvency practitioner might 'arbitrate' disputes falling under the *vis attractiva*. Non-insolvency-related actions, which may fall under the Brussels Ibis Regulation, are presumptively arbitrable. Arbitration may only be obstructed if they become non-arbitrable because of the opening of insolvency proceedings or because the debtor has been replaced by an insolvency practitioner who no longer wants to arbitrate the dispute and the *lex concursus* permits her/him to do so.

Moreover, article 6(2) allows the insolvency practitioners to request the consolidation of insolvency-related and non-insolvency-related actions before the courts of the defendant's domicile, so long as the latter are competent under the Brussels Ibis Regulation. This option is frozen where the non-insolvency-related disputes are to be arbitrated. The arbitration trumps the jurisdiction under the Brussels Ibis Regulation and, hence, a requirement for the disputes to be consolidated under article 6(2) EIR.

Given the above, consolidation would also be debarred if the *lex concursus* allowed the insolvency practitioner to arbitrate an insolvency-related dispute and the practitioner triggered the arbitration indeed.

2.4 *Insolvency Proceedings and Pending Arbitration*

As for pending arbitration, article 18 of the EIR states: 'the effects of insolvency proceedings on [...] pending arbitral proceedings concerning an asset or a right which forms part of a debtor's insolvency estate shall be governed solely by the law of the Member State [...] in which the arbitral tribunal has its seat'.

Evidently, article 18 adopts a conflict-of-law rule whereby the *lex arbitri* governs the effects of the insolvency proceedings on pending arbitrations. Intuitively, such a rule leads to a law other than the *lex concursus* if the arbitral seat lies outside the State of the insolvency proceedings; otherwise, *lex fori concursus* and *lex arbitri* coincide. As a conflict-of-law rule, article 18 binds courts, namely the court of the insolvency proceedings and the court of the arbitral seat. By contrast, arbitral tribunals are not bound by article 18 because they are not as compelled to statutory conflict-of-law provisions as courts are. On the other hand, arbitral tribunals usually apply the *lex arbitri* to evaluate most facts that may expose the award to the risk of annulment, as would happen if the *lex arbitri* were to establish the interruption of arbitration after the opening of insolvency proceedings.

2.5 *Insolvency Proceedings and Exequatur of the Awards*

The EIR does not deal with the effects of the awards. Recital 73 precises that article 18 'should not affect national rules on recognition and enforcement of arbitral awards'. All these issues are settled in the State of the insolvency proceedings according to the *lex fori* in tandem with international rules, such as those established by the 1958 New York Convention. The resulting legal framework covers the *exequatur* as a whole. This means that, despite the arbitration sticking to the rules governing the interplay with the insolvency proceedings, the award may be refused on different grounds.

On the other hand, article V of the New York Convention implicitly relies on insolvency rules when, for instance, the arbitral tribunal does not interrupt the arbitration, notwithstanding the *lex arbitri* required to do so because of the insolvency proceedings. The award might not be recognized, in fact, if the continuation of the arbitration ran against the public policy of the requested State or because the dispute was no longer arbitrable according to article V(2)(b) and article V(2)(a) of the New York Convention, respectively. It may happen, though, that the award is recognized in other States, including that of the insolvency proceedings, whose legal order raises no obstacles like the above.

Since article 18 states that the *lex arbitri* governs the effects of the insolvency proceedings, even if *lex concursus* were to mandate the arbitration's interruption or the dispute's non-arbitrability, such reasons could not be pleaded for barring the recognition of the award if the *lex arbitri* did not provide the same. However, any scenario depends on the right understanding of Article 18 read in conjunction with Recital 73.[24]

3 Insolvency Proceedings and 'Genuine' ADR in the EIR Framework: The Recourse to 'Mediation' in Multinational Group Insolvency

Turning to other ADR instruments, mediation is expressly at the disposal of the group coordinator according to article 72 (2)(b) of the EIR.

The coordination proceedings may be launched when multiple insolvency proceedings are opened vis-à-vis different members of the same group of companies. The coordinator, who is in charge of the coordination proceedings, may 'mediate any dispute arising between two or more insolvency practitioners of group members'. In consistency with its role, the coordinator is seen as the most suitable person to assist insolvency practitioners in their attempt to settle disputes arising out of the coordination proceeding. Disputes may regard, for instance, asset distribution or the implementation of the coordination plan.

24 On this point see extensively Antonio Leandro, *Jurisdiction in EU Cross-border Insolvency Law* (Edward Elgar 2025), Chapter 7, para 2.d.

Coordinators fit this role well because they are appointed among persons qualified to act as insolvency practitioners. Who better than an insolvency practitioner can understand the needs of other insolvency practitioners? Moreover, the coordinator is expressly called to carry out its tasks with impartiality and due care as a mediator usually is. At closer inspection, however, article 72 is not concerned with full-blown insolvency disputes. It addresses conflicting positions that arise out of the coordination proceeding. Consequently, the 'mediation' also is confined to the scope and purposes of such proceeding.

On the other hand, mediation under article 72 looks like the one envisaged in the Singapore Convention, namely a process of reaching an amicable settlement of disputes with the coordinator's assistance. Moreover, it is apparent that, just as the mediator in the Convention, the coordinator in the EIR lacks 'the authority to impose a solution upon the insolvency practitioners'. This is consistent with the fact that coordinators are generally endowed with non-binding powers. Still similarly to the Singapore Convention, 'mediation' under article 72 has a broad meaning irrespective of the expression used in the concrete case.

3.1 *Insolvency Proceedings and 'Genuine' ADR in the EIR Framework: Welcoming ADR under the Lex Concursus*

Apart from the case of article 72, mediation and other ADRs are eligible to settle genuine insolvency disputes or conflicting positions between debtors and creditors or between the creditors if the *lex concursus* so permits.

In other words, while the EIR allows authorities involved in multinational-group insolvency to avail of an alternative way to litigation for disputes arising out of the coordination proceedings, the use of ADR s in insolvency matters generally depends on the *lex concursus*. Whether this option is established by statutes or triggered by courts also depends on the *lex concursus* in question. It is only worth recollecting that the European Commission encourages – if not urges – courts to appoint mediators to assist debtors and creditors in successful negotiations on a restructuring plan.[25] Such 'cheer' for ADR s is equally intended for domestic and cross-border situations.

The fact remains that the difference between insolvency matters, insolvency-related and non-insolvency-related disputes impinges again on the access to ADR s. Moreover, the insolvency may lead to the debtor's 'incapacity' to settle the agreement, its replacement by the insolvency practitioner in the search for ADR s, or even the dispute no longer being eligible for settlement through ADR. Considering once again the wide-ranging competence of the *lex concursus* on

25 Commission Recommendation (n 2), para III.B.

the course of the proceedings, the debtor's divestment, and the powers of the insolvency practitioners, it may be argued that it governs not only the availability of ADRs in insolvency situations or for settling insolvency-related disputes but also the effects of settlement agreements either in the State of the insolvency proceedings or in other Member States.

As regards the effects of the opening of insolvency proceedings on 'pending ADR mechanisms', it is difficult to apply other laws than the *lex concursus*. Article 18 patently works solely for 'pending lawsuit' and 'pending arbitration' unless the first expression is meant to include the use of ADR within foreign judicial proceedings and the second is it for the Med-Arb processes.

4 ADR and the 2019 Restructuring Directive

It seems commonplace that ADR has more room in pre-insolvency scenarios than in full-blown insolvency proceedings. This is why the 2019 Restructuring Directive now deserves attention.

It is well known that the Directive lays down, among others, rules on pre-insolvency restructuring frameworks. It prompts parties to use out-of-court proceedings so that the debtor might oversee the crisis while keeping its activity ongoing. The key advantages of ADR are consistent with such advocacy for out-of-court proceedings if one emphasizes confidentiality, time-cost efficiency, flexibility, and preserving valuable commercial relationships through negotiation. Out-of-court negotiations for debt restructuring are often more satisfactory to debtors and creditors than in-court proceedings.

However, only if the final agreement settles a dispute can we witness a genuine ADR outcome. Otherwise, i.e., when the negotiation aims at restructuring debts rather than resolving disputes, the term ADR is appropriate only in a broad sense. On the other hand, debt restructuring entails the 'composition' of divergent positions, which is at the heart of ADRs' mission. As early as under the proposal of the Directive, the EU's intention was that Member States 'ensure that mediators [...] receive the necessary initial and further training' to better carry out their task in restructuring, insolvency, and second chance matters,[26] without distinguishing between full-blown disputes and 'mere' conflicting positions.

It remains that out-of-court proceedings lack enforceability unless their workouts are sanctioned by courts and, with the dress of court decisions or

26 Article 25 of the Proposal for a Directive of the European Parliament and of the Council on preventive restructuring frameworks, second chance and measures to increase the efficiency of restructuring, insolvency and discharge procedure and amending the Directive 2012/30/EU (COM (2016) 723 final, 22 November 2016).

settlements, or authentic instruments, are recognized and enforced through the EIR, the Brussels Ibis Regulation, or national law depending on the instrument applicable to the case.

Without being judicially sanctioned, the workout is likely to be enforced in the EU space as a contract. This means, *inter alia*, that the agreement would not bind third parties. Moreover, 'new money' claims resulting from the agreement could trigger rank issues if the debtor were subsequently to fall into insolvency proceedings. Such problems need a conflict-of-law solution when the proceedings are opened in a State different from that whose law governed the agreement or where the ADR took place. The *lex concursus* will apply to set the rank unless the agreement has constituted secured claims or other legal rights that the EIR shields from such law.

5 Concluding Remarks

ADRs and business crises are increasingly getting along. The EU consistently urges States and operators to prompt the use of out-of-court mechanisms to achieve outcomes that might be as quick and time-and-cost efficient as satisfactory for debtors and creditors. That is particularly true for pre-insolvency situations.

Moreover, if the Singapore Convention were to enter into force for the EU Member States and be applicable to preventive restructuring, such workouts would benefit from a more efficient regime of recognition and enforcement. On the other hand, a well-settled interplay between the Convention, the EIR, and the 2019 Insolvency Directive is also needed to make this scenario materialise successfully.

The dialogue between ADRs and full-blown insolvency proceedings is at the onset and features more complexities, especially when it comes to liquidation proceedings. Arbitration, mediation, and negotiation might enter the scene as alternative venues to settle insolvency-related or non-insolvency-related disputes, but under the requirements, if any, that *lex concursus* establishes. That is, such dialogue is far from being uniformly regulated in the EU space. Let alone on a global scale.

Views from International Lawyers

The History of the ILA Committee on International Commercial Arbitration

An Assessment of its Contribution to the Codification of the Law of International Arbitration

Luca G Radicati di Brozolo[*]

The International Arbitration Committee is one of the ILA's oldest committees. Over many decades, it has studied a variety of aspects of international commercial arbitration well before this dispute settlement mechanism acquired the central role it now plays in international business transactions and became the subject of intense academic interest. In these few pages, it is worthwhile pausing to consider its work in the last quarter of a century, which is obviously the one most relevant to contemporary international arbitration.

In this period, the Committee addressed six diverse, but all significant, issues of international commercial arbitration, i.e. public policy, *res judicata* and *lis pendens*, the ascertainment of the contents of the applicable law, confidentiality, inherent powers of arbitrators and the reasoning of arbitral decisions. Each of these topics formed the subject of a Final Report and Recommendations

The Final Report and Recommendations on 'Public Policy as a Bar to the Enforcement of International Arbitral Awards'[1] – prepared under the chairmanship of Pierre Mayer and with Audley Sheppard as rapporteur and adopted at the New Delhi Biennial Conference in 2002 – deal with a classic topic of international commercial arbitration, the contours of which were less well understood than nowadays by the arbitration community. The Report and Recommendations are significant because they identify the criteria for the determination of the scope of public policy as a bar to the enforcement of arbitral awards and highlight the need to limit the notion of public policy to principles that are 'sufficiently fundamental', excluding from that notion 'mere "mandatory rules"', so that that recognition and enforcement can only be denied where they would 'manifestly disrupt the essential political, social

* Former Professor of Private International Law and International Arbitration, Catholic University of the Sacred Heart, Milan; Founding Partner, Arblit.

1 Committee on International Commercial Arbitration, 'Final Report on Public Policy as a Bar to Enforcement of International Arbitral Awards' and Resolution 2/2002, both in International Law Association, Report of the Seventieth Conference (New Delhi 2002) (International Law Association, New Delhi 2002).

 | DOI:10.1163/9789004727663_011

or economic interests protected by the rule'. Although these notions are commonly accepted today, their conceptualization in these terms helped to clarify the limits of the control of awards by domestic courts and thus to better define the limits beyond which courts should not interfere with arbitration.

The next Report and Recommendations, on '*Res Judicata* and *Lis pendens* in International Arbitration' – adopted at the 2006 Toronto Biennial Conference – was prepared by the new chairman, Filip de Ly, who chaired the Committee until now, again with Audley Sheppard as rapporteur. These are probably the most significant of the Reports and Recommendations discussed here because they provide an important basis for the development of arbitration-specific rules to determine the preclusive value of arbitral awards. This is a very important issue – both theoretically and practically – usually addressed superficially on the basis of domestic law, both by domestic courts and, more surprisingly, by arbitrators. The Committee's Report and Recommendations survey the approaches to *res judicata* in domestic legal systems, highlighting the differences, particularly between common law and civil law systems, and the fact that domestic rules have been developed for court judgments and are not necessarily suitable for arbitral awards. On that basis, and noting the need for a uniform approach in international arbitration, the Committee recommends a set of rules that tend to adopt a broader notion of *res judicata* than is traditionally held to apply in civil law systems and that, in considerable measure, resembles that of common law systems. The Report notes that *res judicata* should not normally be held to be a component of public policy.

As I have argued elsewhere,[2] despite their undisputable value, the ILA's Report and Recommendations on *res judicata* have not had the impact on the case law that I think they deserve. Arbitrators and courts have been reluctant to apply them or take them into consideration, particularly on the grounds that they do not reflect an approach to *res judicata* common to all, or at least most, jurisdictions.[3] This is disingenuous, essentially because – for *res judicata* as for all other issues that arise in connection to arbitration – there is no need for arbitration-specific rules to reflect an approach that is adopted by all legal systems, which would render the development of autonomous rules virtually impossible given the differences between different systems. The idea is to find rules suited to arbitration, where finality is particularly important to business

2 See Luca G Radicati di Brozolo and Flavio Ponzano, 'How to Assess the *Res Judicata* Effects of International Arbitral Awards: Giving Concreteness to an Autonomous Approach' in (2024) *Arbitration International*, 409–444.

3 With some notable exceptions. For an example, see the 2019 Award by an arbitrator operating under the aegis of the Milan Chamber of Arbitration discussed *infra*, 174.

users and the formalisms of some domestic systems are inappropriate. Also, the due process and access to justice concerns often invoked in support of restrictive *res judicata* approaches are for the most part overblown given the nature of the users of arbitration.

The Committee's recommendations, which take all this into account and propose pragmatic arbitration-specific rules, are ideally suited for international arbitration, and actually today appear perhaps too restrained. This is in part due to the fact that, having been prepared about twenty years ago, they do not consider that there has been an evolution in the approach to *res judicata* in civil law jurisdictions, many of which have moved to a somewhat broader, more pragmatic and less formalistic, one which to a significant extent adopts some of the conceptions that are typical of common law jurisdictions.

The product of the ILA's work on *res judicata* is thus, according to me, the paradigm of the soft-law-making efforts the international arbitration community should engage in more forcefully. A very significant development in this direction is the IBA Arbitration Committee's recent decision to take up the issue of arbitral *res judicata* with a view to proposing the adoption of guidelines on the subject, and that its preliminary report draws heavily on the ILA's Recommendations.

Also the Committee's Final Report and Recommendations on '*Lis Pendens* and Arbitration',[4] adopted at the same Toronto Conference, are important, although they have attracted less attention. The Report contains an exhaustive analysis of law on parallel proceedings in domestic jurisdictions, both with regard to domestic proceedings and with regard to the interactions between court proceedings and arbitral proceedings and different arbitral proceedings. The Recommendations support the principle of positive *Kompetenz-Kompetenz* whereby an arbitral tribunal that considers itself *prima facie* competent should proceed with the arbitration regardless of other proceedings pending before a national court or another arbitral tribunal. The Recommendations then identify various circumstances in which an arbitral tribunal requested to stay an arbitration on the basis that parallel proceedings are pending *may* decline jurisdiction or stay the current arbitration in the interest of avoiding conflicting decisions or preventing costly duplication of proceedings or protecting the parties from oppressive tactics. The Recommendations emphasize that a rigid first-in-time approach is not suitable for arbitration and put considerable store on the case management powers of the arbitrators.

4 Committee on International Commercial Arbitration, 'Final Report on *Lis Pendens* and Arbitration' and Resolution 1/2006, Annex 1, both in International Law Association Report of the Seventy-Second Conference (Toronto 2006) (International Law Association, Toronto 2006).

In its subsequent work the Committee has addressed a number of other topics of considerable interest both for practitioners and scholars of international arbitration.

The Report and Recommendations on 'Ascertaining the Contents of the Applicable Law in International Commercial Arbitration'[5] – adopted at the Rio de Janeiro Biennial Conference on 2008 under the Chairmanship of Filip De Ly, with Mark W. Friedmann and the present author as co-rapporteurs – address a problem with which all arbitrators are confronted when (as is generally the case) they are required to decide according to the law. The Report surveys the different approaches to the question of the ascertainment of the applicable rules in domestic law and in international law and concludes that those approaches do not provide strong guidance for how the content of law should be ascertained by arbitrators. This is not only because of the differences between national legal systems, but also because of the fundamental differences between the position of arbitrators and that of national and international courts. The Report and Recommendations therefore advocate a balanced autonomous and arbitration-specific approach which is articulated in considerable detail. In this emphasis on the need for transnational solutions there is a certain parallelism with the approach of the Recommendations on *res judicata* illustrated above. In respect of the ascertainment of the applicable law, the recommended approach relies heavily on the input of the parties as to the content of the rules to be applied by the arbitrators to decide the issues before them but may require the intervention and guidance of the arbitrators. It presupposes that arbitrators must strike a balance between a strict *iura novit curia* approach (which risks 'taking the arbitration from the parties' and making arbitrators appear partial) and a pure *laissez faire* approach that may leave arbitrators without sufficient guidance with the risk of making an award that is legally incorrect. The Report and Recommendations underscore the importance of always giving the parties the opportunity to be heard on material that goes meaningfully beyond their submissions and of avoiding the introduction by arbitrators of legal issues bearing on the outcome of the dispute not raised by the parties.

5 Committee on International Commercial Arbitration, 'Final Report on Ascertaining the Contents of the Applicable Law in International Commercial Arbitration' and Resolution 6/2008, both in International Law Association Report of the Seventy-Third Conference (Rio de Janeiro 2008) (International Law Association, Rio de Janeiro 2008).

The Report and Recommendations on 'Confidentiality in International Arbitration'[6] – adopted at the 2010 Biennial Conference in The Hague again with Mark W. Friedman and this author as co-rapporteurs – address a topic that arises very frequently in arbitral proceedings, and which is more complex that often assumed. Contrary to the common belief that arbitration is confidential – which is apparently one of the drivers of the choice of arbitration – there is no overarching duty of confidentiality in arbitration. Although certain national laws provide for such an obligation, many do not, and the scope of the obligation differs from one to the other. Arbitration rules too deal with the subject differently. The Report surveys the different sources and identifies the various problems that confidentiality gives rise to, including the identification of the applicable law, the parties bound by the obligation, the scope of the obligation, the exceptions to confidentiality (in particular in the face of competing obligations of disclosure), the lifespan and the enforcement of the obligation. The Recommendations underscore the advisability of specifically addressing the question in arbitration agreements or in the terms of reference, bearing in mind that provisions on confidentiality contained in the contract or other documents forming the subject of the arbitration do not necessarily apply to the confidentiality of the arbitration. The Recommendations also set out a number of model confidentiality clauses.

The Report and Recommendations on 'Inherent Powers of Arbitrators in International Commercial Arbitration'[7] – adopted at the Washington DC Biennial Conference in 2014, with Mark W. Friedmann and the present author as co-rapporteurs – are devoted to the inherent powers of arbitrators, which is to say the powers that arbitrators are generally understood to possess in order to be able to deal with situations (including challenging and controversial matters that may fundamentally affect the outcome of the dispute) not addressed by the parties' arbitration agreement or the applicable curial law and rules. The premise of the Report and Recommendations is the need to define the scope of these non-enumerated powers of the arbitrators, or at a minimum to develop a framework for understanding when they may be properly employed, given the harmful consequences of a wrongful exercise of that authority.

---

6 Committee on International Commercial Arbitration, 'Final Report on Confidentiality in International Commercial Arbitration' and Resolution 1/2010, both in International Law Association, Report of the Seventy-Forth Conference (The Hague 2010) (International Law Association, The Hague 2010).

7 Committee on International Commercial Arbitration, 'Final Report on Inherent Powers and Arbitrators in International Commercial Arbitration', in International Law Association, Report of the Seventy-Sixth Conference (Washington DC 2014) (International Law Association, Washington DC 2014).

The Report provides an overview of the origin of inherent and implied powers and discusses the various situations and circumstances where they may be relevant to international commercial arbitration, providing definitions and classifications of those powers and a framework for analyzing them. The Report highlights that, over time, certain not enumerated powers initially exercised by arbitrators on the basis that they are inherent to their mandate have come to be viewed as routine (cases in point being the power to grant interim measures and *Kompetenz-Kompetenz*). The Report analyzes in detail various categories of implied or inherent powers, and specifically those relating to procedure and the conduct of the proceedings. The most relevant and frequently resorted to are those relating to procedure, to decision-making and to safeguard against misconduct and perceived improprieties, as well as – in some limited cases – the power to reverse decisions, as long as the tribunal is not *functus officio*.

In the final section on the framework of arbitral power, the Report analyzes the different contexts in which the arbitrators' non-enumerated powers can be deployed, which are also a function of the level of detail in the sources governing a particular arbitration. A basic distinction is that between situations in which these powers can be implied by express provisions contained in those sources and those where the arbitrators have to rely on the powers necessary to exercise their basic function of resolving the dispute, which implies in particular the power to oversee and conduct the proceedings and adopt the measure necessary to pursue that goal and to protect the integrity of the proceedings and to render and enforceable award. The Report urges the arbitrators, when exercising their implied powers, to do so with attention, including by identifying the grounds for exercising those powers and hearing the parties as to how they intend to exercise them and adopting any measure only if strictly required and proportionate to the aims to be achieved.

The Report and Recommendations on 'Reasoning of Arbitral Decisions'[8] – prepared by co-rapporteurs Georgios Petrochilos and Matthew Gearing and adopted at the 2022 Lisbon Biennial Conference – focuses on the best practices to be followed by arbitrators in drafting their awards. This is an important subject, given the frequent criticism of the drafting and reasoning of arbitral decisions, which are sometimes accused of excessive length and detail or, conversely, of being too succinct and difficult to understand (and sometimes even of being extremely lengthy but of providing only minimal reasoning on crucial issues). On this point the Report and Recommendations note that there is no

8 Committee on International Commercial Arbitration, 'Final Report on Reasoning of Arbitral Decisions' and Resolution 6/2012, both in International Law Association, Report of the Eightieth Conference (Lisbon 2022) (International Law Association, Lisbon 2022).

one size fits all and that the extent to which reasons are required depends on the circumstances of the case. What is important is that in each case the reasons are sufficient to satisfy the expectation of the parties that the decision of the arbitrators enable the reader, primarily the parties themselves, to understand the reasoning upon which it is based.

The Report discusses the approaches to reasoning in different legal cultures, observing that the requirements of domestic law on reasoning provide little guidance for arbitrators, due to the reluctance of national courts to involve themselves in debates about adequacy of reasoning. The requirement of adequate reasoning applies not only to all types of awards, irrespective of the basis of the decision (law, fact or equity) but also to procedural orders on important contested issues, particularly if involving due process. Also, decisions on quantum must be reasoned, especially when the methodology for the calculation is the subject of dispute.

To conclude, the ILA's Committee on International Commercial Arbitration contributes effectively to the development of thinking on international arbitration. Its reports provide thorough analysis of the topical issues, based on a survey of the current law and practice and focusing on identifying practical solutions specifically tailored to arbitration. In some cases – and this is particularly the case of *res judicata* – they form the basis for establishing arbitration-specific rules that allow arbitration better to fulfill its role as a true transnational dispute settlement mechanism for commercial disputes. It is regrettable that the ILA's contribution to the development of international arbitration is not more at the center of debates on arbitration.

How to Be(come) an International Lawyer

*Cameron Miles**

1 Introduction[1]

In November 2010, I was sitting in a place much like this one, in a position similar to the one you occupy now. It was a seminar, and I was a (comparatively) young master's student undertaking dedicated study in international law for the first time. I had, I think it fair to say, absolutely no idea what I was doing.

The subject of the seminar was State responsibility, and the discussion had swung round to the law of remedies. Asked by the instructor to name the leading authority on the concept of full reparation in international law,[2] and having done the reading for a change, I answered with confidence: 'Chor-zow Factory'.[3] The instructor was not impressed by my mangled pronunciation of the name of a small city in Silesia, and corrected me: 'Chorzów'.[4] To which, not wishing to be rude, I promptly responded: 'bless you'.

The situation becomes worse when I add that the location of this episode was the Finley Library in the Lauterpacht Centre for International Law at the University of Cambridge, and the instructor was Professor (and later Judge) James Crawford.

This incident swam to mind, unbidden from deep memory, when I sat down to pen these remarks. I have been a student, scholar, or practitioner of international law going on 15 years – a number that horrifies me now that I have said it out loud. I cannot pretend that the story that underpins it has been an unbroken narrative of unstoppable achievement, and it would do you all a disservice for me to try. But, as my father says, almost everyone can teach you one of two things. They can teach you *what* to do; and they can teach you what *not* to do.

---

* Barrister, 3 Verulam Buildings, London; Fellow, Centre for International Governance and Dispute Resolution, Kings College London.

1 These remarks were delivered to a group of students in the Law Faculty of the University of Bologna on 15 April 2024, as part of a series of lectures convened under the auspices of the Italian branch of the International Law Association. With discrete amendments and additions, the text is as spoken on that day.

2 *Factory at Chorzów* (*Germany v Poland*), Judgment (1928) PCIJ Ser A No 17.

3 This anecdote works much better when said aloud than read on the page, but it got a laugh, so it stays where it is. Suffice to say, in 2010 I said it phonetically, in a fairly heavy Australian accent.

4 Being the correct Polish pronunciation, which is closer to 'Khozh-oof'. Believe me when I tell you that, to the untrained or half-listening ear, it *could* sound like a sneeze.

 | DOI:10.1163/9789004727663_012

In the time we have together today, I am going to try to teach you a little bit of both, starting with the advice that: (a) if you are going to try to pronounce something in Polish that you have only ever read as an English speaker, ask a Polish person for help first; and (b) most mistakes, while potentially embarrassing, do not matter in the long run, and you should embrace the opportunities for self-improvement that they offer.

I propose to structure my remarks – in a manner that would doubtlessly please the French academy – under three headings, each of them containing three subheadings. First, the basic qualities that I found helpful in becoming a practicing international lawyer.[5] Second, the development of professional profile necessary to practice international law with a measure of regularity. And third, the technical and personal skills required to be a successful international lawyer once you become one.

Before I get into that, a word of warning, and possibly of comfort. It is not easy to become an international lawyer. Law itself is hard enough to excel at, and international law, given its obvious attractions, has an additional degree of difficulty attached thereto. 'Many are called, but few are chosen', as Judge Crawford later cautioned me. But (and this is the comforting bit) it is far from impossible. As any mountaineer will tell you, there are many routes to the summit. What I tell you today is only one way to climb the mountain, and it is the way that I have found – through painstaking trial and error – over a decade and a half of professional life. If you, as individuals, dedicate yourselves to becoming international lawyers, you may well find a path that is more uniquely yours, and be all the better for it.

2 Starting Out

We start with those basic qualities that must be cultivated to become an international lawyer. The first of these is very simple: *be a good lawyer*. By this, I do not mean be skilled in the tropes and techniques of international legal analysis, although that certainly helps. I mean be a good *domestic* lawyer, in whatever tradition you have been raised.[6]

---

5 By a practicing international lawyer, I mean an international lawyer in private practice (whether in a law firm or as a sole practitioner) as opposed to a staff attorney in a foreign ministry, international organization, or non-governmental organization. I have not been any of the latter, and so any insights I could offer would be limited.

6 James Crawford, 'Deference or Difference? The Relationship Between English and International Courts and Tribunals', in Stephen Moriarty (ed), *The Commercial Bar Association (COMBAR) 1989–2014: Celebrating the First 25 Years* (Hart Publishing 2016) 82.

International law has, in the past half century, advanced in leaps and bounds, but its practice and process remain tethered to national concepts of what law is and how it behaves. It is not and cannot be, despite attempts by some to argue otherwise, a complete legal system in the way that a domestic legal system is a complete legal system. International law must rely on domestic law from time – to time to fill its gaps, directly or by analogy, and give it form and substance.

But beyond this, a good understanding of domestic law will make you a better and more distinctive international lawyer. An example of this arises from the generations of lawyers that built international law as we know it from the dawn of the United Nations in 1945 to the end of the Cold War in 1990. For most of that time, a junior international law academic would not be permitted to teach *just* international law – there wasn't enough of it going around. Rather, they would be expected to teach a useful legal discipline and do international law essentially as a side hustle. But when you discover exactly what these leading figures were doing while treating international law as a passion project, you see how it influenced their scholarship. Ian Brownlie was a tort lawyer. Rosalyn Higgins was an oil and gas lawyer. James Crawford was a public lawyer. Myres McDougal was a property lawyer. And Roberto Ago specialised in the conflict of laws.

The scholarship and advocacy of each of these titans was improved by having a thorough grounding in their preferred domestic fields, enabling them to bring fresh insights to bear. There may come a time where it is possible to create an international lawyer essentially from scratch, but that time is a long way off – and I am by no means convinced that such an international lawyer will be an improvement on the current model.

A second basic concept: *be more than just a good lawyer*. Law is fundamentally a means for the organization of community action. International law is no different, it is simply that the communities are larger; although, as Sir Hersch Lauterpacht observed, its basic unit remains the individual.[7] In order to be an effective international lawyer, therefore, you need a grounding in other aspects of these communities, not least so that you can make the law intelligible to them. People dislike lawyers not for practicing law, but for thinking and speaking like lawyers.

More to the point, cases are rarely about just the law – other areas of human endeavour have a habit of intruding. These annoying interlopers are called 'facts'. A wider education will help you deal with them. So, studying science

7 Hersch Lauterpacht, *International Law and Human Rights* (Stevens & Sons 1950) 62–63.

will mean you are better equipped to understand climate change. Studying economics will mean you can better understand international trade. And the experience of one of my present cases, concerning the construction of hydroelectric powerplants in Indian-administered Kashmir, and their compliance with the terms of the Indus Waters Treaty,[8] would be greatly improved if I had studied engineering.

But if I had to pick an area of additional study that is of the greatest utility to a practicing international lawyer, it would be the humanities. As with everything I say today, I speak from selfish personal experience. Having spent my final year of high school in a committed effort to do as little work as possible, I failed to secure the grades required for admission to Monash University as a law student. And so, instead, I embarked on a broad-based humanities degree combining aspects of history, archaeology, and anthropology, studying law later. I have never regretted this mishap. If law is a means for the organisation of community action, a study of those communities will open your mind to how law is made and applied. Invariably, this is not because this or that legal rule can derived from first principles as a universal net good. It is because a particular element of the community wants it to be created and has the persuasive power, soft or hard, to ensure it is created.[9] I would like to think that my time in the humanities gave me a greater awareness of these processes, and how they can be applied in the real world.

My third basic concept: *speak and write in English.* A century ago, the advice may have been to speak and write in English and French, as well as in your native language, if it was different. No longer. It is not for nothing that Otto von Bismarck, when asked on his deathbed in 1898 to nominate the most significant development in modern political history, is reported to have said: 'the inherent and permanent fact that North America speaks English'.[10]

The simple and brutal truth is this. Globalization, coupled with the cultural influence of the Anglosphere, have meant that English now stands alone as the dominant language of international law,[11] at least as practiced in international courts and tribunals. To take one reductive and anecdotal example, look

8 *Indus Waters Treaty Arbitration* (*Pakistan v India*), PCA Case No 2023–01, Award on the Competence of the Court, 6 July 2023; Indus Waters Treaty Neutral Expert Proceedings (India v Pakistan), PCA Case No 2023-14, Decision on Certain Issues Pertaining to the Competence of the Neutral Expert, 7 January 2025.

9 On related themes, see also Robert Caro, *The Power Broker: Robert Moses and the Fall of New York* (Vintage Press 1975).

10 George L Beer, *The English-Speaking Peoples, Their Future Relations, and Joint International Obligations* (Macmillan Press 1918) 186.

11 Anthea Roberts, *Is International Law International?* (Oxford University Press 2017) 260–267.

at the composition of many counsel teams in contested cases before the International Court of Justice ('ICJ'). Beyond the Agent and any other party representatives, you will usually see some mixture of an American law firm, two or three English (or sometimes Australian) barristers, and a single French professor, included as an equal to the others, but also as a nod to the fact that article 39(1) of the ICJ Statute provides that '[t]he official languages of the Court shall be French and English'. All bar the professor will be pleading in English. And when the professor stands up to plead in French, most of the Bench will reach for the simultaneous translation.

From this, we may draw a simple lesson. If you want to have the greatest possible reach as an international legal practitioner, you need to have English at your disposal. That we are now conversing in English is testament to that fact. I am privileged to be able to address you today, in the heart of Italian legal scholarship, in my native language. I venture to say that I would be able to do so almost anywhere in the world. But, if you were to attempt to give a lecture on international law in London, or Dubai, or Islamabad, or Jakarta, or Tokyo, or Santiago, or Nairobi in Italian, or even in French, comprehension between speaker and audience may be difficult to come by. English is the world's great second language – so great that I can persist in wretched monolingualism without paying any appreciable professional price.

On that blunt note, I conclude my first heading. On to my second: the development of professional profile.

3 Developing Professional Profile

In 1908, an English classicist by the name of Francis Cornford produced a pamphlet on academic politics. It was called *Microcosmographia Academica*.[12] In it, he adumbrated many useful rules for the young academic politician, none more so than the so-called 'principle of the dangerous precedent'. It boils down to this: 'Every public action which is not customary, either is wrong, or, if it is right, is a dangerous precedent. It follows that nothing should ever be done for the first time'.[13]

I mention this because when I once asked Judge Crawford how to be briefed to appear before the ICJ, he airily replied, 'Oh, it's very easy: you just have to

12 Translated: *Study of a Tiny Academic World.*

13 Francis M Cornford, *Microcosmographia Academia, being a guide for the young academic politician* (Metcalfe & Co 1908) §VII.

have been there before'. This kind of Zen riddle did not strike me as particularly helpful then. I hope to be of greater assistance to you now.

At the outset, I will note this. You are all very fortunate. We are, at this moment, living through one of the periodic deaths of multilateralism. Problems that States ought to be able to solve with diplomacy are instead being solved through litigation, which is, remarkably, still seen as a useful tool of international relations.

In this, the current practice of international law is very different to what took place in earlier multilateral dark ages. Judge Christopher Greenwood is fond of quoting from a volume of the *ICJ Reports* that he inherited from the previous occupant of his chambers at the Court.[14] In his account, the volume for 1977 contained only four pages: two pages in English and two pages in French on the same point. The inside cover of the volume stated rather sadly that 'this volume contains neither an index nor a table of contents'. Underneath, someone had written in pencil: 'nor anything else'.

That situation does not persist today. When I checked the ICJ's website this morning, it listed 23 pending cases,[15] more than at any other point in its history or that of its predecessor. There has never been a better time to become an international lawyer.

So, how do you get your first case? There are innumerable ways to skin this particular feline but I can tell you what worked for me. The first and most basic principle is this: become known as someone with expertise in international law. You will note that I did not say just to *obtain* expertise in international law. I said to *become known* for it, which is altogether more difficult.

The basic foundation of this is well understood, which is obtaining the necessary (or, at any rate, desirable) postgraduate qualifications, namely an LLM or a PhD in international law from a reputable university. I hate to belabour the point, but the language of instruction should be English, if possible.

But this alone is not sufficient. Before I obtained my postgraduate degrees, I was a nobody. After, I was a nobody with a passable CV. If I reflect on what I did to become recognised as an international lawyer, it was using the skills I had learned to publish academic writing. The reason why this is effective is

---

14 Christopher Greenwood, 'The Highways, Byways and Dark Alleys of International Law' (2020) 60 *Middle Templar* 106, 106.

15 International Court of Justice, 'Pending Cases': <https://www.icj-cij.org/pending-cases> [accessed 15 April 2024]. Admittedly, one of them is the *Gabčíkovo-Nagymaros* case, judgment in which was rendered in 1997: *Gabčíkovo-Nagymaros Project* (*Hungary/Slovakia*), Judgment [1997] ICJ Rep 7. An additional procedure commenced by Slovakia was discontinued in 2017: ICJ Press Release No 2017/31 (21 July 2017). What the case is still doing on the Court's docket is one of the enduring mysteries of international law.

simple. International lawyers – in government service, in international or non-governmental organizations, in private practice – are busy people with difficult problems. If, in the course of investigating one of those problems, they come across something written by you that provides them the answer they're looking for, then I guarantee you will be remembered, and positively.

But, of course, the fact of writing is not enough. What you write must be useful to people who actually *do* international law. At the risk of being an absolutist, this means that anything you write should approach a question from a positivist, black letter perspective, or at least something adjacent to that perspective. While sociological, ontological, or eschatological enquiry into this or that foundational principle of international law may be interesting, that is not the same thing as being useful – and while I may admire the writings of some critical legal scholars (and those of other, more esoteric, movements) I would never think to cite them in legal advice or argument.

Beyond this, two more pieces of advice. First, make sure that anything you write can be found by the people you want to read it – which means publishing it with a prominent journal or blog. Full many a flower is born to blush unseen and waste its sweetness on the desert air[16] – or, alternatively, in something like the *East Anglia Journal of International Law and Animal Husbandry*.[17] Second – and you will be surprised how many people forget this – have an opinion. There is nothing more frustrating than reading a detailed treatment of an issue you have been tackling for weeks, only to discover that its author, when it comes time to draw their triumphant conclusion, has taken the coward's way out, and said that both sides of the argument have their merits. A firm opinion tells me more than the author has done their research. It tells me that they are their own person – and willing to take a public position on a difficult issue, without heed to professional consequence, because they feel it is right. When it comes to being recognised, there are worse reputations to have.

I turn to the second tool of professional development. This is perhaps a challenging one: *go where the work is*. As you will have gathered by now, although I live and practice in London, I am not from there. I am from Melbourne – a place about as far away from London as it is possible to be. But I am in London because the number of international lawyers in private practice in Melbourne generally hovers around zero. And so, I have gone where the work is.

When I tell you to go where the work is, however, I do not necessarily mean you need to uproot yourself from home and family in order to live somewhere

16 Thomas Gray, 'Elegy, Written in a Country Churchyard', in John Mitford (ed), *The Works of Thomas Gray*, vol I (William Pickering 1836) 94.

17 This is not a real publication but sounds like it should be.

with extortionate housing prices. Going where the work is may mean joining your State's Foreign Ministry or Attorney-General's office. It may mean joining a committee in your local Bar association or other professional body. Or it may mean becoming a member of (*inter alia*) the International Law Association, the International Bar Association, or the European or American Societies for International Law, and participating in one of their working groups. The important thing is being around people who are engaged in the day-to-day technical reality of international law. In this way you will become known to them as a good and knowledgeable colleague, the kind of person who you want to be with, shoulder to shoulder at 3 a.m. in a hotel in The Hague, trying frantically to come up with a response to the rather pointed question that a tribunal sitting in the Peace Palace asked the previous afternoon.

This brings me to the third and most important tool of professional development: *get a mentor*. None of us got here alone. All of us had the benefit of someone who said to themselves, 'I like this young person, and I am going to help them'. That mentor, once found, will help you hone your skillset. They will introduce you to their colleagues. They will write endless letters of support. And, if they are themselves an international law practitioner, they will get you your first case.

As you may have gathered, despite our somewhat rocky start, I was fortunate enough to count Judge Crawford as my mentor.[18] I am not the only one. He had more than 70 doctoral students over the years, and he considered them an achievement on the same level as the others of his glittering career.[19] And yes, he got me my first case, which was a supporting role in a small investment arbitration against Papua New Guinea, which we ultimately lost spectacularly.[20]

But it is not necessary to have the support of a Judge Crawford to get that first brief. All you need is to have someone with connections to the world you want to be in, who believes in you, and is willing to share their experience. The only *quid pro quo* is this: when you finally reach the summit and stand atop it, weeping for there are no more worlds to conquer, leave the ladder down. There may be someone that you, in your own way, can help up behind you.

18 I have had others, whom I do not mention here. But they know who they are, and they have my eternal gratitude.

19 Douglas Guilfoyle et al, 'James Crawford: His Legacy and Impact on International Law in Australia and Globally' (2022) 40 *Australian Year Book of International Law* 25, 35–37. For an act of filial piety, see Cameron Miles, 'James Crawford and the Law of State Immunity' (2022) 40 *Australian Year Book of International Law* 115.

20 *PNG Sustainable Development Program Ltd v Independent State of Papua New Guinea*, ICSID Case No ARB/13/33, Award, 5 May 2015.

Speaking of the summit, this brings us to my final heading: how to do international law once you get there.

4 Atop the Mountain

F Scott Fitzgerald once defined personality as 'an unbroken series of successful gestures'.[21] The same might be said of a career as an international lawyer, especially in private practice. It is not enough to get your first case – you need to get the next one as well.

Again, I start with an item of basic advice that is forgotten with a surprising measure of regularity: *do a good job*. By this, I don't mean to make sure you win. Not every case is winnable, and any lawyer who says otherwise is either a fool or trying to sell something to a potential client. But give yourself the time and space to ensure that your performance – even in an unwinnable case – is that of a competent legal technician.

There is a tendency among some legal practitioners to start looking for their new brief the moment their previous one is confirmed, as though professional success is measured by line items on a CV. I don't necessarily criticise that: ambition is a good thing to have. But where chasing your next case means not giving proper care and attention to the one that you have, then we start to have a problem.

You see, the market for international legal services is ultimately quite intelligent, as herd creatures sometimes are. Worse than that, the community of international lawyers is very small and they are all, seemingly, incurable gossips. It does not take long for word of underperformance to circulate, and when it does, it sticks. If you do 10 good pieces of work and one bad piece of work, guess which one will be remembered?

My second piece of advice: *understand that international litigation is not like domestic litigation.* In domestic litigation – particularly commercial litigation – the object of the game is to obtain a judgment stating either that everything your client did was entirely proper, and/or everything that the other guy's client did was entirely improper, and that your client is owed a fabulous sum of money as a consequence.

International litigation, and especially inter-state litigation, is not like that. It is litigation conducted in the service of a set of wider diplomatic and policy

21 Francis Scott Fitzgerald, *The Great Gatsby* (Charles Scribner's Sons 1925) 2.

priorities – the greater game of international relations – in which the judgment is very rarely the final, or even a necessary, objective. Understanding your place within those priorities is the key to being a good practicing international lawyer. You are rarely, if ever, the main event. You are a cog in a large and complex machine, and usually not a very big one.

I should add, there is a satisfaction to this. Very rarely as citizens do we get to see how decisions of international importance are made. By showing you understand international law as the helpmate of international policy, you become trusted to help shape that policy, in ways you never thought possible. Sometimes, this is a thrill – you are working some of the most sophisticated minds in global relations. Sometimes, it is not – what you thought was feigned incompetence concealing some wider master plan turns out to be actual incompetence. But at least you know what you're dealing with.

What this means at the coalface is that you may have to advance some points that you don't like, sacrifice points that you do, and generally do things that you don't think assist in winning the case for reasons you don't think are very good or even completely understand. And that's just fine – provided the client's wider strategic vision is adhered to and realised. This surrender of the self can be found in some domestic cases, but rarely as acutely.

That being said, this subordination of ego is not absolute. Professional standards exist for a reason, and while they will provide unimpeachable justification for behaviour that wider society may consider distasteful, they have their limits. Just as one must provide good service to one's client, one must also provide good service to oneself. Where professional society would look askance at your conduct, it is time to walk away. You can always afford to lose a bad client; you can never afford to lose a good reputation.

I come now to the final piece of advice. By it, I hope to liberate you. Understand that the three most powerful words in any international lawyer's arsenal are these: *I don't know*. Too often we are told – especially when we are junior lawyers – that we are expected to be perfect. To know how to prepare a witness, draft a pleading, or manage a client automatically. To understand law and procedure instinctively. To be brilliant advocates from Day 1. I can tell you from painful, personal experience: to buy into that lie invites disaster, and that disaster becomes all the more fraught when you realise how easily it could have been avoided.

There are very few things in this job that cannot be remedied, provided they are recognized and dealt with quickly. If you do not know something, ask for help, and ask for it early. And keep asking for help throughout your careers. One of the joys of this profession is that there is usually someone smarter than you nearby, ready and willing to assist.

5 Conclusion

So, there you have it. Nine rules for becoming (or being) a practicing international lawyer:

1. Be a good lawyer.
2. Be more than just a good lawyer.
3. Speak and write in English.
4. Get a reputation for expertise.
5. Go where the work is.
6. Get a mentor.
7. Do a good job.
8. Understand your role.
9. Ask for help.

These are my principles. And as Marx once said,[22] if you don't like them, I have others. Indeed, despite my professed commitment to the Francophone rule of threes, I have one additional principle, which brings us to a nice, round Anglophone ten. It is this: *above all, be kind.*

Be kind to your colleagues. Be kind to your clients, and to your adjudicators. Be kind to your opponents. And be kind to yourself. Ultimately, we are all studies in human frailty. We are people doing a job, albeit one that will consume you if you let it. One day, we will need to hang up our robes and reckon with what we have done. Life is too short to wonder then if you might have been a better person. Better to err on the side of caution, and be that better person from the start.

In closing, what you do with what I've said is entirely up to you. As I've tried to stress, there's more than one route to the summit. My way may not be open to you – and, equally, your way may not have been open to me. But when you do locate your path, be sure to tell others. Fifteen years from now, one of you may be in front of a group like this one, speaking on the same subject. And when you find yourself there, I can guarantee two things.

First, you will be telling your audience something different. And second, you will know how to pronounce *Chorzów* Factory.

---

22 Not that one; another one: Fred Shapiro (ed), *The Yale Book of Quotations* (Yale University Press 2006) 498.

Reports by ILA Italy Committees and Study Groups Members

1 Introduction by the Section Editors

The Committees and Study Groups represent the core of the International Law Association (ILA). They convene members of the Association and conduct research and studies on a range of topics within the domains of international law. Committees assist the ILA in achieving its statutory objectives of 'study, clarification and development of international law, both public and private, and the furtherance of international understanding and respect for international law'. They prepare reports and make recommendations for adoption at the ILA's biennial conferences. Study Groups offer a more flexible and informal framework for collaboration within the Association. Unlike Committees, Study Groups are established to evaluate the relevance of topics for potential future Committee work, provide swift responses to pressing issues, or address matters that may not be well-suited for consideration by a Committee.

Over the years, members of the Italian branch of the ILA have actively engaged in these efforts. They ensure a continuous contribution to the furtherance of the mandates assigned to Committees and Study Groups, also in view of the preparation of final reports for consideration by the membership, in the case of Committees.

This section of the Yearbook of the Italian Branch of the ILA provides an insight into the most recent activities of several ILA Committees and Study Groups which involve Italian scholars and practitioners. Each section provides a brief introduction to the Committee/Study Group's mandate, the main issues that have been addressed in recent years (including discussions held at the ILA Biennial Conference in Athens in June 2024), the content of final reports or resolutions presented at the Conference, and finally, the plans for future initiatives.

The aim is to offer an account of the dynamic intellectual engagement of Italian members, as well as to highlight emerging topics and subtopics that warrant the attention of the Italian Branch.

Giovanna Adinolfi and Mirko Sossai

2 Alternative Dispute Resolution in International Law

The ILA Committee on Alternative Dispute Resolution (ADR) was established on 7 May 2022. It was chaired by Gabrielle Marceau (Swiss Branch) and Davinia Aziz (Singaporean Branch) until Spring 2024, when Amy Porges (American Branch) and Serena Forlati (ILA Italy) were appointed as Co-Chairs. The current Rapporteur is Ottilia Anna Maunganidze (South African Branch). Amy

 | DOI:10.1163/9789004727663_013

Porges (American Branch), Facundo Perez-Aznar (Argentinian Branch) and Ohiocheoya Omiunu (British Branch) also held this office until 2024. Among the other 35 Members is Chiara Tondini (ILA Italy).

The Committee's mandate[1] is, in a nutshell, to identify common features and definitions of ADR procedures; assess which procedures work best and for which kinds of disputes, with the goal of facilitating 'Appropriate Dispute Resolution' (namely, resolution practices that are tailored to disputes); identify any underlying principles; and elaborate best practices in the field. The focus is on the settlement of disputes in which at least one party is a State, including investor-state disputes and some transitional justice cases. Neither arbitration nor disputes between private parties are as such included, although references thereto may be included in specific cases.

The Committee begun its activities in December 2022. It has since worked at the elaboration of an ADR taxonomy which helps analyzing and systematizing case studies, with the aim of identifying commonalities, best practices, and factors contributing to success of failure in each instance. Members have engaged in completing 35 case studies so far, that are organized around three main clusters: international trade disputes, international investment disputes, and other public international law disputes. Most case studies were discussed collegially in two virtual meetings, held respectively on 7 June and 18 August 2023. During the former, Members Martin Doe and Tamada Dai informed the group on the activities of the International Council for Commercial Arbitration Panel of Experts to Develop a Paris Agreement Conciliation Annex. A third virtual meeting was organized on 16 October 2023 in partnership with the International Dispute Resolution Programme at the Centre for International Law (CIL) of the National University of Singapore under the Chatham House Rule; the first part of the meeting was a 'fireside conversation' with Professor Tommy Koh on a broad range of topics, including his role in cases included in the committee's survey. Three sessions followed, dealing respectively with the Taxonomy, the role of resources in ADR and the Committee's future work. On 16 November, Co-Repporteur Facundo Perez-Aznar reported on the Committee's activities at the 5th ILA Italy Biennial Conference (see page 47–63) and a Preliminary Report was discussed within the group in November-December 2023.

In 2024, the new co-chairs organized a closed meeting of the Committee at the Athens ILA Conference and a further online meeting on 16 July 2024, to discuss the future work of the committee. These will include studying process

1 Available at www.ila-hq.org/en_GB/documents/2023-approved-mandate.

design and dispute systems design in ADR and engaging with experienced ADR practitioners and neutrals on best practices in ADR in international disputes. The Committee has organized a conference on "Shaping Appropriate ADR in International Law", to be held on 7 April 2025. Thereafter, and in keeping with its Mandate (para. 13), the Committee will 'shift from research to concrete guidance for practitioners and governments in their choice of procedure in resolving international disputes', elaborating guidelines and principles that may be adopted as a resolution of the ILA.

The Committee has obtained an extension of its mandate, so as to present its Interim Report in 2025 and conclude its work by 2028.

Serena Forlati

3 Global Health Law

The Global Health Law Committee was established in October 2014 and is co-chaired by Professor Frederick Abbott (Florida State University, American Branch) and Professor Brigit Toebes (University of Groningen, Netherlands Branch). ILA Italy is represented within the Global Health Law Committee by Professor Pia Acconci (University of Teramo, since 2015) and Professor Stefania Negri (University of Salerno, since 2016).

The mandate of the Committee is to identify and describe 'Global Health Law' as a separate branch of international law by investigating relevant rules and practices in several specific subject-matters, including, but not necessarily limited to:

1. international legal norms relevant to addressing threats to international health security, which include norms addressing the prevention, containment and control of health security threats caused by the spread of infectious disease, as well as environment-related threats and natural or man-made disasters;
2. international legal norms relevant to conflicts among subject-matter priorities, including the tensions between trade, finance, investment and health;
3. international legal norms that may be used to address health disparities that arise from economic and social differences, both between developed and developing states and within societies, in particular including persistent failures to address health needs of women.

Since the outbreak of the COVID-19 pandemic, the Committee has focused its work on global health emergencies caused by the spread of infectious diseases and explored the role of international law norms and principles in prevention, preparedness and response to pandemics.

In April 2020, the Committee adopted a "Statement of the Global Health Law Committee of the International Law Association (ILA) regarding the COVID-19 pandemic".[2] This **statement** restated the fundamental principles and rules of international law that could contribute to containing and ending the pandemic, safeguarding the rights of individuals and groups and restoring the normal functioning state of the international society.

The Third Report to the Kyoto Conference (29 November – 13 December 2020) expanded on the importance of international law in addressing the COVID-19 pandemic and discussed relevant key topics, such as artificial intelligence, access to medicines and human rights protection, together with related legal challenges and policy options. It also formulated recommendations in this respect.

On the occasion of the Kyoto Conference, the Committee approved resolution No. 2/2020 adopting an updated and integrated version of the April 2020 "Statement regarding the Covid-19 pandemic".[3]

The Fourth Report to the Lisbon Conference (19–24 June 2022) laid special attention on the law-making processes still ongoing at the World Health Organization, namely the revision of the International Health Regulations (2005) and the negotiation by the Intergovernmental Negotiating Body of a Pandemic Treaty, and also on related issues, including pathogens and data sharing, and equitable access to benefits. Pia Acconci contributed to this section, on account of her related research activities and publications. Another section of the report focused on climate change and public health and the role of the right to health in climate action, which relied to a large extent on a previous publication by Stefania Negri.[4]

On 30 March 2023, the Committee adopted a "Note on the negotiation of a Pandemic Accord and amendments to the International Health Regulations" (IHR) which provided for some observations on the developments of the two ongoing parallel law-making processes and the inherent complex questions raised by the interaction of the two regimes. The Committee's main aim was to encourage the negotiating member states to prioritize a set of allocation

2 Available at www.ila-hq.org/en_GB/news-articles/statement-ila-global-health-law-committee-regarding-covid-19-issued-5-april-2020.

3 Available at www.ila-hq.org/en_GB/documents/resolution-2-kyoto-2020-global-health-law-final.

4 Stefania Negri, 'Climate Change and Global Health. Exploring Regime Interaction and the Role of the Right to Health Argument in International Climate Litigation' (2021) 23 International Community Law Review 219.

principles or methodologies for placing the relevant subject matters into one or the other negotiating basket.[5]

In view of the Athens Conference (24–28 June 2024), the Committee worked on its Fifth Report. The first draft Report was circulated in February 2024, as it included, among others, recommendations for the negotiations related to a Pandemic Treaty and amendments to the 2005 International Health Regulations (IHR). A revised draft of the Report was published on 19 June 2024, shortly before the Athens Conference, to duly take into account the results of the 2024 77th World Health Assembly, which approved a set of amendments to IHR and extended the negotiations for a Pandemic Treaty to 2025.

The final version of the Fifth Report was presented at the Athens Conference by the Committee's co-chairs and discussed by a group of Committee members (Pedro Villarreal, Siobhan Wills and Morten Walloe Tvedt). The panel was chaired by H.E. Judge Yuji Iwasawa and attended by other Committee members (including Stefania Negri and remotely Pia Acconci) and several interested ILA Members. As approved on 25 June, the Fifth Report consists of three major sections: the first addresses post-COVID-19 pandemic legal developments with respect to pandemic preparedness, surveillance and response; the second addresses One Health and Planetary Health, including a discussion of climate and health issues following the recent adoption of the COP Declaration on Climate and Health; the third addresses social determinants of mental health and related subject matter. Pia Acconci contributed to the Report by focusing on the interplay between investment and health under the perspectives at the root of the three sections, while Stefania Negri contributed to the second section, by focusing on environmental health and the One Health approach.

During the Athens Conference, the Committee also organised a "Global Health Law" panel session dedicated to the topic "Surviving Animal Diseases: One Health in International and European Law". The panel was held on 26 June 2024, chaired by Brigit Toebes, with the participation of Gian Luca Burci (Geneva Graduate Institute) and Stefania Negri as main speakers and Catherine Brölmann (University of Amsterdam) as discussant. Stefania Negri gave a presentation on "One Health as a strategic priority of the EU Global Health Strategy".

Pia Acconci and Stefania Negri

5 Available at <https://frederickabbott.com/ila_global_health>.

4 Human Rights in Times of Emergency

In recent years, several States have declared or invoked a state of emergency, using it as a means to derogate from specific rights guaranteed by the international human rights treaties to which they are parties. Notably, under the European Convention on Human Rights (ECHR), countries like Ukraine, France, and Turkey have both notified and extended states of emergencies. These States have also invoked Article 4 of the International Covenant on Civil and Political Rights (ICCPR). Moreover, the COVID-19 pandemic has prompted a massive resort to measures severely restricting human rights, leading around 35 states to derogate from the ECHR, the American Convention of Human Rights (ACHR), and the ICCPR.

As is known, the invocation of a state of emergency permits the executive to suspend certain obligations under the constitution and to derogate from the corresponding rights under international human rights treaties, in order to impose exceptional and temporary measures deemed necessary to preserve the life of the nation. However, states of emergency are often the setting for egregious violations of human rights, including forced disappearances, summary or arbitrary executions, widespread and systematic torture, abrogation of the right of association, and other unjustified limitations on individual rights and freedoms.

Against this background, the ILA decided in 2017 to establish a Committee devoted to the topic of Human Rights in States of Emergency, appointing Christina Cerna (USA) and Stefan Kadelbach (Germany) as its chairpersons. The Committee is composed of around 50 members. ILA Italy is represented by Elena Sciso and Emanuele Sommario.

Human rights in times of emergency is not a new topic for the ILA, having been studied in the 1980s by the ILA Committee on the Enforcement of Human Rights Law, which drafted the Paris Minimum Standards of Human Rights in a State of Exception[6] (adopted by the 61st Conference of the ILA in 1984) and the Queensland Guidelines for Bodies Monitoring Respect for Human Rights during States of Emergency[7] (adopted by the 64th Conference of the ILA in 1990). The present Committee had to take this important work into account while developing its research.

6 Richard B Lillich, 'The Paris Minimum Standards of Human Rights Norms in a State of Emergency' (1985) 79 American Journal of International Law 1072.

7 Richard B Lillich, 'Queensland Guidelines for Bodies Monitoring Respect for Human Rights During States of Emergency' (1991) 85 American Journal of International Law 716.

The Committee's mandate consists of two parts. The first part deals with the existing practice of international human rights bodies and regional human rights bodies, including the Human Rights Committee and its less formal bodies. The aim was to examine and systematize practice related to emergencies, taking the last 30 years into account. The second part will instead focus on State practice with respect to emergency situations, considering both *de jure* and *de facto* emergencies.

The work of the Committee has been directly affected and slowed down by the COVID-19 emergency. A meeting planned in Strasbourg in March 2020 to discuss a draft of the Interim Report had to be cancelled. However, before the pandemic started, the Committee had the opportunity to hold an interim meeting at the Scuola Superiore Sant'Anna in Pisa, on 24–25 July 2019, to prepare the work assignments for the Interim Report, which was presented at the 79th Conference of the ILA in Kyoto, in 2020.[8]

The Committee reconvened in June 2022, on the occasion of the ILA 80th Biennial Conference in Lisbon. During the Conference, an open workshop was held in which some of the Committee members introduced their work related to the Final Report. Emanuele Sommario presented on the topic of "Restrictions of Human Rights in Emergencies caused by Disasters".[9]

A second interim meeting was held at the Johann Wolfgang Goethe University in Frankfurt, on 24–25 March 2023. Fourteen members of the Committee met to discuss the plans for their final report to be presented at the 2024 ILA Conference. Committee members were called upon to draft a short report addressing different types of emergencies (e.g., war, terrorist campaigns, pandemics) in different countries. To facilitate a comparative approach, all reports had to take into account certain given aspects, including a description of the gravity of the situation, the emergency measures introduced, the judicial and/or parliamentary control on such measures, their necessity and proportionality, the non-derogability of certain rights, and aspects concerning non-discrimination. Twenty-four country and thematic reports were compiled, upon which the co-rapporteurs based the initial draft of the final document. This draft was subsequently discussed during an interim meeting of the Committee held at the University of Vienna in February 2024. Following these discussions, the Final Report was adopted and presented at the ILA Conference in Athens in June

8 International Law Association, Report of the Seventy-Ninth Conference (Kyoto 2020) (International Law Association, Kyoto 2020) 686.

9 International Law Association, Report of the Eightieth Conference (Lisbon 2022) (International Law Association, Lisbon 2022) 633.

2024.[10] The report provides a comprehensive analysis of the emergency measures implemented by States and their impact on human rights. Additionally, it evaluates State practices against both procedural and substantive standards set by regional and international supervisory bodies. The Report concludes with several recommendations addressed to States and treaty monitoring bodies.

Elena Sciso and Emanuele Sommario

5 International Law and Sea Level Rise

The Committee on International Law and Sea Level Rise was established by the ILA Executive Council in November 2012. The Committee was tasked with a two-part mandate:

1. to study the possible impacts of sea level rise and the implications under international law of the partial and complete inundation of State territory, or depopulation thereof, in particular of small island and low-lying States; *and*
2. to develop proposals for the progressive development of international law in relation to the possible loss of all or of parts of State territory and maritime zones due to sea level rise, including the impacts on statehood, nationality, and human rights.

Giuseppe Nesi (University of Trento) is the Italian Member of the Committee since January 2022.

A first report was presented in 2018 during the 78th ILA Biennial Conference in Sidney. The report and two pertinent resolutions were adopted. During the 80th ILA Biennial Conference held in Lisbon in June 2022, an interim report was submitted, and it was decided to extend the term of the mandate of the Committee until 2024.

In its 2022 interim report, the Committee identified the following key questions to be examined further in the context of climate change-induced sea level rise:

1. What are the implications for statehood of diminishing State capacity and diminishing resident populations?
2. What are the implications of different potential forms of State transformation – including confederation, federation, condominium, lease – on the protection of affected populations?

10 Available at https://www.ila-hq.org/en_GB/committees/human-rights-in-times-of-emergency.

3. Taking as a starting point the principle that all persons affected by sea level rise will, at all times, remain rights holders under international human rights law, what does existing international human rights law (and other relevant bodies/principles of international law, such as the law on statelessness) say about the distribution of obligations between States towards these persons as rights holders – especially under different scenarios likely to emerge during the process of sea level rise? Where are there gaps, and how might international law be developed to address such gaps?

After the 2022 Biennial Conference, the Committee held a first intersessional meeting in Lisbon on 18 and 19 November 2022; another meeting took place in Bern, on 10 June 2023. On the former occasion, the Committee discussed and adopted two syllabi containing a significant part of the work plan of the Committee through 2024. Syllabus 1 was on statehood and the rights of the affected population; syllabus 2 was on the law of the sea.

These syllabi serve as the guide for the Committee work towards the completion of the final report due for presentation at the 2024 ILA Biennial Conference.

The work is divided into two parts, each corresponding to the relevant syllabus.

The main emphasis is on the themes elaborated in syllabus 1 (on statehood and the rights of affected populations), for which purpose a Working Group (WG) has been formed and members were invited to join and contribute to designated themes with short papers.

The WG met in Bern on 10 June 2023 to discuss the drafts prepared in accordance with the syllabus. The meeting was preceded by a half-day public event on 9 June, a conference aimed at presenting the work of the Committee to the interested public.

Another intersessional meeting of the Committee was planned in November 2023, in Trento, thanks to the availability of the ILA Italian branch and of the University of Trento. Due to unforeseeable reasons, at the very last moment the Committee decided to continue its work online in view of the 2024 ILA Biennial Conference. The debate within the Committee was finalized at the eve of the 2024 ILA Biennial Conference, that took place in June in Athens, where the Final Report was adopted.

In the 50 pages Final Report the Committee examined all issues at stake, starting from those regarding statehood and the rights of affected population. As regards statehood, the Report assesses that since States bear the important responsibility to ensure the protection of their population, the question of statehood is fundamentally linked to that duty of protection and its continuous implementation. While all coastal States are potentially affected by sea level rise, low-lying small island developing States (SIDS) are disproportionally impacted in the context of statehood, considering that the decrease or loss of (habitable) land territory, substantial parts of their populations may have to move abroad and build new lives in other States that admit them.

With regard to the challenge of safeguarding statehood in the face of sea level rise, the Committee agreed that continuity of statehood should be presumed. Affected States not only have the right but to some extent also the duty to provide for their own preservation using the various means at their disposal. Such duty can be derived from States' human rights obligation to protect the life, security and health of affected members of their population, guarantees that may require taking physical measures to safeguard territory. The principle set out in Article 6 of the 1933 Montevideo Convention on Rights and Duties of States, that the recognition of a State is 'unconditional and irrevocable', provides for and supports the objective of international law to facilitate legal certainty and stability. In this regard continued membership of the United Nations is one of the crucial indicia of the continuing existence of affected States.

Measures to safeguard the effectiveness of the international legal personality of the affected States have been indicated: physical measures to safeguard territory and their legal implications; legal measures concerning State territory in consequence of sea level rise; and the right to self-determination of peoples affected by sea level rise. In relation to the responsibility of affected States and third States, it is important to recognise the following principles of international human rights protection to address these challenges and to act in accordance with them. *First*, individuals affected by sea level rise are always rights holders under international law. *Second*, as long as affected States are able to safeguard substantial parts of habitable territory, the primary responsibility to respect, protect and fulfil the human rights of the members of their population remains with them. *Finally*, at the point where an affected State has lost most of its habitable territory, and most of its population has moved abroad, but still retains its statehood, the primary responsibility to respect, protect and fulfil the human rights of those affected shift to the State(s) where they now live. In some situations, this might raise complex questions of overlapping jurisdictions. The Committee did not venture into adopting conclusions about a hypothetical issue of whether the concept of 'territory' might be extended *de lege ferenda* to include submerged lands which have become inundated by sea level rise and took the view that potential future legal rights based on fully submerged territories will ultimately have to be decided in the policy sphere and on a background of factual changes conceivable in a rather long-term perspective. The Committee did agree, however, to the two propositions concerning the maritime entitlements of the affected low-lying SIDS in the process of the diminishing habitability and gradual submergence of their land territory in consequence of climate change-related sea level rise. *First*, that baselines and limits of maritime zones that are in compliance with the LOSC and deposited with the UN Secretary General should continue in place even if the territory involved gradually changes as a result of climate change-related impacts including sea level rise in the process or submergence. And *second*, that existing maritime boundaries, whether agreed or adjudicated, should continue in force and represent the legal extent of maritime zones, even if the territory from which the boundaries were originally calculated gradually changes in the process of submergence.

Giuseppe Nesi

6 International Tax Law

After the establishment in 2017 in the form of a Study Group, ILA set up the Committee on International Tax Law in 2020. The Committee is chaired by Juliane Kokott and co-chaired by Pasquale Pistone (ILA Italy), with the participation of another member of the Italian branch, Maria Cecilia Fregni.

The Committee's mandate is articulated in three phases. Phase 1 focused on taxpayers' rights as non-State actors under international law and was completed before the 2022 ILA Conference held in Lisbon with the publication of a book.[11] Phase 2 started before the Lisbon Conference with focus on the establishment of a fair and equitable international tax nexus. Phase 3 is expected to complete the works of the Committee with emphasis on international tax enforcement.

After some preliminary research conducted from 2020 onwards, the 80th Conference held in Lisbon in 2022 marked the real start of Phase 2 of the research project of the Committee. Professor Pistone chaired two sessions of the event and Professor Fregni presented her views on citizenship, residence and taxation.

Three hybrid events/webinars have followed since then. An online event held on 11 January 2023 focused on selected issues, including the link between democracy and taxation (with a presentation by Pasquale Pistone), taxation and sovereignty, sustainable taxation, and geographical focus; an hybrid event hosted by the New York University (3–4 April 2023) for a dialogue between the

11 J Kokott, P Pistone, Taxpayers in International Law. International Minimum Standards for the Protection of Taxpayers' Rights (Bloomsbury 2022).

US international law scholars and the international tax community. Eminent scholars such as José Alvarez and Rob Howse held reports. The experience of the closest nexus under private international law was used as a possible model for international tax law. The event was also attended by officials of the United Nations and was held in parallel with the meetings of the UN Economic and Social Council that preceded the first report by the UN Secretary General on matters of international tax cooperation (August 2023). Finally, a webinar held on 12 January 2024 served different purposes. First, it reviewed fairness and equity of international tax nexus in the light of the fragmentation of international law and focused on the implications of international nexus arising at the crossroads between climate nexus and tax nexus. Second, it critically reviewed an interim article that serves as the basis for the expected interim report to be prepared for the Athens Conference. Third, it broadened the geographical focus of the Committee's works on Africa, Latin America and the Middle East with the participation of local speakers.

Moreover, two events linked with the activities of the Committee took place in 2023. First, the scientific event giving rise to the Regional Platform for Tax Cooperation in Latin America and the Caribbean took place in Bogotá (Colombia) on 2–3 May 2023. The Co-chair of the Committee Pasquale Pistone was involved in the planning of the event, which also involved several other members. The focus was on the need for an equity inter-country allocation of taxing rights based on the criteria of the closest connection. Second, within the framework of the 150th anniversary of ILA, the tax session (held on 14 November 2023) co-chaired by the chair Juliane Kokott and involving several members of the Committee analysed the developments of international tax law across the past century with emphasis on selected points related to the ongoing work by the ILA Committee.

The Tax Committee intends to present its final report of Phase II at the 82nd ILA Conference in 2026, which will include either recommendations or, if possible, a restatement of international tax nexus. The ongoing distribution of questionnaires (one of which was answered by over 60 countries) allowed for empirical based fact-finding, which is being processed by the five rapporteurs (from five continents) and by the authors of a context book, which sets the systematic theoretical framework for the possible future of international tax nexus.

The 82nd Biennial Conference, to be held in Vienna in 2026, will also be the opportunity to present an interim report of Phase III of the activity of the TaxCommittee, with focus on international tax enforcement.

The ILA TAX Committee reiterates the wish to achieve a stronger involvement of ILA members with a background on public international law, private international law and international economic law, as well as on international tax law.

Pasquale Pistone and Maria Cecilia Fregni

7 Space Law

Since 2013 the ILA's Space Law Committee has been working on the topic of the legal regulation of private commercial suborbital spaceflights. Over the years, several reports have been presented on the topic by Rapporteur Professor Stephan Hobe, current Chair of the Committee substituting Professor Silvia Maureen Williams, and recently assisted by rapporteurs Dr. Philip de Man and Dr. Rada Papova. LA Italy is represented by Sergio Marchisio and Marco Pedrazzi.

After several years of tests, suborbital flights became operational in 2021, with several launches of Blue Origin's New Shepard, carrying the first paying tourists. More time is needed for these flights to become a routine activity. Such flights are challenging from a legal perspective, as it is not clear whether, and to what extent, they are subject to international space law and/or to international air law. In fact, inasmuch as they reach outer space (their destination is considered to be outer space, and their purpose 'space tourism'), these flights are subject to space law, which applies to the activities conducted by means of objects launched into outer space. But one challenge derives from the fact that the boundary between airspace and outer space has never been defined. Not only do States disagree on where the boundary is, they do not even agree on whether such a boundary is necessary or not. The most one can say is that a number of States consider the limit between airspace and outer space to be around 100 km above sea level. In any case, what distinguishes suborbital flights from other space flights is that, whatever altitude they reach (and some of them certainly reach outer space), their velocity is not sufficient to let them enter into orbit.

As for air law, it is applicable to aircrafts, to the extent they are used for a part of suborbital flights' journeys (as happens in certain scenarios, such as the horizontal take off and horizontal landing of Virgin Galactic's SpaceShip Two). Apart from that, suborbital flights not reaching outer space would seem to take place in an international legal void.

Some States have begun enacting laws covering suborbital flights, providing authorisation of such flights on the basis of compliance with certain requirements, and requiring the informed consent of individuals participating in such flights. However, a more uniform approach is advisable, at least to some degree.

The Space Law Committee has elaborated a set of draft model rules over the past several years, to be proposed to national legislators and to international regulators as well. The purpose of such rules is to provide some uniform standards to be followed by States, enabling them to comply with international obligations and to pursue certain public policy objectives, such as safety, coordination with aviation activities, transparency, and, it is hoped, protection of the environment. The rules will provide for authorization of the activity and the vehicle by the territorial or national State, based on compliance with certain criteria; for registration of the suborbital space vehicle; for liability of the authorising State for damage caused to third parties; for a differentiation of the roles of commander, crew members and spaceflight participants; and for a regulation of facilities (spaceports) from which suborbital activities are undertaken.

An advanced version of the rules was discussed at the Lisbon ILA Biennial Conference in June 2022 and was subjected to further, online consultations over the following year and a half. The intention was to approve the final version at the Athens Biennial Conference of June 2024.

The Italian members have actively contributed to the discussions of the Committee, both online and in person, and to the elaboration of the draft rules. Professor Pedrazzi participated in the Committee meeting in Lisbon in June 2022.

Another important event in the process leading up to the finalisation of the Rules was the workshop on The Legal Framework of Suborbital Flights – Perspectives from Air Law and Space Law, which took place on 19–20 October 2023 at the University of Vienna. The workshop was organised by Committee member Professor Irmgard Marboe, jointly with Committee Chair Professor Stephan Hobe, and its conclusions are going to be published in a volume by Brill. The workshop was attended by several Committee members and other experts and provided the occasion for further reflection, in view of the completion of the Committee's work on the topic. Professors Sergio Marchisio and Marco Pedrazzi actively participated in the workshop by analysing, respectively, the legal situation and the current developments relating to the construction and operation of spaceports in Europe, with special reference to, *inter alia*, the relevant Italian ENAC (National Civil Aviation Authority) regulation, and the legal status of astronauts and its relevance for suborbital flights, specifically looking at the duties of assistance in the event of accident or distress.

Then, the ILA Space Law Committee used the intersessional period between the ILA Biennial Conference in Lisbon and the following one in 2024 to discuss and agree on the commonalities and differences between international space law and air law, and completed the final draft of the Rules on non-orbital spaceflight activities to serve as a reference for national legislators and as a guidance for international organisations deliberating on the regulation of such activities. Finally, the 81st Conference of the ILA held in Athens, Greece, 25–28 June 2024, considered the Report prepared by the Space Law Committee, and adopted the model rules on non-orbital spaceflight activities, which may guide the interpretation and reform of national legislations as well as regional and international instruments, and can contribute to the building of a more reliable and predictable legal framework (Resolution 05/2024).

Sergio Marchisio and Marco Pedrazzi

8 Urbanisation and International Law – Potential & Pitfalls

Our planet continues to urbanise. Already today, more than half of the world's population is living in cities. This number is expected to rise further in the next decades. Metropolises in the Global South face daunting challenges with respect to adequate housing, urban poverty, access to basic services and a healthy environment. Digital urban infrastructure and surveillance systems are reshaping our cities. Until recently, cities have been perceived as irrelevant to international life and invisible in international law and governance. If planetary urbanisation is a major challenge to the rebalancing of the Earth system and cities necessary partners to this rebalancing and to addressing global challenges generally, a crucial question for international law and governance arises: how is urbanization changing international law – its norms, institutions, processes, practices, and argumentation?

In November 2023, the new Committee on "Urbanisation and International Law – Potential & Pitfalls" has been established. It is co-chaired by Professors Helmut Aust (Germany) and Janne Nijman (The Netherlands), who will coordinate the work together with two co-rapporteurs, Anel Du Plessis (South Africa) and Mirko Sossai (Roma Tre University), member of the Italian branch. The Committee will study and clarify how existing international law develops and is developed in urban contexts and in turn why and how cities participate at the level of international law and governance. The mandate includes taking stock of the existing legal framework; studying the normative processes in which cities and other urban actors engage in and with international law; evaluating how their involvement in institutional practices shape law, policy and its implementation, and assessing what patterns of argumentation or discourse constitute the urban turn in international law and governance and the politics of this discourse.

The relationship between the urban and the international holds both potential and pitfalls: a potential that pressing questions of urban governance are addressed through the means of international law, but also the pitfalls that follow from unmediated contacts between the global and the local and the power dynamics that might work to the detriment of local governments and urban citizens alike.

This Committee builds on the work of the ILA Study Group on the role of cities in international law, which examined the legal ramifications of the rise of the city as an actor on the international stage. In the period between 2019 and 2022, the Study Group (SG) has contributed significantly to the establishment of a new research field in public international law. When the SG was established, the connection between cities and international law might still have seemed to be rather esoteric to many in the field. In terms of substantive output, the SG has launched a website collecting "city reports" on how local governments engage with international law. Moreover, the work of the SG has contributed to but reciprocally also benefitted considerably from the publication of the *Elgar Research Handbook on International Law and Cities* in 2021 which includes a significant number of contributions from the members of the SG.

The mandate of the Committee expands the work of the SG: the focus is broader as the theme of "urbanization and international law" has repercussions across a wide range of different fields of international law. This will allow this Committee to study in more depth how urban space is structured by law, how questions of urban sustainability are addressed by international law or how international humanitarian law addresses the reverberating effects of urban warfare on the civilian population and infrastructure. With the 2030 Agenda for Sustainable Development and SDG 11 the international community has committed to make cities and human settlements inclusive, safe, resilient and sustainable. Cities are organising in transnational networks and developing city diplomacy initiatives to influence, for example, norm- and policy creating processes at the international level. The specificities of norm-application in urban contexts challenge existing bodies of international law.

As urbanisation affects various areas of public international law, the mandate of the Committee touches upon the work undertaken in other ILA Committees. In this regard, its work would complement the activities on human rights in times of emergency; global heritage in armed conflict; international migration and international law. The establishment of a committee holds the promise to also broaden the membership base of the existing group of ILA members previously involved in the SG. At the ILA's Biennial Conference in Athens, Committee officers noted the growing interest in this topic, as national branches from the Global North and South became more closely involved through the nomination of new members. Both the open and closed sessions at the Conference provided valuable opportunities to further refine the Committee's work programme. Given its global reach, the ILA offers a unique platform for collaborative research on the intersection of urbanization and international law.

Mirko Sossai

9 Use of Force: Military Assistance on Request

The third iteration of the Use of Force Committee was formed and had its mandate ('Military Assistance on Request') confirmed by the ILA Executive Council in November 2018, although the majority of nominations were only confirmed, and thus the Committee properly composed, in early 2020. The officers initially had intended to deliver the Committee's Final Report at the ILA Biennial Conference in 2022. However, unfortunately the onset of the COVID-19 pandemic delayed the Committee's work. Committee activity nonetheless continued throughout 2020–2021, and notable progress has been made. In 2022, the ILA Executive Council approved an extension of the mandate until 2026 to allow the Committee to complete its work.

The Committee on the Use of Force currently includes two Italian members: Dr Chiara Redaelli and Professor Antonio Bultrini.

In the course of 2023, the Committee examined and discussed several background papers, submitted by Committee members, on a variety of topics that are relevant to the main theme of the current mandate. Such topics ranged from internal self-determination to proportionality, violations of both *ius in bello* and *ius contra bellum* stemming from or connected to various possible forms of foreign military assistance (or military action with consent), and so on.

Two meetings took place in 2023: the first one in person in Warsaw and a remote one at the end of the year. On the occasion of the Warsaw meeting, Chiara Redaelli presented a background paper on "Provision of Weapons and Training, Non-Lethal-Assistance".

The Committee then held two meetings in person in Athens in June 2024, in the context of the ILA Biennial Conference. The first was a closed meeting, while the second was open to all ILA members attending the Conference. On this occasion, Antonio Bultrini presented a report addressing the concrete impact of foreign interventions in civil wars, based on empirical findings from conflict studies, and including also a number of policy and *de lege ferenda* related implications.

The Committee met again remotely in October 2024 and then a very important in-person meeting, aimed at discussing a full draft report, will take place in Cape Town (South Africa) in February 2025. The latter will be followed by a final online meeting at the end of 2025.

The work of the Committee has definitely proved to be more complex and challenging than originally foreseen, and this too explains why its mandate has been extended. A lot of work is still needed on key substantial issues (notably in terms of *lex lata/lex ferenda* distinctions and with regard to civil wars), before the Committee can adopt a final report. The Committee is also discussing the possibility to approve a Resolution and possibly a set of recommendations. The Final Report will likely be presented at the Biennial Conference to be held in Vienna in 2026.

It is worth adding that an edited book, collecting developed versions of the various background papers, is under preparation.

Antonio Bultrini and Chiara Redaelli

Judicial and Arbitral Practice

Taking Stock of the ILA's Influence Over Disputes on International Law

*Carlotta Ceretelli**, *Donato Greco***, *Mariangela La Manna****, *Giuliana Lampo***** *and Andrea Mensi******

1 Introduction

The actual relevance of international legal teachings for the purposes of the clarification, codification, and further development of international law is a subject scholars systematically keep engaging with,[1] besides from being a topic that even international institutions are interested in.[2] The notion of the teachings of publicists is more complex than one might deem at first sight,[3] as it encompasses, together with individual scholars, also those entities that have been empowered by States to elaborate on international law, such as the International Law Commission (ILC), and expert groups or learned societies lacking a specific mandate from States. This is notably the case of the International Law Association (ILA) and the *Institut de droit international* (IDI), among others. An overall assessment of the impact produced by the teachings of publicists on the international legal order, its subjects, and actors is beyond the scope of this Section, whose focus – consistently with the approach underlying the Yearbook – will entirely be on the contribution of the ILA in the development of international law, pursuant to the statutory goals envisaged under its Constitution.[4]

* Postdoctoral Research Fellow in International Law, University of Padua.
** Assistant Professor of International Law, University of Naples Federico II.
*** Assistant Professor, Catholic University of the Sacred Heart, Milan.
**** Postdoctoral Research Fellow in International Law, University LUISS Guido Carli, Rome.
***** Adjunct Professor of International Law, Catholic University of the Sacred Heart, Milan.

1 Sondre Torp Helmersen, The Application of Teachings by the International Court of Justice (Cambridge University Press 2021).

2 ILC, 'First report on subsidiary means for the determination of rules of international law, by Charles Chernor Jalloh, Special Rapporteur' (13 February 2023) UN Doc A/CN.4/760.

3 For an accurate account, Sandesh Sivakumaran, 'The Influence of Teachings of Publicists on the Development of International Law' (2017) 66(1) ICLQ 1, 5.

4 International Law Association, 'Constitution of the Association' (adopted at the 77th Conference, 2016) para 3.1: 'The objectives of the Association are the study, clarification and development of international law, both public and private, and the furtherance of international understanding and respect for international law'.

 | DOI:10.1163/9789004727663_014

As for some methodological underpinnings, a clear-cut choice in favour of an empirical approach to case-law is made here. The influence of the work produced by the committees and study groups created under the auspices of the ILA will, thus, be assessed – both in quantitative and qualitative terms – through the lens of international judicial and arbitral practice, with a view to answering the main research question underlying the Section, namely whether and up to what extent the work of the ILA is able to influence the development of international law.

The present research covers approximately the last two decades. This temporal scope is far from casual as it was, in fact, identified pursuant to a very significant trend in the international society, namely the proliferation of international courts and tribunals, which appears to have been particularly conspicuous in this timespan.

A large gathering of jurisdictions, spanning from the International Court of Justice (ICJ) to regional human rights systems as well as arbitral tribunals – in the areas of both investment claims and commercial disputes –, is addressed in the research. However wide its scope, though, some significant exclusions are to be pointed out. The treaty bodies of the United Nations (UN) as well as the Dispute Settlement Mechanism of the World Trade Organization (WTO) were, in fact, deliberately carved out. The former were excluded due to their *quasi-judicial* nature, while the latter was set aside due to the ongoing crisis of its Appellate Body. In addition, the WTO, as is known, is a relatively closed regime, not very receptive of norms and acts originated in other contexts. Thus, there appears to be no significant and recent instance of this system referring to the work of the ILA. The case-law collected is classified according to the subject-matter dealt with, pursuant to a scheme resulting from the empirical set of data gathered.

2 *Res Judicata* in International Arbitration (Carlotta Ceretelli and Giuliana Lampo)

The survey conducted in this Section focuses on international investment and commercial arbitration, including some related decisions of domestic jurisdictions.[5] At a first sight, indeed, sporadic, and brief references to the ILA Final

5 For a general overview on ILA's contribution to private international procedural law see Patrick Kinsch and Vincent Richard, 'L'influence des travaux de l'ADI sur le développement du droit international en matière de procedure civile et commerciale' in Catherine Kessedjian, Olivier Descamps and Teodolinda Fabrizi (eds), *Au service du droit*

Report on Public Policy and to the Recommendations adopted in New Delhi with Resolution 2/2002 are made by national courts.[6]

However, it is the work of the ILA on the principle of *res judicata* that seems to bear the most significance for the present analysis. In the case of *GPF v Poland* of 2020, administered by the Stockholm Chamber of Commerce (SCC), for instance, the core issue was whether a ruling on jurisdiction could constitute *res judicata*, thus depriving the respondent State of the possibility to raise new jurisdictional objections after the issuance of the judgment of the Court of Justice of the European Union in the *Achmea* case.[7] The tribunal, before finding that this was not the case, relied on the work of the ILA by concisely stating that '[t]he meaning of *res judicata* under international law is reflected in the recommendation of the International Law Association' and using the words of the ILA to describe the effects of *res judicata*.[8]

More recently, the requirements for the application of the *res judicata* principle have been discussed by arbitral tribunals in light of the ILA Recommendations on *Res Judicata* and Arbitration, adopted in Toronto by the Committee on International Commercial Arbitration with Resolution No 1/2006. In the case of *Rutas de Lima v Municipalidad Metropolitana de Lima (II)*, decided in 2022 by an *ad hoc* arbitral tribunal operating under the Arbitration Rules adopted by the United Nations Commission on International Trade Law (UNCITRAL) in 2010,[9] it was discussed whether a previous award rendered in 2020 between the same parties[10] had the effect of *res judicata* so that the tribunal was barred from reconsidering questions relating to the same contract. The tribunal, in

---

international – Les 150 ans de l'Association de droit international (Éditions Panthéon-Assas 2023) 521. For a comprehensive investigation on international arbitration and its relationship with ILA studies see Julie Spinelli, 'L'influence des travaux de l'ADI sur la pratique de l'arbitrage international', ibid 623.

6 *BCB Holding Limited, Belize Bank Limited v Belize*, Caribbean Court of Justice [2013] CCJ 5 (AJ) (26 July 2013); *Republic of Kazakhstan v Ascom Group SA, Anatolie Stati, Gabriel Stati, Terra Far Trans Traiding LTD*, Court of Appeal of Luxemburg, Judgment No 133/19 (19 December 2019); *VEB RF State Development Corporation v Ukraine*, Kyiv Court of Appeal, Proceedings No 2-vk/824/4/2020 (15 September 2020), all citing Committee on International Commercial Arbitration, 'Final Report on Public Policy as a Bar to Enforcement of International Arbitral Awards' in International Law Association, Report of the Seventieth Conference (New Delhi 2002) (International Law Association, New Delhi 2002).

7 *GPF GP Sàrl v Republic of Poland*, SCC Case No V 2014/168, Award (29 April 2020).

8 Ibid para 284.

9 *Rutas de Lima SAC v Municipalidad Metropolitana de Lima (II)*, Award (16 December 2022).

10 *Rutas de Lima SAC v Municipalidad Metropolitana de Lima (I)*, Award (11 May 2020).

addressing the issue, dealt with the requirements to be satisfied for an award to have *res judicata* effects. In this respect, it stated that

> the recommendations of the International Law Association, which reflect developments from multiple jurisdictions, state that: 'An arbitral award has conclusive and preclusive effects in further arbitral proceedings if: it has become final and binding in the country of origin and there is no impediment to recognition in the country of the place of the subsequent arbitration; it has decided on or disposed of a claim for relief which is sought or is being reargued in the further arbitration proceedings; it is based upon a cause of action which is invoked in the further arbitration proceedings or which forms the basis for the subsequent arbitral proceedings; and it has been rendered between the same parties'.[11]

The tribunal then underlined that both the *lex arbitri* (that of Washington, D.C.) and the law applicable to the merits (Peruvian) adopted the same approach,[12] before finding that only certain claims were barred.[13]

Support for the ILA's approach to the issue of *res judicata* was also expressed by a sole arbitrator operating under the aegis of the Milan Chamber of Arbitration in 2019.[14] In particular, the arbitrator considered that it was inapposite to apply domestic bodies of law to the issue of *res judicata* and preferred to 'adopt a transnational approach, based on uniform rules, having regard to the specificity of the arbitration process', as authoritatively suggested, among others, by the ILA.[15] The arbitrator, indeed, considered ILA's work on *res judicata* as 'a useful guidance for arbitrators', and proceeded to apply the requirements therein enshrined to ultimately find that the triple identity test was not satisfied.[16]

One of the requirements for the application of *res judicata* envisaged by the ILA, i.e. the one according to which the previous award should be final and binding and capable of recognition in the country where the subsequent proceedings have its seat, was specifically discussed by the arbitral tribunal in the

11 *Rutas de Lima (II)* (n 9) para 223.

12 Ibid para 224.

13 Ibid paras 226 ff.

14 Excerpts from the award are published in 29 *Rivista dell'Arbitrato* 931, with a comment by Pasquale Mazza.

15 Ibid 934. On this issue see also Jim Yang Teo, 'Transnational Res Judicata in International Commercial Disputes and Potential Influences for BRI Dispute Resolution' (2024) 20 *Journal of Private International Law* 437.

16 Ibid.

case *Iberdrola v Guatemala* (*II*),[17] in which the issue was whether a Permanent Court of Arbitration (PCA) tribunal had to recognise *res judicata* effects to a previous award rendered between the same parties and in which a tribunal established under the auspices of the International Centre for Settlement of Investment Disputes (ICSID) found that it did not have jurisdiction.[18] The PCA tribunal stated that such a requirement was added by the ILA in its work on *res judicata* and, although it had not been discussed by the parties, it felt the need to note that it was actually satisfied.[19]

Conversely, an instance where the ILA's stance on the relevance of previous or contemporary proceedings was only partially upheld can be found in the ICSID case of *Helnan v Egypt*.[20] In this case, the issue was whether a domestic award rendered in Egypt could be said to have *res judicata* effects before an ICSID tribunal. The latter tribunal answered in the negative, recognising that a decision by a national court or arbitral tribunal can be opposed as *res judicata* only within the legal order to which it belongs.[21] This position seems to find support in the Final Report on *Lis Pendens* and Arbitration of the ILA Committee on International Commercial Arbitration, where it is stated that there is no *lis pendens* as between national and international proceedings, since an international tribunal is considered to be hierarchically superior to any national court or private arbitral tribunal'.[22] The tribunal in *Helnan*, as mentioned, agreed with the conclusion but rejected the argument supporting it:

> It is admitted that '*there is no effect of* res judicata *from the decision of a municipal court so far as an international jurisdiction is concerned*'. This is not so much because, as pointed out by the International Law Association '*an international tribunal is considered to be hierarchically superior to any national court or private arbitral tribunal*', but essentially because

17 *Iberdrola Energía,* SA *v The Republic of Guatemala* (*II*), PCA Case No 2017–41, Award (24 August 2020).

18 *Iberdrola Energía* SA *v Republic of Guatemala*, ICSID Case No ARB/09/5, Award (17 August 2012).

19 *Iberdrola* (*II*) (n 17) para 273.

20 *Helnan International Hotels A/S v Arab Republic of Egypt*, ICSID Case No ARB/05/19, Award (3 July 2008).

21 Ibid para 125.

22 Committee on International Commercial Arbitration, 'Final Report on *Lis Pendens* and Arbitration' in International Law Association, Report of the Seventy-Second Conference (Toronto 2006) (International Law Association, Toronto 2006) para 3.2, citing Douglas Reichert, 'Problems with Parallel and Duplicate Proceedings: The Litispendence Principle and International Arbitration' (1992) 8 *Arbitration International* 237.

> although the subject matter may be substantially the same, the causes of action are different.[23]

Another interesting aspect of ILA's approach to *res judicata* which has been debated by arbitral tribunals relates to the extension of the principle. According to the Recommendation 4.2 of the ILA Resolution No 1/2006, in the case of arbitral awards the preclusive effect of *res judicata* covers the 'determinations and relief contained in its dispositive part as well as in all reasoning necessary thereto'. In the well-known proceedings administered by the PCA between Chevron-Texaco and the Republic of Ecuador, finally decided in 2011, the claimants implicitly followed ILA Recommendation by claiming that the partial award of 2010 already settled the issue of damages quantification and that, as a result, Dr Cordero Ordóñez's Expert Opinion was to be considered inadmissible.[24] The respondent State contested ILA's approach to *res judicata* as being 'broader than what is usually allowed in civil law practice, where *res judicata* effect tends to be reserved to the dispositive',[25] while the tribunal avoided to take a position on the matter and limited itself to observe that 'it is disputed whether and to what extent the reasoning of an arbitral award may be vested with *res judicata* effect independently of the *dispositif*'.[26]

A major openness towards ILA's studies has been registered in the field of commercial arbitration. In particular, in the final award on quantum pertaining to the proceedings *Conproca v Pemex*, the ICC arbitral tribunal noted that

> the award constitutes *res judicata*. Such characteristic applies to both its ruling and all the aspects of the factual grounds, which constitute the basis for the decision contained in the ruling, in other words, its *ratio decidendi*, since all of that is part of the decision adopted by the Tribunal.[27]

To support the statement, ILA Recommendation 4.2 on *res judicata* was expressly recalled, together with a dated decision by the Supreme Court of Justice of Mexico.[28] Due to this assumption, the final award of the tribunal entirely aligned with both the rulings and the reasoning of the previous award on quantum.

---

23 *Helnan* (n 20) para 124, emphasis in the original, footnotes omitted.

24 *Chevron Corporation (USA) and Texaco Petroleum Company (USA) v The Republic of Ecuador*, PCA Case No 34877, Final Award (31 August 2011) paras 250–251.

25 Ibid para 262.

26 Ibid para 273.

27 *Conproca, SA de CV v Petroleos Mexicanos and Pemanex Refinacion*, ICC Case No 11760/KGA/CCO/JRF, Final Award on Quantum (23 December 2011) paras 116–117.

28 Ibid paras 118–119.

Contrary to this trend, the broad extension of *res judicata* suggested by the ILA found a severe opposition in domestic jurisdictions, particularly in Switzerland. On a few occasions, indeed, an arbitral award was appealed before the Swiss Federal Tribunal claiming the violation of procedural public policy since the arbitral tribunal which issued the award failed to correctly apply the principle of *res judicata*. More precisely, in the case *A LLP v B* of 2015, an ICC arbitral tribunal was criticised for not having followed the reasoning of a previous award on preliminary issues, rendered in a case between the same parties, with the same *causa petendi* and on a similar *petitum*.[29] The appellant argued that the principle of *res judicata* extended to the reasoning by mentioning the ILA Report of 2009 on the topic, but the Federal Tribunal rejected this broad interpretation of the concept as being incompatible with Swiss law.[30] The opposite situation emerged in 2021 in the appeal proceedings of the *Actis v Rakesh Malhotra* award, where an arbitral tribunal established under the London Court of International Arbitration was accused of having improperly treated as *res judicata* some decisions of the British High Court of Justice, reasoning included.[31] Consistently with the precedent of 2015, the Federal Court rejected the broad interpretation of the principle 'tout en concédant que les Recommandations de l'ILA et la doctrine de l'*issue preclusion* ne se sont pas véritablement imposées dans la pratique internationale'.[32] The appeal was then dismissed.

Finally, it bears noting that a tepid support to ILA's broad concept of *res judicata* has been recently showed by the ICJ under specific conditions. In the case concerning the *Delimitation of the Continental Shelf Beyond 200 Nautical Miles*, indeed, the Judgment on preliminary objections of 2016 admitted that 'in order to ascertain what is covered by *res judicata*, it may be necessary to determine the meaning of the operative clause by reference to the reasoning set out in the judgment in question'.[33] However, the ICJ made no references to ILA's studies.

In conclusion, the work of the ILA on procedural issues, and in particular the work on *res judicata*, has proven to be very useful for arbitral tribunals, despite the fact that references do not seem to be numerous.[34] This is probably

29 *A v B*, Federal Tribunal, 4A_663/2014 (29 May 2015) para 3.1.

30 Ibid para 3.2.5.

31 *A, Société B v Z*, Federal Tribunal, 4A_530/2020 (15 June 2021) para 6.1.

32 Ibid para 6.3.

33 *Question of the Delimitation of the Continental Shelf between Nicaragua and Colombia beyond 200 Nautical Miles from the Nicaragua Coast* (*Nicaragua v Colombia*) (Preliminary Objections) [2016] ICJ Rep 100, para 61.

34 In this respect, see the contribution by Luca G. Radicati di Brozolo in the present volume, *supra* at 133.

due to the gaps characterising international procedure, particularly the procedure of non-institutionalised dispute settlement bodies. Be that as it may, tribunals have shown deference towards the positions adopted by the Association in its reports and recommendations. This has sometimes been done to clarify the notion of *res judicata* and the requirements of the test for recognising preclusive effects to a certain decision. In some cases, on the contrary, tribunals have explicitly engaged with the position of the ILA to depart from or to only partially uphold it. Even in these cases, however, what seem to emerge from the brief survey conducted above is that ILA's stance on complex questions of procedural law, despite being seldom cited, is highly regarded by arbitrators and national judges.

3 Foreign Direct Investment Protection (Carlotta Ceretelli and Giuliana Lampo)

The purpose of this Section is to highlight the contribution offered by the ILA to the international protection of foreign direct investment (FDI) by looking at the judicial practice of international arbitral tribunals.[35] A survey of the case-law from the last two decades has revealed a contained but noteworthy application of the ILA'S studies, mostly to interpret the standards of protection of FDI enshrined in international investment agreements.

A first example in this respect is the case *Big Sky Energy v Kazakhstan*, arising out of actions of the respondent State which the claimant framed as an expropriation of its interests in a company owning licenses to explore, develop and exploit a number of oil fields.[36] In particular, the claimant argued that Kazakhstan had failed to protect its investment and breached, *inter alia*, the standard of full protection and security. More in detail, the claimant argued that the State had a duty to take all measures it could reasonably be expected to take as part of a duty of due diligence, not limiting to the protection of investors against denial of justice. In arguing this, the investor extensively relied on

35 For a detailed account of the influence that the ILA has had on the evolution of international investment law see August Reinisch, 'Investment Law' in Catherine Kessedjian, Olivier Descamps and Teodolinda Fabrizi (eds) (n 5) 567. See also Philippe Kahn, 'Etat actuel du droit des investissements etrangers dans les pays en voie de développement' in Maarten Bos (ed), *The Present State of International Law and Other Essays Written in Honour of the Centenary Celebration of the International Law Association 1873–1973* (Springer 1973) 283.

36 *Big Sky Energy Corporation v Republic of Kazakhstan*, ICSID Case No ARB/17/22, Award (24 November 2021).

the work of the ILA on due diligence.[37] Interestingly, also the tribunal, when describing the obligations of due diligence, relied on the work of the ILA and, namely, on the Second Report of the Study Group on Due Diligence in International Law:

> The International Law Association, cited by both Parties, describes such due diligence in the following manner: 'In international law obligations of conduct are far more common than obligations of result. This means that international law tends to focus primarily on the behaviour of States rather than the outcomes of that behaviour. Due diligence standards preserve for States a significant measure of autonomy and flexibility in discharging their international obligations. Rigid application of international rules, mandating results, or imposing liability in the event of breach in any circumstance cuts against the grain of notions of State sovereignty and domains of non-interference'.[38]

According to the tribunal, however, even assuming the standard of full protection and security to impose on States an obligation of 'legal' protection in addition to that of 'physical' protection of the investment, this should be considered to entail exclusively the existence of a functioning system of courts and legal remedies available to investors.[39]

Taking a step back in time, a crucial clarification on the meaning of another standard, and namely the 'fair and equitable treatment' one, has been offered by the *Grand River* Award of 2011, rendered by an arbitral tribunal established under Chapter 11 of the North American Free Trade Agreement (NAFTA).[40] At the core of the dispute there was the lack of consultation of First Nations investors belonging to the Canadian indigenous peoples of Haudenosaunee, an omission that, according to the claimants – among which there were individuals belonging to the group –, determined a violation of article 1105 NAFTA. The latter, indeed, sets forth in paragraph 1 the obligation for States to 'accord to investments of investors of another Party treatment in accordance with international law, including fair and equitable treatment and full protection and security'. Once observed that 'the content of the obligation imposed by

37 Ibid para 292.

38 Ibid para 551. See ILA Study Group on Due Diligence in International Law, Second Report, 2016.

39 Ibid para 553.

40 *Grand River Enterprises Six Nations, LTD, et al v United States of America*, Award (12 January 2011).

article 1105 must be determined by reference made to customary international law',[41] the tribunal admitted the existence of a customary rule imposing on governmental authorities the obligation to consult indigenous peoples on every project affecting them. To support this position, a reference was made to article 19 of the United Nations Declaration of the Rights of Indigenous Peoples and, at the same time, to the 2010 Interim Report of the ILA Committee on the Rights of Indigenous Peoples:

> [A] recent study by a committee of several international law experts assembled under the auspices of the International Law Association, after an exhaustive survey of relevant state and international practice, found a wide range of customary international law norms concerning indigenous peoples, including 'the right to be consulted with respect to any project that may affect them'.[42]

However, the investors' claim was dismissed for two reasons. Firstly, the tribunal noted that due to the collective nature of indigenous rights, consultations were required only with indigenous representatives and not with all the members of the community.[43] Secondly, and more generally, the customary minimum standard of treatment codified by article 1105 was found incompatible with specialised rights protecting only a limited group of people.[44]

Far from being absolute, the safeguard that arbitral tribunals offer to FDI is usually subject to investors' *bona fides* in the establishment of the investment.[45] The *World Duty Free* case, decided by an ICSID Tribunal in 2006, is emblematic in this respect, as the Republic of Kenya contested the validity of the investment contract procured by the payment of a bribe under both the applicable laws (Kenyan and English) and international public policy.[46] Interestingly,

41 Ibid para 176

42 Ibid para 210. For a general reference on the contribution of the ILA to the codification of the set of rules applicable to indigenous peoples' rights see Timo Koivurova, Federico Lenzerini and Siegfried Wiessner, 'The Role of the ILA in the Restatement and Evolution of International and National Law Relating to Indigenous Peoples' in Katja Karjalainen, Iina Tornberg and Aleksi Pursiainen (eds), *International Actors and the Formation of Laws* (Springer 2022) 89.

43 *Grand River* (n 40) para 211.

44 Ibid para 213.

45 Attila Tanzi, 'The Relevance of the Foreign Investor's Good Faith' in Andrea Gattini, Attila Tanzi and Filippo Fontanelli (eds), *General Principles of Law and International Investment Arbitration* (Brill Nijhoff 2018) 193.

46 *World Duty Free Company Limited v Republic of Kenya*, ICSID Case No ARB/00/7, Award (4 October 2006) paras 106–108.

beside the idea of international public policy traditionally invoked as a bar to the enforcement of foreign judgments, the arbitral tribunal recognised that:

> The term 'international public policy' (…) is sometimes used with another meaning, signifying an international consensus as to universal standards and accepted norms of conduct that must be applied in all fora. It has been proposed to cover that concept in referring to 'transnational public policy' or 'truly international public policy'.[47]

In mentioning the concept of 'transnational public policy', an explicit reference was made to the ILA Report on International Commercial Arbitration on Public Policy as a Bar to the Enforcement of International Arbitral Awards, adopted on the occasion of the Seventieth Conference in 2002.[48] Then, after a wide analysis of the domestic laws and international conventions dealing with corruption, as well as of the national and international jurisprudence on the subject, the Tribunal concluded that bribery was contrary to international public policy and dismissed the claim.[49]

Quite differently, on another occasion, a reference has been made to the ILA's work on public policy with the purpose of strengthening the protection offered to a foreign investor. In the *Frontier Petroleum* case, decided under the UNCITRAL Rules, actually, the claimants alleged that the refusal to enforce commercial arbitral awards due to them being contrary to public policy amounted to a breach of the Canada-Czech Republic Bilateral Investment Treaty.[50] Faced with the argument of the respondent State that the claim was inadmissible, as it would have required the tribunal to improperly act as a court of appeal against domestic decisions, the arbitrators decided that they did have the power to review the interpretation and application of the concept of public policy as a bar to the enforcement of arbitral awards under the 1958 New York Convention on the Recognition and Enforcement of Foreign Arbitral Awards and to scrutinise whether such interpretation and application was 'an abuse of rights contrary to the international principle of good faith'.[51] The tribunal went on to answer in the negative, finding that the decision by Czech's courts was not a violation of treaty obligations owed to investors. In doing so, it referred

47 Ibid para 139.

48 'Final Report on Public Policy as a Bar to Enforcement of International Arbitral Awards' (n 6).

49 *World Duty Free* (n 46) para 157.

50 *Frontier Petroleum Services Ltd v The Czech Republic*, UNCITRAL, Final Award (12 November 2010).

51 Ibid para 525.

to the work of the ILA on public policy as a bar to the enforcement of international arbitral awards to interpret the extent of the concept of *ordre public*:

> It is widely accepted that while the reference to 'public policy' in Article V(2)(b) of the New York Convention refers to international public policy, it is nonetheless a reference to the particular national conception of international public policy that is relevant rather than to a conception of public policy that is in some way detached from the legal system at the place where recognition and enforcement is sought.[52]

The survey conducted above reveals that the works of the ILA are sparingly mentioned and used by investment tribunals that have to address issues on which the Association has had the opportunity to express its position. In particular, the tribunals sitting in the cases reported in this Section have used the work of the ILA on quite different topics to define and give content to highly debated notions, such as due diligence obligations, the rights of indigenous peoples and public policy. It is certainly true that the application of ILA's work in the field of the protection of FDI is not as consistent as the one made by tribunals in other areas (and namely, in procedural law matters). However, at a closer look, the references to this work, although scarce, reveal that the stance of the ILA on questions of both public and private international law is regarded as highly authoritative.

4 Human Rights (Andrea Mensi)

This section outlines the ILA'S contribution in the ongoing evolution of international human rights law and, particularly, in the jurisprudence of the Inter-American Court on Human Rights (IACtHR). First, it focuses on the consideration of the Burgh House Principles on the Independence of the International Judiciary, adopted by the ILA Study Group on the Practice and Procedure of International Courts and Tribunals in 2004,[53] in two recent judgements of

52 Ibid para 526, referring to Committee on International Commercial Arbitration, 'Interim Report on Public Policy as a Bar to Enforcement of International Arbitral Awards' in International Law Association, Report of the Sixty-Ninth Conference (London 2000) (International Law Association, London 2000).

53 Study Group of the International Law Association on Practice and Procedure of International Courts and Tribunals, and the Project on International Courts and Tribunals, '*The Burgh House Principles on the Independence of the International Judiciary*' (2004). For a general overview on the Burgh House Principles see Philippe Sands, Ruth Mackenzie, and

the IACtHR.[54] Furthermore, it examines the Advisory Opinion of 17 September 2003 on the Juridical Condition and Rights of Undocumented Migrants,[55] where the Concurring Opinion of Judge Cançado Trindade, who was serving as President of the IACtHR at the time of the decision, referred to the ILA Declaration of Principles of International Law on Mass Expulsion, adopted by consensus at the ILA 62nd Conference in Seoul in 1986.[56]

The ILA'S works have been considered by the IACtHR in the recent decisions *Aguinaga Aillòn v Ecuador* of 30 January 2023 and *Rìos Avalos et al v Paraguay* of 19 August 2021. The first case concerned alleged violations of the right to judicial guarantees, judicial protection, as well the principles of freedom from *ex post facto* laws and judicial independence after the dismissal of a judge of the Ecuadorian Supreme Electoral Tribunal.[57] The latter case concerned the removal of two judges from the Supreme Court of Justice of Paraguay in 2003, including alleged violations of the rights to a competent and impartial authority and to a previously established procedure, guarantees of due process, the right to duly reasoned decisions and to legality in relation to the principle of judicial independence, as well as the rights to appeal the decision and to judicial protection.[58] In both decisions, the IACtHR declared how judicial independence is a prerequisite of the rule of law and democracy and how the lack of independence is a synonym of arbitrariness.[59] The Court, therefore, found how judicial independence is a principle guaranteed at the international and regional level.[60]

Among international and regional instruments considered to demonstrate the general acceptance of the duty to guarantee judicial independence, the

---

Campbell McLachlan, 'The Burgh House Principles on the Independence of the International Judiciary' (2005) 4(2) *Law and Practice of International Courts and Tribunals* 247; Jean-Pierre Cot, 'The Hague vs. Burgh House' (2011) 10(1) *Law and Practice of International Courts and Tribunals* 25.

54 *Aguinaga Aillòn v Ecuador (Merits, Reparations and Costs)* Inter-American Court of Human Rights Series C No 483 (30 January 2023); *Rìos Avalos et al v Paraguay (Merits, Reparations and Costs)* Inter-American Court of Human Rights Series C No 429 (19 August 2021).

55 *Juridical Condition and Rights of Undocumented Migrants*, Advisory Opinion OC-18, Inter-American Court of Human Rights Series A No 18 (17 September 2003) (hereinafter 'Advisory Opinion OC-18/03').

56 'Declaration of Principles of International Law on Mass Expulsion' in International Law Association, *Report of the Sixty-Second Conference* (Seoul 1986) (International Law Association, Seoul 1986) 13.

57 *Aguinaga Aillòn v Ecuador* (n 54) para 1.

58 *Rìos Avalos et al v Paraguay* (n 54) para 1.

59 *Rìos Avalos et al v Paraguay* (n 54) para 91; *Aguinaga Aillòn v Ecuador* (n 54) para 68.

60 *Rìos Avalos et al v Paraguay* (n 54) para 92; *Aguinaga Aillòn v Ecuador* (n 54) para 69.

IACtHR mentioned the Burg House Principles on the Independence of the International Judiciary. These have been developed considering specifically the characteristics of international courts and tribunals,[61] but they include some general norms that are, nevertheless, applicable also to domestic courts. The Principles state, indeed, how judges 'shall exercise their functions free from direct or indirect interference or influence by any person or entity'.[62] As a proof of the importance of such rule under international law, in both judgements, the IACtHR found the responding States responsible for violating, *inter alia*, the right to judicial independence under article 8(1) of the American Convention on Human Rights.

The works of the ILA have also been considered in the Concurring Opinion of Judge Cançado Trindade to the Advisory Opinion of the IACtHR on the *Juridical Condition and Rights of Undocumented Migrants*. The Advisory Opinion dealt with the deprivation of the enjoyment and exercise of certain labour rights of migrant workers and its compatibility with the duties of the American States to guarantee legal equality, non-discrimination, and the equal and effective protection of the law as part of international human rights instruments. The request submitted by Mexico also referred to the subordination or conditioning of the observance of human rights law obligations, including of *erga omnes* nature, and to the meaning that legal equality, non-discrimination, and the equal and effective protection of the law have in the context of the progressive development of international human rights law and its codification.[63] The Concurring Opinion of Judge Cançado Trindade emphasised how the forced displacement and vulnerability of migrant workers intensified during globalisation and raised several fundamental rights questions.[64] These included forms of labour exploitation, the increase in poverty, as well as social exclusion and marginalisation. In considering how these issues involved the whole international community, Judge Cançado Trindade mentioned the ILA Declaration of Principles of International Law on Mass Expulsion as a means for the identification of *opinion juris communis*:

> On this last point, it may be recalled that, in 1986, the International Law Association adopted (in its 62nd. session, in Seoul), by consensus, the Declaration of Principles of International Law on Mass Expulsion, in

61 'The Burgh House Principles on the Independence of the International Judiciary' (n 53) Preamble.

62 Ibid Principle 1.1.

63 Advisory Opinion OC-18/03 (n 55) para 1.

64 Concurring Opinion of Judge Cançado Trindade to the Advisory Opinion OC-18/03 para 20.

which, *inter alia*, it expressed its 'deep concern' with 'the vulnerabilidad and precarious position of many minorities', including migrant workers.[65]

The ILA Declaration was drafted by the ILA Committee on the Legal Status of Refugees and addressed the refugee problem from the perspective of the country of origin, dealing with the causes of refugees and their solutions. The ILA Declaration states, for example, the obligation of the country of origin to adequate compensation to refugees, combined with their right to return, to negate any incentive to these countries to force, directly or indirectly, their citizens to become refugees. As underlined by the Concurring Opinion, according to the ILA Declaration, the principle of non-refoulement is applicable even if refugees have been legally admitted in the receiving State, and independently of having arrived individually or massively.[66] The ILA Declaration is, however, relevant also for migrant workers. It affirms, indeed, in its Preamble the 'deep concern' on the vulnerabilities and precarious conditions of many minorities, including migrant workers,[67] and in Principle 17 on mass expulsions it considers also migrant workers.[68] Judge Cançado Trindade highlighted the influence of the ILA Declaration in the development of international human rights law in this field, considering the adoption four years later of the 1990 International Convention on the Protection of the Rights of All Migrant Workers and Members of Their Families.[69] Overall, the ILA Declaration has been conceived by the Concurring Opinion as part of 'the universal juridical conscience' on the need to reconceptualise the bases of the international legal order on refugees, displaced persons and undocumented migrants and for the necessity of prevalence of the dignity of the human person in any circumstances,[70] which mirrors the findings of the Advisory Opinion.[71]

The jurisprudence of the IACtHR demonstrates the influence of the ILA's instruments on the evolution of international human rights law. The Burg House Principles represented an initial effort to establish principles of general

65 Ibid para 21.

66 'The Burgh House Principles on the Independence of the International Judiciary' (n 53) Principle 12. Furthermore, as observed by the IACtHR, at Principle 19 the Declaration urged States to terminate any expulsion of a massive character and to establish a system of 'early warning'.

67 Ibid Preamble.

68 Ibid Principle 17.

69 Concurring Opinion of Judge Cançado Trindade (n 64) para 20. See also Committee on the Legal Status of Refugees, 'Declaration of Principles of International Law on Compensation to Refugees' in International Law Association, Report of the Sixty-Fifth Conference (Cairo 1992) (International Law Association, Cairo 1992).

70 Concurring Opinion of Judge Cançado Trindade (n 64) paras 25 and 28.

71 Advisory Opinion OC-18/03 (n 55) para 173.

application concerning judicial independence and impartiality in international tribunals, which are now commonly respected, as demonstrated by recent IACtHR decisions. Furthermore, as noted by Judge Cançado Trindade, the ILA Declaration of Principles of International Law on Mass Expulsion served to identify *opinion juris communis* and influenced the successive adoption of the International Convention on the Protection of the Rights of All Migrant Workers and Members of Their Families. Although references to these instruments are not abundant, nor consistently considered across different regional human rights tribunals, they nonetheless underscore the authority and influence of the ILA's works before international courts and their contribution to the general acceptance of international human rights principles.

5 State Jurisdiction to Adjudicate: Scope and Limits (Mariangela La Manna)

The present Section is especially thought of in order to offer an overview of the treatment by international judicial instances of the work of the ILA on the subject-matter of State jurisdiction to adjudicate, the limits thereof, and a few related matters (*e.g.* immunity, etc.). More precisely, the Section will describe those cases whereby international courts and tribunals assessed the greater or lesser compatibility with international law of States' exercise of jurisdiction also by citing and quoting reports, resolutions, and guidelines crafted under the auspices of the ILA. Such materials would, in fact, be resorted to from time to time as further proof of the existence of a rule under general international law, as well as for the purposes of corroborating or contesting a line of argument.

In truth, not many examples of international judicial instances explicitly recalling the work of the ILA in the area of State jurisdiction are to be found. Quite on the contrary, in this area there are but a few sets of proceedings hosting either express or indirect references to ILA'S documents. However, the scarce quantity of such references appears to be more than made up for by the latter's poignancy and sheer relevance.

The most relevant case for the purposes of the present Section is certainly the *Jurisdictional Immunities of the State* case,[72] where several references to the ILA and its work can be found both in the submissions of the parties to the

72 For a broad account of the relevance of the work of the ILA with reference to this case, see Photini Pazartis, 'Le droit à la réparation des victimes de violations du droit international humanitaire' in Catherine Kessedjian, Olivier Descamps and Teodolinda Fabrizi (eds) (n 5) 551.

case, that would eventually shape and inform the reasoning of the Court in its Judgment of 3 February 2012, and in the Dissenting Opinion appended by Judge Cançado Trindade to the judgment itself. As for parties' submissions, one will want to mention an intriguing (albeit indirect) reference to the ILA made by Germany in its memorial,[73] whereby a scholarly publication[74] presenting the work carried out by the Committee on International Human Rights Law and Practice over a period of four years, including the Committee's Final Report, was explicitly recalled.[75] This was done in order to purport that, contrary to the position of the Italian Supreme Court of Cassation in its *Ferrini* judgment,[76] there is no conflict whatsoever between the mandatory rule prohibiting gross violations of human rights and the one establishing State immunity from the civil jurisdiction of other States. It is precisely against such background that the Court would eventually build its contention concerning the 'logical problem' in its 2012 judgment and separate 'substantive' from 'procedural' rules.[77]

At a later stage in the proceedings, Germany mentioned in its reply to the written observations presented by Italy[78] yet another important document prepared by an ILA Committee, *i.e.* the Draft Declaration of International Law Principles on Reparation for Victims of Armed Conflicts (Substantive Issues),[79] adopted by the Committee on Reparation for Victims of Armed Conflicts, under the chairmanship of Natalino Ronzitti. The reference was intended to further demonstrate that the provision establishing victims' right to reparation under article 6 ('Victims of armed conflict have a right to reparation from the responsible parties') was not so much the codification of an established

73 *Jurisdictional Immunities of the State* (*Germany v Italy*) (Memorial of the Federal Republic of Germany of 12 June 2009).

74 Thilo Rensmann, 'Impact on the Immunity of States and their Officials' in Menno T Kamminga and Martin Scheinin (eds), *The Impact of Human Rights Law on General International Law* (OUP 2009) 151–170.

75 Committee on International Human Rights Law and Practice, 'Final Report on the Impact of International Human Rights Law on General International Law' in International Law Association Report of the Seventy-Third Conference (Rio de Janeiro 2008) (International Law Association, Rio de Janeiro 2008).

76 Italian Court of Cassation, Judgment No 5044 of 11 March 2004.

77 *Jurisdictional Immunities of the State* (*Germany v Italy: Greece intervening*) [2012] ICJ Rep 99, para 82.

78 *Jurisdictional Immunities of the State* (*Germany v Italy*) (Reply of the Federal Republic of Germany of 5 October 2010).

79 Committee on Reparation for Victims of Armed Conflict, 'Draft Declaration of International Law Principles on Reparation for Victims of Armed Conflict (Substantive Issues)' in International Law Association Report of the Seventy-Fourth Conference (The Hague 2010) (International Law Association, The Hague 2010) 3.

principle but had rather to be conceived in terms of progressive development of international law.[80] It was, in fact, claimed that:

> It is clear from the explanations given by the Rapporteur that his proposal is meant to introduce new rules, rules that to date have no firm foundation in international law.

Also, the subsequent reference to article 15 in the Declaration ('Non-Retroactivity') was envisaged to exclude any possible retroactive effect of victims' right to reparation, thus denying its application to international crimes committed by the German army during WWII:

> This is also corroborated by Article 15(1) of the draft declaration according to which the rights and obligations reflected in the text shall have no retroactive effect. Whatever the justifiability of the suggested reform, the reformers themselves acknowledge quite openly that they would turn a historic page in the history of international law.[81]

Judge Cançado Trindade's Dissenting Opinion provides for ample references to the work of the ILA,[82] which are referred to in order to uphold the thesis revolving around the inapplicability of the customary rule on State immunity from the civil jurisdiction of another State whenever the underlying compensation claim is based on State conduct amounting to gross violations of human rights. First, the Dissenting Opinion quotes the Final Report on the Exercise of Universal Jurisdiction in Respect of Gross Human Rights Offences,[83] by recalling that:

> One of the 'conclusions and recommendations' (No 4) reached by that ILA Committee was that: 'No immunities in respect of gross human rights offences subject to universal jurisdiction shall apply on the grounds that crimes were perpetrated in an official capacity' (p. 21).

---

80 Reply of the Federal Republic of Germany (n 78) para 42.

81 Ibid.

82 *Jurisdictional Immunities of the State* (*Germany v Italy: Greece intervening*) (n 77), Dissenting Opinion of Judge Cançado Trindade paras 50 ff.

83 Committee on International Human Rights Law and Practice, 'Final Report on The Exercise of Universal Jurisdiction in Respect of Gross Human Rights Offences' in International Law Association Report of the Sixty-Ninth Conference (London 2000) (International Law Association, London 2000) 403–431.

Subsequently, Judge Cançado Trindade would move on to quote the Draft Declaration of International Law Principles on Reparation for Victims of Armed Conflict mentioned above and the commentaries thereto,[84] in order to emphasise the support of international legal scholarship for an individual right to reparation not only under international human rights law, but also pursuant to the law of armed conflict.

Another seminal case where the ICJ borrowed amply from the works of the ILA is the *Arrest Warrant* case.[85] More precisely, in her Dissenting Opinion,[86] Judge Van den Wyngaert quoted the abovementioned Final Report on the Exercise of Universal Jurisdiction[87] for the purposes of corroborating the approach purporting the compatibility of universal criminal jurisdiction *in absentia* with international law:

> There is a massive literature of learned scholarly writings on the subject of universal jurisdiction. I confine myself to three studies, which emanate from groups of scholars: the Princeton principles, the Cairo principles, and the Kamminga report on behalf of the ILA, and look at one point: do the authors support the Congo's proposition that universal jurisdiction *in absentia* is contrary to international law? The answer is no.

Another extremely significant reference to the work of the ILA is to be found in the case-law of the European Court on Human Rights (ECtHR). This is all the more relevant since, far from being expressed in dissenting or separate opinions or in parties' submissions, the reference was made by the Grand Chamber itself. In its 2018 judgment in the *Naït-Liman* case,[88] the Grand Chamber mentioned in fact a resolution adopted by the ILA Committee on International Civil Litigation and the Interests of the Public.[89] Interestingly enough, the

84 'Draft Declaration of International Law Principles on Reparation for Victims of Armed Conflict' (n 79).

85 *Arrest Warrant of 11 April 2000 (Democratic Republic of the Congo v Belgium)* [2002] ICJ Rep 3.

86 *Arrest Warrant of 11 April 2000 (Democratic Republic of the Congo v Belgium)* [2002] ICJ Rep 3, Dissenting Opinion of Judge Van den Wyngaert para 57.

87 'Final Report on The Exercise of Universal Jurisdiction in Respect of Gross Human Rights Offences' (n 83).

88 *Naït-Liman v Switzerland* App No 51357/07 (ECtHR, 15 March 2018) paras 64–66.

89 Committee on International Civil Litigation and the Interests of the Public, *Resolution No 2/2012 on 'International Civil Litigation and the Interests of the Public'* in International Law Association *Report of the Seventy-Fifth Conference* (Sofia 2012) (International Law Association, Sofia 2012) 38 ff. See also Andrea Saccucci, 'The Case of *Naït-Liman* Before the European Court of Human Rights. A *Forum non Conveniens* for Asserting the Right of Access to

contribution of the ILA Committee is thoroughly addressed in the judgment and the relevant provision on *forum necessitatis* jurisdiction under Resolution No 2/2012 is quoted in full:

> At its Sofia Session in 2012, the 'Committee on International Civil Litigation and the Interests of the Public' of the International Law Association (hereafter, 'the ILA') adopted Resolution No 2/2012. This Resolution addresses problems of coordination between different jurisdictions and is limited to claims against individuals, corporations, and other non-State actors (…). Among the elements which could serve as grounds for State jurisdiction, the Resolution proposes, inter alia, the forum of necessity. The relevant paragraphs are worded as follows: (1) Scope '1.1 These Guidelines apply to civil claims against corporations, individuals and other non-State actors arising out of or brought to redress conduct constituting a human rights violation, in view of the nature of the norm allegedly violated or the gross or systematic nature of the breach alleged'.
>
> 2.3. Forum of necessity '2.3(1) The courts of any State with a sufficient connection to the dispute shall have jurisdiction in order to avert a denial of justice. 2.3(2) A denial of justice in the sense of paragraph 2.3(1) occurs if the court concludes upon hearing all interested parties, and after taking account of reliable public sources of information, that: (a) no other court is available; or (b) the claimant cannot reasonably be expected to seize another court. (3) A sufficient connection in the sense of paragraph 2.3(1) consists in particular in: (a) the presence of the claimant; (b) the nationality of the claimant or the defendant; (c) the presence of assets of the defendant; (d) some activity of the defendant; or (e) a civil claim based on an act giving rise to criminal proceedings in the court seized of those proceedings, to the extent that that court has jurisdiction under its own law to entertain civil proceedings'.

Finally, also the judicial practice of the Court of Justice of the European Union has occasionally resorted to the work of the ILA. This happened back in 2017 in the famous *Schrems* case.[90] In the conclusions of Advocate General Bobek,[91] a reference to yet another important document adopted by the Committee

---

a Court in Relation to Civil Claims for Torture Committed Abroad?' in Serena Forlati and Pietro Franzina (eds), *Universal Civil Jurisdiction. Which Way Forward?* (Brill 2021) 3.

90 Case C-498/16 *Maximilian Schrems v Facebook Ireland Ltd* [2018] ECLI:EU:C:2018:37. See also Kinsch, Richard (n 5) 529–530.

91 Ibid Conclusions of Advocate General Bobek [2017] ECLI:EU:C:2017:863, para 120 fn 37.

on International Civil Litigation and the Interests of the Public, namely the Paris-Rio Guidelines of Best Practices for Transnational Group Actions can be found.[92] While pointing out the advantages of collective redress for the purposes of effective judicial consumer protection (i.e. preventing parallel proceedings), Advocate General Bobek recalled in a footnote that in the context of transnational group actions the Guidelines above had pursued the same policy goal via the provision of an alternative forum to the defendant's forum, based on the close connection to the parties and the transactions:

> See for example the Resolution No 1/2008 on Transnational Group Actions, of the International Law Association, adopted at its Rio de Janeiro Conference. Point 3 of this resolution is devoted to jurisdiction. According to 3.1: 'A transnational group action may be brought in the defendant's forum'. According to 3.3: 'A transnational group action may also be brought in the courts of another country closely connected to the parties and the transactions, provided that trial of the action in that country is reasonably capable of serving the interests of the group and has not been selected to frustrate those interests'.

In conclusion, it appears that the work produced by ILA Committees on the subject matter of jurisdiction and related issues was highly regarded by international courts and tribunals, not to mention States parties to proceedings, that would sometimes build their argument around them. Though the collection above is not particularly conspicuous in purely quantitative terms, the variety of instances further confirms the authoritativeness and prestige of codification under the auspices of the ILA.

6 Delimitation of Maritime Boundaries and Status of International Watercourses (Donato Greco)

Another area of international adjudication in which ILA acts have been cited with some frequency over the past decade concerns contentious interstate jurisdiction over disputes over both the delimitation of marine areas and the status of watercourses. Indeed, while international courts and tribunals

92 Committee on International Civil Litigation and the Interests of the Public, Resolution No 1/2008 on 'Paris-Rio Guidelines of Best Practices for Transnational Group Actions' in International Law Association Report of the Seventy-Third Conference (Rio de Janeiro 2008) (International Law Association, Rio de Janeiro 2008) 26 ff.

generally appear more reluctant to rely upon ILA acts explicitly, States parties to a dispute do not show a similar reluctance and expressly cite such sources in support of their arguments.

In this respect, a first example is the *Nicaragua v Colombia* case, in which the applicant State sought the ICJ to clarify 'the delimitation of the boundaries between, on the one hand, the continental shelf of Nicaragua beyond the 200-nautical-mile limit from the baselines from which the breadth of the territorial sea of Nicaragua is measured, and on the other hand, the continental shelf of Colombia'.[93]

At the core of the issue was the normative relevance to attach to paragraph 2 ff of article 76 of the United Nations Convention on the Law of the Sea (UNCLOS), which govern the delimitation of the continental shelf beyond 200 nm from the coast since these provisions were invoked on the assumption that they reflected settled rules of customary international law. Relying upon them, Nicaragua claimed that its continental shelf, following the natural prolongation of its land territory, extended far enough beyond 200 nm to overlap with Colombia's 200 nm entitlement to the continental shelf, measured from the latter's mainland coast.

On the contrary, the respondent State objected that paragraph 2 ff of article 76 UNCLOS governed different cases – those in which it is necessary to delimit the boundary between the continental shelf of a State and the Area subject to the regime of the common heritage of mankind. It thus contended that those rules are not applicable in cases where beyond 200 nm from the coast of a State lies the continental shelf of another State. To support this interpretation, Jean-Marc Thouvenin, pleading in his capacity as counsel for Colombia,[94] referred to a speech given by Rüdiger Wolfrum when he was President of the International Tribunal for the Law of the Sea (ITLOS) at the 73rd ILA Biennial Conference.[95] According to this authority, while paragraph 2 ff of article 76 UNCLOS did govern the delimitation of the boundary between the continental

93 *Question of the Delimitation of the Continental Shelf Between Nicaragua and Colombia Beyond 200 Nautical Miles from the Nicaraguan Coast* (*Nicaragua v Colombia*) (Application Instituting Proceedings Filed in the Registry of the Court on 16 September 2013) [2013] ICJ Rep 1.

94 *Delimitation Beyond 200 Nautical Miles* (*Nicaragua v Colombia*) (Oral Proceedings: Verbatim Record of 6 December 2022) para 8 fn 89.

95 'The Outer Continental Shelf: Some Considerations Concerning Applications and the Potential Role of the International Tribunal for the Law of the Sea', Statement by H.E. Judge Rüdiger Wolfrum, President of the International Tribunal for the Law of the Sea at the Seventy-Third Conference of the International Law Association (Rio de Janeiro 2008) 12–15.

shelf of a State and the Area, they could not provide the legal basis for the delimitation of the continental shelves between States with opposite or adjacent coasts. In its 2023 final judgment, the ICJ agreed with the interpretation offered by Colombia.[96]

In other proceedings initiated according to one of the UNCLOS dispute settlement procedures, States parties to the dispute have cited the works of the ILA to clarify the nature and function of the Commission on the Limits of the Continental Shelf, provided for in article 76(8) UNCLOS and established under the Annex II (hereinafter 'Commission' or 'CLCS').

As to the first aspect, it is worth mentioning the case *Bangladesh v Myanmar*, in which the former State instituted arbitral proceedings under UNCLOS Annex VII to secure the delimitation of Bangladesh's maritime boundaries with Myanmar in the territorial sea, the exclusive economic zone and the continental shelf.

Representing the applicant State, Payam Akhavan argued that the ITLOS should indeed exercise jurisdiction since 'the adjudicative role of Part XV compulsory procedures is in no way diminished by the expert technical advisory role of the Commission'.[97] To this end, he mentioned the First Report of the ILA Committee on Legal Issues of the Outer Continental Shelf, which states that '[i]f Article 76 were to be completely excluded from the procedures of Part XV, the absence of legal expertise in the Commission would seem to be problematic, as there then would be hardly any possibility to submit questions of interpretation raised by a submission to legal scrutiny'.[98]

In the end, the arbitral tribunal clarified that since article 76 UNCLOS 'contains elements of law and science, its proper interpretation and application requires both legal and scientific expertise. While the Commission is a scientific and technical body […], the Tribunal can interpret and apply the provisions of the Convention, including article 76'.[99] Thus, the Tribunal reached the conclusion that '[a]s the question of the Parties' entitlement to a continental

---

96 *Question of the Delimitation of the Continental Shelf Between Nicaragua and Colombia Beyond 200 Nautical Miles from the Nicaraguan Coast* (*Nicaragua v Colombia*) (Judgment of 13 July 2023) para 76.

97 *Dispute concerning the delimitation of the maritime boundary between Bangladesh and Myanmar in the Bay of Bengal* (*Bangladesh/Myanmar*) (Verbatim Record of 12 September 2011 pm) 25 and 26.

98 Committee on Outer Continental Shelf, 'Report on Legal Issues of the Outer Continental Shelf' in International Law Association Report of the Seventy-First Conference (Berlin 2004) (International Law Association, Berlin 2004) 4 and 12.

99 *Dispute concerning delimitation of the maritime boundary between Bangladesh and Myanmar in the Bay of Bengal* (*Bangladesh/Myanmar*) (Judgment of 14 March 2012) ITLOS Reports 2012, para 411.

shelf beyond 200 nm raises issues that are predominantly legal in nature, the Tribunal can and should determine entitlements of the Parties in this particular case'.[100]

A further example which is relevant for the present purposes is the dispute between Mauritius and Maldives over the delimitation of the maritime boundaries between the two countries. In this context, Payam Akhavan, this time representing the respondent State, argued that the UNCLOS does not regulate the case where there is a continuing disagreement between the coastal State establishing its continental shelf and the CLCS.[101] To support this view, he invoked Conclusion No 17 of the Second Report of the ILA Committee on Legal Issues of the Outer Continental Shelf.[102]

> In this regard, the Second Report of the ILA Committee on Legal Issues of the Outer Continental Shelf, from 2006, is instructive. Its members included Judge Dolliver Nelson, Judge Jean-Pierre Cot, and [...] observed that: 'The Convention does not indicate how a continued disagreement between a coastal State and the Commission is to be resolved'. They observed further that: 'The dispute settlement procedures entailing binding decisions under Part XV of the Convention are not available' – not available – 'to resolve such a difference'. Scholars have presented two views on such an eventuality. Some, such as Professor McDorman, suggest that the process could go on indefinitely. Others, such as Professor Caflisch, suggest that in case of continued difference, the coastal State might eventually establish the outer limits in accordance with its submission, though he, and others such as Professor Treves, recognize that in such a case, the outer limits will not be opposable to other States.

In addition, to clarify the scope of article 76(8) UNCLOS, the Maldives then cited Conclusion No 11 of the same ILA Second Report.[103] In its opinion,

> Article 76, paragraph 8, is unambiguous: 'The limits of the shelf established by a coastal State on the basis of [CLCS] recommendations shall

100 Ibid para 412.

101 *Dispute Concerning Delimitation of the Maritime Boundary Between Mauritius and Maldives in the Indian Ocean* (*Mauritius/Maldives*) (Verbatim Records of 20 October 2022 am) 14.

102 Committee on Legal Issues of the Outer Continental Shelf, 'Second Report on Legal Issues of the Outer Continental Shelf' in International Law Association, Report of the Seventy-Second Conference (Toronto 2006) (International Law Association, Toronto 2006) 21, Conclusion No 17.

103 (*Mauritius/Maldives*) (Verbatim Records of 20 October 2022 am) (n 101) 15.

> be final and binding'. Its meaning and consequence are made clear by the ILA Report of 2006. The term 'final' means that the outer limits shall no longer be subject to change. The term 'binding' implies an obligation to accept the outer limits as established. If the outer limits of the continental shelf have been established in accordance with the substantive and procedural requirements of Article 76, they will be final and binding on the coastal State concerned and other States Parties to the Convention. Outer limits lines that have not been established in accordance with these requirements will not become binding on other States.

Furthermore, in the case at hand, both Parties had made submissions to the CLCS, but the latter found itself unable to make recommendations to them under article 76(8) UNCLOS because neither party had given its consent, in accordance with paragraph 5(a) of Annex I to the Rules of Procedure of the CLCS, for the Commission to consider the other party's submission. Therefore, the Maldives made the argument that the ITLOS Special Chamber should not exercise jurisdiction over the delimitation of the continental shelf beyond 200 nm,[104] since 'the CLCS has the final word, not the Part XV procedures. That was the intention of the drafters'. In this respect, it noted that[105]

> [t]he ILA Committee does suggest that '[a] court or tribunal may, in a judgment on a dispute between States Parties to the Convention, find that a recommendation or another act of the CLCS is invalid'.[106] But that does not mean that it is entitled to substitute the scientific and technical functions of the CLCS. This incidental jurisdiction merely applies to questions such as, for instance, 'the Commission has acted within the limits of its competence or *ultra vires*, or that an act of the Commission is invalid for other reasons, such as procedural irregularities or material error'.[107]

The ITLOS Special Chamber accepted this argument, finding that it was not in a position to determine the entitlement of Mauritius to the continental shelf beyond 200 nm in the Northern Chagos Archipelago Region and, in turn, to delimit the continental shelf between Mauritius and the Maldives beyond 200 nm.[108]

104 Ibid 15 and 17.

105 Ibid 15.

106 'Second Report on Legal Issues of the Outer Continental Shelf' (n 102) 28, Conclusion No 22.

107 Ibid 28, Conclusion No 21.

108 *Dispute Concerning Delimitation of the Maritime Boundary Between Mauritius and Maldives in the Indian Ocean (Mauritius/Maldives)* (Judgment of 28 April 2023) para 466 point 4.

In the same case, Mauritius also relied on acts of the ILA.[109] Replying to the Maldives' contention that in law the continental shelf is a single notion and so is the method of delimitation within and beyond 200 nm from the baseline of the coastal State,[110] Mauritius argued that the method of delimitation is inevitably connected to the basis for entitlement. In its words,

> [u]nder Article 76, entitlement to a continental shelf within 200 Miles is still based exclusively on the distance criterion. Entitlement to the continental shelf beyond 200 Miles is still based exclusively on geology and geomorphology. And, the delimitation of the continental shelf within and beyond 200 Miles must still give effect to these different sources of title. […] In other words, in the view of the ILA Committee, Maldives is wrong to argue that the fact that there is a single continental shelf means that the method for delimiting the continental shelf within 200 Miles should also be the delimitation method beyond 200 Miles. [… T]he Committee went on to state […] that since '[d]istance does not play the same role in the establishment of entitlement over and the outer limit of the outer continental shelf', this 'may have an impact on the rules applicable to the delimitation of this part of the continental shelf', that is, beyond 200 Miles. […] Maldives' approach to delimitation of the Parties' overlapping continental shelf entitlements therefore proceeds on the fundamentally erroneous premise that there is no linkage between the method of delimitation and the basis for entitlement. That is wrong, as both the Court and the ILA Committee have said.

Lastly, the works of the ILA have been cited by States parties in disputes concerning international watercourses.[111] In *Chile v Bolivia*, for example, the former

109 Committee on Legal Issues of the Outer Continental Shelf, 'Interim Report on Legal Issues of the Outer Continental Shelf' in International Law Association, Report of the Seventieth Conference (New Delhi 2002) (International Law Association, New Delhi 2002) 9.

110 *Dispute Concerning Delimitation of the Maritime Boundary Between Mauritius and Maldives in the Indian Ocean (Mauritius/Maldives)* (Verbatim Records of 22 October 2022 pm) 30.

111 For some general authorities on the ILA's contribution to the development of International Water Law see Joseph W Dellapenna, 'The Contribution of the ILA to the Development of International Water Law' in Catherine Kessedjian, Olivier Descamps and Teodolinda Fabrizi (eds) (n 5) 499; Salman MA Salman, 'The Helsinki Rules, the UN Watercourses Convention and the Berlin Rules: Perspectives on International Water Law' (2007) 23 Water Resources Development 625; Charles B Bourne, 'The International Law Association's Contribution to International Water Resources Law' (1996) 36 NAT RES J 155; Attila Tanzi et al., *The UNECE Convention on the Protection and Use of Transboundary*

State instituted proceedings before the ICJ, asking it, *inter alia*, to ascertain the status of the Silala River as an international watercourse and, consequently, to declare its right to equitable and reasonable utilisation of the river's waters.

In response to Bolivia's claim to sovereign rights over the 'artificially enhanced flow' of the Silala River, as resulting from installations built on Bolivian territory, Chile invoked article 25 of the 1997 Convention on the Law of the Non-navigational Uses of International Watercourses as an example of a 'general and widespread practice of installing infrastructure in international watercourses that may have the effect of increasing the volume of such watercourses'.[112] According to this provision, 'States of watercourses shall cooperate, where appropriate, to meet the needs or opportunities for regulation of the flow of water in an international watercourse'.

On this basis, Chile maintained that infrastructures aimed at increasing the volume of the Silala River were legitimate regulatory measures within the meanings of paragraph 3 of article 25, which makes it clear that '[f]or the purposes of this article, "regulation" means the use of hydraulic works or any other continuing measure to alter, vary or otherwise control the flow of the waters of an international watercourse'.[113] In support of its interpretation, Chile referred to article 1 of the ILA Regulation of the Flow of Water of International Watercourses of 1980, which the ILC, in turn, had taken into account during the preparatory works of article 25 of the 1997 Convention. Article 1 clarifies indeed that '"regulation" means continuing measures intended for controlling, moderating, increasing, or otherwise modifying the flow of the waters in an international watercourse for any purpose'. However, the ICJ did not address the issue, noting that Chile did not contest Bolivia's sovereign rights over the infrastructure and the 'enhanced flow'.[114]

On the other hand, Bolivia initially attempted to argue that customary international law on transboundary watercourses was not applicable in the case because 'Silala [...] forms an artificially enhanced watercourse'.[115] In its view, the matter should have been regulated by a special agreement, in the absence of which the Bolivian State, from which the waters of the Silala River originate,

---

Watercourses and International Lakes: Its Contribution to International Water Cooperation (Brill Nijhoff 2015).

112 *Dispute over the Status and Use of the Waters of the Silala* (*Chile v Bolivia*) (Additional Pleading of Chile of 16 September 2019) para 2.26.

113 Ibid para 2.28.

114 *Dispute over the Status and Use of the Waters of the Silala* (*Chile v Bolivia*) [2022] ICJ Rep 614, paras 153–155.

115 *Dispute over the Status and Use of the Waters of the Silala* (*Chile v Bolivia*) (Counter-Memorial of Bolivia of 3 September 2018) paras 103–104.

would have had no obligations towards Chile. To this end, the respondent State referred to article 5(1) of the ILA Regulation of the Flow of Water of International Watercourses,[116] according to which '[t]he construction of dams, canals, reservoirs or other works and installations and the operation of such works and installations required for regulation by a basin State in the territory of another can be carried out only by agreement between the basin States concerned'.[117]

In its judgment, the ICJ found the claim no longer had any object, as it later emerged during the proceedings that 'the Parties agree with respect to the legal status of the Silala River system as an international watercourse and on the applicability of the customary international law on non-navigational uses of international watercourses to all the waters of the Silala'.[118]

The contentious cases analysed above include State to State disputes before the ICJ, ITLOS and an UNCLOS Annex VII arbitral tribunal and concern either the delimitation of maritime boundaries or, in one case, the use of an international watercourse. In the four cases examined, it is always the parties to the proceeding, often both of them, who invoke the ILA documents in support of their arguments, specifically, to substantiate a certain interpretation of the treaty provision relevant for the resolution of the dispute. On the contrary, international courts and tribunals tend not to expressly cite the works of the ILA, even when they accept the argument one of the parties had elaborated on the basis of those acts.

7 Conclusions (Donato Greco)

The present contribution aimed to take stock of the influence of the ILA over a period roughly corresponding to the last two decades, by reviewing the judicial and arbitral practice of (mainly) international courts and tribunals and also of the parties to a dispute litigating before them. For this purpose, it examined several jurisdictions including the ICJ, ITLOS and UNCLOS Annex VII arbitral tribunals, regional human rights courts like the IACtHR and the ECtHR, investment and commercial arbitral tribunals as well as, to a very limited extent, municipal courts.

Selected cases can be traced back to five macro-areas: procedural law issues, with a particular focus on the principle of *res judicata*, human rights,

116 Committee on International Water Resources Law, 'Regulation of the Flow of Water of International Watercourses' in International Law Association Report of the Fifty-Ninth Conference (Belgrade 1980) (International Law Association, Belgrade 1980) 5–15.

117 (*Chile v Bolivia*) (Counter-Memorial of Bolivia of 3 September 2018) (n 115) para 105 fn 152.

118 (*Chile v Bolivia*) (n 114) paras 54–59.

investment protection, State jurisdiction to adjudicate as well as the delimitation of maritime boundaries and the status of international watercourses. Except for the first topic, the analysis shows that international courts and tribunals are generally reluctant to openly cite the work of the ILA, as well as, more generally, other pieces of scholarship, even when they agree on the merits with the arguments that a party has built based on the ILA documents. In this sense, the ICJ's self-referential approach appears emblematic of this general attitude. International courts and tribunals seem to be indeed jealous of their own jurisdiction and, except in rare cases, do not wish to endorse the authority of anyone else who might challenge the primary role the *iura novit curia* principle grants to them.

Greater attention towards teachings, particularly those of the ILA, is paid by judges and arbitrators in their dissenting or separate opinions. In an interesting study from 2019, the author points out that '[i]ndividual ICJ opinions contain a total of 191 references to "institutional" teachings: 85 to the IDI, 29 to the ICRC, 18 to the ILA, 15 to the American Law Institute and 14 to Harvard Law School'.[119] It is understandable that, being in the minority, they feel the need to counter the majority's view with arguments supported by other learned authorities. More frequently, however, it is the parties to the dispute who invoke external sources deserving some deference, in an attempt to persuade judges or arbitrators of the validity of their arguments.

In contrast to this general picture stands the matter of procedural law, where ILA acts have been cited relatively more frequently. This is understandable, first of all, if one takes into account the fact that in international investment and commercial arbitral proceedings, arbitrators are often confronted with highly informal procedures and, consequently, may often face normative gaps. While they enjoy a certain margin of discretion in ensuring that the procedure runs smoothly and efficiently, more often than not they feel the need to justify their choices by invoking external authorities such as the ILA, but also the International Bar Association or UNCITRAL. In addition, from a purely numerical point of view, investment and commercial arbitration proceedings are significantly more frequent than interstate litigation cases. This circumstance provides more opportunities for adjudicators and parties to corroborate their decisions or arguments through recourse to pieces of scholarship.

Finally, while it is true that benches of international courts and panels of arbitral tribunals are often composed of international law scholars, access to these positions is overall very limited. Contrarywise, a phenomenon of double

119 Sondre Torp Helmersen, 'Finding "the Most Highly Qualified Publicists": Lessons from the International Court of Justice' (2019) 30(2) EJIL 509, 525.

hatting between scholarly members of the ILA and adjudicators is more common in international investment and commercial arbitration. It thus results that in these areas, academics may be tempted to seek to accredit their own theses when serving as adjudicators.

As to the use that international courts and tribunals (and parties to the dispute) actually make of ILA works, it emerges that most of the time these documents have been invoked to clarify the scope of application of a norm of international law or its status among the sources of the international legal system. As an example of the former case, one may recall the decisions interpreting the principle of *res iudicata* and identifying the requirements for its application or the elements of a decision which must be considered as covered by the preclusive effect of the *ne bis in idem* principle. In the same direction stand cases which, dealing with the rule on State immunity from civil jurisdiction of other States, had to determine whether or not it applies to compensation claims based on gross violations of human rights.

In other cases, the works of the ILA have been used to clarify the status of a norm rather than its content. An emblematic example in this respect is the *Grand River Enterprises v United States* case, in which ILA works have been mentioned among the authorities supporting the customary nature of a rule prescribing the consultation of indigenous peoples on every project affecting their rights. In the same regard, another relevant instance could certainly be the reference made by Germany in the context of the *Jurisdictional Immunities of the State* case to disprove the existence of an established rule of international law on the right to reparation of victims of armed conflicts, at least at the time of the relevant facts.

Despite this general picture, which may appear somehow disappointing, one should note that jurisprudence is only one of the parameters to test the ILA's influence which, in fact, extends far beyond the judicial dimension, as its work has often provided an authoritative point of departure for the ILC in the drafting of codification agreements and other instruments. Indeed, among 'teachings of the most highly qualified publicists of the various nations' within the meanings of article 38(1)(d) of the ICJ Statute, ILA acts are often cited alongside the works of the ILC and those of the IDI, *i.e.* the other two institutions that have traditionally contributed most to the codification of international law and its progressive development.

According to categorisations well-established in the literature,[120] unlike the ILC, which represents a 'state-empowered body', the 'twins institutions' the

120 Sandesh Sivakumaran (n 3) 7.

ILA and the IDI constitute 'private expert groups', whose authority is independent of an official mandate within an intergovernmental organisation or other public body, but rests on the very quality of work, the authority and representativeness of its members.[121] Among the bodies belonging to the category of 'private expert groups', the ILA presents all those structural elements that help to justify the authority of its acts. This stance can be easily grasped through a comparison with the representativeness requirements provided for the composition of the ILC. Article 8 of the Commission's Statute reproduces, in almost identical terms, article 9 of the ICJ Statute, insofar as it provides that 'the persons to be elected to the Commission should individually possess the *qualifications required* and that in the Commission as a whole representation of the *main forms of civilisation* and of the *principal legal systems of the world* should be assured' (emphasis added).

Similarly, the ILA has the peculiarity of having a regional structure as, at present, it counts sixty-six national or regional branches. According to paragraph 8.3 of the Constitution of the Association, 'Branches are regional'.[122] The ILA's membership, around 4.500 members, shows a significant diversity in cultural and professional backgrounds as it ranges from lawyers in private practice, academia, government and the judiciary, to non-lawyer experts from the commercial, industrial and financial spheres, and representatives of bodies such as shipping and arbitration organisations and chambers of commerce.

Furthermore, the scientific activity of the ILA revolves around committees specifically established 'to carry out research, surveys and investigations on selected areas of international law and to prepare reports for consideration by the membership and other interested parties at the biennial conferences and recommendations for adoption by the Conference Plenary'.[123]

According to the ILA Committee Rules & Guidelines,[124] a committee must be composed of 'members with *relevant expertise*' (paragraph 1.1) and, more generally, 'Persons nominated for an International Committee must have *sufficient expertise* in the subject of the Committee in question, either as academics or practitioners' (paragraph 4.3), with the consequence that 'the Chair may reject a nomination for lack of *demonstrated expertise*; […] the requirement of *balanced representation*' (emphasis added). The meaning of 'balanced

121 Fritz Münch, 'L'influence de l'International Law Association sur la doctrine et la pratique du droit international' in Maarten Bos (ed) (n 35) 23.

122 International Law Association, 'Constitution of the Association' (n 4).

123 International Law Association, 'ILA Committee Rules & Guidelines' (Adopted by the Executive Council in November 2024) para 1.1.

124 Ibid.

representation' can be inferred from the context as in paragraph 5.1 the notion is associated with the composition of the committee's membership. The latter should indeed represent 'academics, practitioners, geographical regions, different legal systems, gender, younger members'.

In conclusion, this inquiry seems to confirm, with regard to the ILA, certain assumptions on the relevance of teachings that have emerged in the practice of international adjudication. International courts and tribunals as well as parties to a dispute seem to select pieces of scholarship to be cited in support of their grounds based on criteria such as the overall quality of the work, the expertise and official capacity of the drafters, or, as in the case of judicial decisions, the existence of consensus or disagreement among the authors of a collective work.[125]

Although the ILA is an NGO, the very fact that its scientific activity has been organised in an international apparatus of committees and that its works sometimes take the name of 'resolutions', 'principles' and 'rules' adopted at international conferences shows the Association's ambition to establish itself as an actor capable of imposing its voice in the debate on what international law is. As is confirmed by the multiple references to its acts contained in the ongoing works of the ILC on subsidiary means for the determination of rules of international law,[126] just over 150 years after its foundation, the ILA remains one of the main players in that community of international lawyers, which, though 'dispersed throughout the world and engaged in diverse occupations, constitutes a kind of invisible college dedicated to a common intellectual enterprise'.[127]

---

125 Sondre Torp Helmersen (n 119) 515 ff.

126 ILC, 'First report on subsidiary means for the determination of rules of international law' (n 2).

127 Oscar Schachter, 'Invisible College of International Lawyers' (1977–1978) 72(2) Nw U L Rev 217.

Book Review

Catherine Kessedjian, Olivier Descamps, Teodolinda Fabrizi (eds), *Au service du droit international/To the Benefit of International Law* (Edition Panthéon-Assas 2023) pp. 5–704, 70€.

This volume celebrates the 150th anniversary of the International Law Association, founded in Brussels in 1873. There is no better way for the Yearbook to inaugurate its Review Section, especially considering the undoubted richness, appealing style and originality of the book.

Apart from the forewords by Christine Chinkin and Franck Latty, the Introduction by the Editors, and an essay on the position of the ILA Director of studies by Alfred HA Soons, the book is divided into three parts.

The first part ('The Moment 1873') describes the history and the origin of the International Law Association. Inspired by the ideals of some pacifist movements, as highlighted especially by Mark Weston Janis' contribution, the ILA was established by a group of lawyers and academics, whose goal was to foster an 'international spirit' throughout the world and to push forward a new international legal order, more suitable for a modern and a liberal world. Such an ambition was universal, even if at the time universality was of course intended limitedly, as referred to relations among the 'civilised' countries.

In 1873, international law was in fact largely a European affair while 'special rules' – such as those about extraterritoriality or consular jurisdictions, harbinger of the colonial law – were applied to the rest of the world. Various contributions give account of the 'state of the art', dwelling also on nationalistic claims, economic interests and ideal aspirations influencing the legal norms (Jean-Louis Halpérin, Martti Koskenniemi). Depicting this scenario in a global context, including the views from Africa (Jean-Pierre Bat), Latin America (Paulo Borba Casella), and Asia (Frédéric Constant), is a special merit of the book. The same holds true for framing the described legal issues in the cultural environment of the period, by paying particular attention to history (Isabelle Dasque), philosophy (Laurent Fedi, Mathias Girel), economics (Jean-Pierre Williot) and even arts (Annamaria Cascetta, Dominique Lobstein). This choice makes the reading particularly enriching and enjoyable for curious lawyers.

The second part of the book gives a picture of a lot of the national branches of the Association. As Christine Chinkin points out (p 5), the federal structure of the Association, comprising an international headquarters and national branches, is its primary strength. This is a sparkling and lively section. It is not only full of episodes of the life of the members (in some cases true 'makers' of the modern international law), but in some cases also acquaints readers with the historical events of the countries themselves, with special regard to their

 | DOI:10.1163/9789004727663_015

impact on the attitude towards international law and its 'way of living' within the domestic systems. As ILA Italy is concerned, Professor Gabriella Venturini, former President of the Branch (2013–2021), recounts the involvement of the Italian legal community since the inception of ILA, mainly thanks to Pasquale Stanislao Mancini, and the subsequent continuous strong engagement in the activities of the Association up to the present day (see also Gabriella Venturini, in this volume, p 1).

The third part of the volume is devoted to the contribution to the development of international law through the works of the international Committees and the resolutions adopted by the biennial Conferences. Here the international lawyer is at ease as he/she finds a vast bulk of study material in the various subjects dealt by the Committees. The substantive rules of international trade law, human rights, protection of cultural heritage, sustainable development, space law, reparation for victims of violations of humanitarian law, investment law, State immunity, climate change, securities regulation as well as some aspects of private international law such as international civil procedure law, are soundly investigated especially in the perspective of the progressive development of international law. The influence of some of these works in shaping rules or standards is noteworthy.

In this vein of dedication to reality, questions on the future challenges of ILA and its role cannot be missed. A short but incisive contribution at the end of the book (*Building Tomorrow's ILA. From the perspective of the ILA s younger members*, p 667 ff) lists a number of recommendations that should be followed in order to ensure the relevance of the organisation in the coming years, among which the promotion of diversity and the participation of younger members. In this regard, significant changes have recently already occurred.

The book is a wealth of information for any scholar or practitioner of international law. In times of conflicts in many parts of the world the strong commitment of a non-governmental organisation pursuing peace and justice through the study of international law is a wave of optimism.

It only remains to thank the 'small band of visionaries' who met the first time in Brussels on a morning in October 1873 (see Franck Latty, p 9), not only for their legacy, but also for beginning the process of making international law a field of academic specialization and a professional career, shaping the lives of many people in the future, including those who write and read these lines.

Alberto Malatesta
Professor of Private International Law, LIUC University, Castellanza
Secretary General, ILA Italy

ILA *Italy Activities*

ILA Italy Activities in 2024

5th ILA Italy Biennial Conference. Alternative Dispute Resolution in International and EU Law: Recent Trends, 16 November 2023, University of Ferrara.

Multilateral Legal Frameworks to Address Climate Change: Implementation Challenges and Responses, opening lecture, 18 January 2024, organised by ILA Italy in the context of the ILA Italy Environmental Transition Series (January–March 2024).

The International Framework on Climate Change and the Energy Transition: An Overview, seminar, 18 January 2024, organised by ILA Italy in the context of the ILA Italy Environmental Transition Series (January–March 2024). Keynote speech: prof. Tomoko Ishikawa (Nagoya University; Advisory Board of the Investment Treaty Forum - British Institute of International and Comparative Law).

Litigating in the Energy Transition Era, seminar, 15 February 2024, organised by ILA Italy in the context of the ILA Italy Environmental Transition Series (January–March 2024).

Legal Tools to Advance Construction of New Energy Infrastructure, seminar, 14 March 2024, organised by ILA Italy in the context of the ILA Italy Environmental Transition Series (January–March 2024).

La *soft law* nel sistema di fonti del diritto internazionale, workshop, 15 March 2024 organised by prof. Pia Acconci (University of Teramo), under the auspices of ILA Italy.

Biodiversità e mare: il traguardo dell'Accordo BBNJ, conference, 21 March 2024 organised by prof. Gian Maria Farnelli (University of Bologna Alma Mater) under the auspices of the Ministry of Foreign Affairs and International Cooperation and ILA Italy.

Ethical Standards for International Arbitrators, workshop, 12 April 2024, organised by Anna De Luca (Of Counsel, Macchi di Cellere Gangemi) and Gian Paolo Coppola (Partner, LCA Studio legale) under the auspices of ILA Italy.

 | DOI:10.1163/9789004727663_016

Interessi delle future generazioni e cambiamento climatico alla luce del recente contenzioso interno e internazionale, webinar, 9 May 2024 organised by prof. Micaela Frulli (University of Firenze) in the context of the National Research Project (PRIN) "FUEL-IT: Future Generations and International Law: Boosting and Italian Response" (2022), under the auspices of ILA Italy.

«So do You Want to Be an International Lawyer?», seminar, 15 April 2024 organised by prof. Attila Tanzi (University of Bologna Alma Mater) and dr. Ludovica Chiussi Curzi (University of Bologna Alma Mater), under the auspices of ILA Italy. Guest speaker: Cameron Miles (Barrister, 3VB Chambers).

Human Rights in Times of Crisis: A View from the Global South, symposium, 16 April 2024, organised by prof. Attila Tanzi (University of Bologna Alma Mater) and dr. Ludovica Chiussi Curzi (University of Bologna Alma Mater) under the auspices of ILA Italy. Guest speaker: S.E. Suljuk M. Tarar, Pakistan's Ambassador to the Netherlands.

Full Protection and Security in International Investment Law: Old and New Challenges, seminar, 13 May 2024, organised by prof. Attila Tanzi (University of Bologna Alma Mater) and dr. Ludovica Chiussi Curzi (University of Bologna Alma Mater) under the auspices of ILA Italy.

One Health. International, Supranational, Regional and National Experiences, conference, 10–14 May 2024, organised by prof. Gianluca Contaldi (University of Macerata).

The European Union and Global Health (Jean Monnet Eu4gh Summer School), conference, 3–7 June 2024, organised by prof. Stefania Negri (University of Salerno) in cooperation with the European Association of Health Law, the Global Health Law Consortium and the Observatory on Human Rights: Bioethics, Health, Environment, under the auspices of ILA Italy.

International Law before Domestic Courts: Comparative Approaches from Chile and Italy, webinar, 26 June 2024, co-organised by ILA Italy and ILA Chile under the auspices of the Sociedad Chilena de Derecho Internacional (SOCHIDI) and the interest group "Diritto interno e diritto internazionale" of the Società italiana di diritto internazionale (SIDI).

Presentazione del libro: Giorgio Bosco, *La Croce Rossa Internazionale e il diritto umanitario*, 26 June 2024, organised by Sen. Giuliomaria Terzi di Sant'Agata, President of the European Union Policies Committee of the Senate of the Republic, and sponsored by prof. Gabriella Venturini (University of Milan Statale).

Sentenze e atti stranieri in materia di diritto di famiglia e cittadinanza. Avvocati e ufficiali di stato civile a confronto, conference, 19–20 September 2024, organised by prof. Elisa Baroncini (University of Bologna Alma Mater), dr. Marco Argentini (University of Bologna Alma Mater), prof. Roberta Clerici (University of Milan Statale), and prof. Alberto Malatesta (University Carlo Cattaneo, LIUC), in cooperation with ILA-Italy, Camera degli Avvocati Internazionalisti and Associazione Nazionale degli Ufficiali di Stato Civile e d'Anagrafe (ANUSCA).

International Law, Food and Water, webinar, 15 October 2024, co-organised by ILA Italy and ILA Chile under the auspices of the Sociedad Chilena de Derecho Internacional (SOCHIDI) and the Universidad de Chile.

La tutela della biodiversità marina dopo l'Accordo BBNJ, seminar, 25 October 2024 organised by dr. Donato Greco (LUISS Guido Carli) under the auspices of ILA Italy; Guest speaker: Vito De Lucia, Director of the Norwegian Centre for the Law of the Sea (Arctic University of Norway, Tromsø).

From Fossils to Renewables: How Climate Change Is Shaping the Future of Investment Arbitration, seminar, 29 October 2024, organised by Irene Petrelli (Partner, Curtis, Mallet-Prevost, Colt & Mosle LLP; ArbIt) and Bianca Berardicurti (Counsel, Legance) in cooperation with ILA-Italy.

Le sfide del contenzioso climatico dinanzi alle corti italiane: prospettive di diritto internazionale, seminar, 31 October 2024, organised by dr. Donato Greco (LUISS Guido Carli) under the auspices of ILA Italy; Guest speaker: Luca Saltalamacchia (Lawyer, Dini-Saltalamacchia), Napoli.

The Many Shades of Climate Change. Through the Lenses of Dispute Settlement, conference, 8 November 2024, organised by prof. Maria Chiara Malaguti (University Cattolica del Sacro Cuore) in cooperation with University of RomaTre, UNIDROIT Centre on Transnational Commercial Law and International Arbitration, and Banca d'Italia Eurosistema, under the auspices of ILA Italy and SIMEST.

Immunità giurisdizionali dello Stato, riparazione delle gravi violazioni del diritto internazionale e legalità costituzionale: a dieci anni dalla sent. 22 ottobre 2014, n. 238, conference, 22 November 2024, organised by dr. Donato Greco (LUISS Guido Carli) under the auspices of ILA Italy.

The European Parliament, EU Trade Policy, and Civil Society, conference, 25 November 2024, organised by prof. Elisa Baroncini (University of Bologna Alma Mater) under the auspices of ILA Italy.

Sponsorship Credits